60 HIKES *within* 60 MILES
SAN DIEGO
INCLUDING NORTH, SOUTH, AND EAST COUNTIES

60 Hikes *within* 60 MILES

SAN DIEGO

INCLUDING NORTH, SOUTH, AND EAST COUNTIES

Sheri McGregor

MENASHA RIDGE PRESS
Birmingham, Alabama

Copyright © 2004 Sheri McGregor
All rights reserved
Printed in the United States of America
Published by Menasha Ridge Press
Distributed by The Globe Pequot Press
First edition, first printing

Library of Congress Cataloging-in-Publication Data

McGregor, Sheri, 1961-
60 Hikes within 60 miles, San Diego/Sheri McGregor,--1st ed.
p. cm.
ISBN 0-89732-554-0
1. Hiking--California--San Diego County--Guidebooks. 2. San Diego
(Calif.)--Guidebooks. I. Title: Sixty hikes within sixty miles, San Diego. II. Title.

GV199.42.S24M34 2003
796.52'09794'985--dc22   2003059259

Cover design by Grant M. Tatum and Travis Bryant
Text design by Karen Ocker
Cover photo copyright Sheri McGregor, photo location Lake Morena
Author photo by William Kordela
All other photos by Sheri McGregor
Maps by Scott Roush and Steve Jones

Menasha Ridge Press
P.O. Box 43673
Birmingham, AL 35243
www.menasharidge.com

To those who love to commune with nature. May you do so
with utter respect, deep appreciation, and a sense of joy . . .
always joy.

TABLE OF CONTENTS

TABLE OF CONTENTS

ACKNOWLEDGMENTS

Many people provided a wealth of information for this book in impromptu phone conversations, along the trail, or through published information made available in brochures or on Web sites by departments working within San Diego County. These "official" rangers and many others were helpful.

The lion's share of thanks goes to my hiking partners Brian and Mia, for their tireless legs and willing attitudes. If it weren't for Brian's quiet presence and unwavering strength, I couldn't have finished this book. Mia's joyful marvel about the world rivals my own—her chatty nature surpasses mine!

My secondary hiking partners also deserve thanks. Henry makes a long, hot hike a comedy sketch, so we shared laughs. Hilary hunkers down to the task when she's needed, and I appreciate her pinch-hitting. Even Sam put in a dose of trail time. . . .

Others who provided support and assistance include Rory—for his sympathetic ear—I hope he'll join me on the trail soon. Julie, Lori, and Matt offered continuing feedback on the writing in progress—and lots of laughs. And a high-five to my Menasha Ridge editors, Russell Helms and Mopsy Gascon, for their patience and encouragement during the trials I faced in completing this guidebook. I also want to thank Tricia Parks at Menasha for her enthusiasm in promoting the final product.

—*Sheri McGregor*

FOREWORD

Welcome to Menasha Ridge Press's *60 Hikes within 60 Miles,* a series designed to provide hikers with information needed to find and hike the very best trails surrounding cities usually underserved by good guidebooks.

Our strategy was simple: First, find a hiker who knows the area and loves to hike. Second, ask that person to spend a year researching the most popular and very best trails around. And third, have that person describe each trail in terms of difficulty, scenery, condition, elevation change, and all other categories of information that are important to hikers. "Pretend you've just completed a hike and met up with other hikers at the trailhead," we told each author. "Imagine their questions, be clear in your answers."

An experienced hiker and writer, author Sheri McGregor has selected 60 of the best hikes in and around the San Diego metropolitan area. From the rail trails and urban hikes that make use of parklands to flora- and fauna-rich treks along the numerous area lakes and hills in the hinterlands. From urban hikes that make use of parklands and streets to aerobic outings in the mountains, McGregor provides hikers (and walkers) with a great variety of hikes—and all within roughly 60 miles of San Diego.

You'll get more out of this book if you take a moment to read the Introduction explaining how to read the trail listings. The "Topographic Maps" section will help you understand how useful topos will be on a hike, and will also tell you where to get them. And though this is a "where-to," not a "how-to," guide, those of you who have hiked extensively will find the Introduction of particular value.

As much for the opportunity to free the spirit as well as to free the body, let these hikes elevate you above the urban hurry.

All the best,
The Editors at Menasha Ridge Press

ABOUT THE AUTHOR

As a child growing up in San Diego, Sheri McGregor remembers lying in the grass watching tiny bug–worlds crawl by. Today, with five children of her own, McGregor still watches bugs . . . and sometimes feels just as tiny among the towering trees, majestic mountains, and free-flowing waters of San DiegoCounty. Authoring this hiking guide allowed McGregor to enjoy the local wilderness with a purpose—sharing her love of nature with readers. Out on the trails, even the shadows fall into intricate patterns that display the poetry of the natural world.

In addition to writing about nature and the outdoors, McGregor has published two novels and writes about a variety of subjects. From psychology and fitness to travel and home decor, her over 1,000 nonfiction articles, essays, and short fiction have appeared in themed anthologies, a supplemental textbook, and national/international publications including *The Washington Post,* Salon.com, Reader's Digest's Publications, *LA Parent,* InfoWeek, Sunset Publications, and *San Jose Magazine.* She also assists with companies' communication needs.

PREFACE

In San Diego County, a variety of exquisite outdoor escapes awaits you. Stand at the ocean's edge and let the cool breeze ruffle your hair as the surf foams up around your ankles. An hour's drive takes you to the mountains where the pine air always smells like Christmas. Yet, from an eastern bluff, you can look out over the gaping mauve-brown expanse of the Anza Borrego Desert. This diverse topography is a paradise for hikers looking for quick getaways from the city bustle and for healthy variety in their wilderness treks.

County hiking experiences range from an easy stroll over well-defined paths to strenuous peak treks gaining 1,000 feet within a few short miles of rocky trail. With more than two dozen lakes in San Diego County, and several land preservation groups working to keep open spaces safe from urban development, hiking opportunities abound. Marshland and lagoon areas provide homes to rare or endangered types of terns, and scrub areas provide nesting sites for others, such as the endangered Least Bell's Vireo.

▶ ENJOYING THE GREAT OUTDOORS

Getting out among the trees has beneficial effects. In recent years, studies at respected institutions such as Johns Hopkins have shown that merely looking at a beautiful meadow or hearing a babbling brook can reduce one's perception of pain. People in hospital rooms with windows allowing a view to the sky fared better than those in rooms without such views. Nature's restorative powers, found within an hour's drive and a few steps into the wilderness, made preparing this book about San Diego's backyard a joy.

Amid the routine struggles of life, just driving out of the city toward a favorite destination brings a sense of release. Once on the trail, whatever irritations remain to cloud the mind are swept away by the music of wind rushing through the trees, or carried off on the dark-tipped tail of a mule-deer spotted bounding off into the woods. Even a honey bee seems to carry away burdens—collected in the fat yellow pollen pockets on hind legs he drags heavily behind as he buzzes off to a distant flower. Make a conscious effort to put aside your concerns and troubles, and let yourself lighten up and take a break while on the trail. With a relaxed mind and an easy spirit, you may be surprised at the tiny wonders you'll see.

HIKING RECOMMENDATIONS

▶ 1 TO 3 MILES

Batiquitos Lagoon Trail
Bayside Trail
Clevenger Canyon South: West Trail
Crest Canyon Open Space Preserve Loop
Discovery Lake and Hills Loop
Elfin Forest Recreational Reserve: Botanical
  Loop
Elfin Forest Recreational Reserve: Way Up Trail
Famosa Slough Trail
Heller's Bend Preserve Trail
Hosp Grove Loop
La Jolla: Coast Walk

La Jolla: Tide Pools Walk
Lake Wohlford: North, Kumeyaay Trail
Lake Wohlford: South Trails
Los Jilgueros Preserve Trail
Palomar Mountain: Fry Creek Campground
  Loop
Rancho Carrillo Loop
Stelzer Park Loop
Sunset Cliffs Park Trail
Torrey Pines State Reserve: Combined Trails
  and Points Loop

▶ 3 TO 6 MILES

Anza Borrego State Park: California Riding
  and Hiking Trail
Blue Sky Trail to Lake Ramona
Clevenger Canyon South: East Trail
Cowles Mountain Loop
Cuyamaca Rancho State Park: Stonewall
  Peak Trail
Daley Ranch: Engelmann Oak Loop
Guajome Regional Park Trail
Highland Valley Trail
Laguna Mountains: Sunset Trail
Lake Dixon Shore View Trail
Lake Hodges: North Shore Trail
Lake Morena Trail
Lake Poway Loop

Mission Trails Regional Park: Combined
  Trails Loop
Monserate Mountain Trail
Mount Woodson East Trail
Palomar Mountain Overview Loop
Piedras Pintadas Interpretive Trail
San Elijo Lagoon Trail
Santa Margarita River Trail
Sweetwater Reservoir: Riding and Hiking Trail
Three Sisters Waterfall Trail
Tijuana Estuary Trail
Volcan Mountain Preserve Trail
Wilderness Gardens Preserve: Combined
  Trails Loop
William Heise County Park: Combined Trails

▶ 6 TO 8 MILES

Agua Caliente Creek Trail
Daley Ranch: Combined Trails
Iron Mountain Peak Trail
Iron Mountain to Ramona Overlook and Pond
Laguna Mountains: Penny Pines to Pioneer
  Mail

Lake Hodges: West Trail
Lake Poway to Mount Woodson Peak
Los Penasquitos Canyon Preserve: West End
  to Waterfall Loop
Sycamore Canyon: Goodan Ranch Open
  Space Preserve Loop

HIKING RECOMMENDATIONS

▶ 8 TO 10 MILES

Clevenger Canyon North: East Trail
Lake Poway to Mount Woodson Trail
  (through Warren Canyon)

Los Penasquitos Canyon Preserve: East End
  to Waterfall Loop
San Pasqual Valley: Mule Hill Trail

▶ STEEP HIKES

Bayside Trail
Clevenger Canyon North: East Trail
Clevenger Canyon South: East Trail
Cowles Mountain Loop
Cuyamaca Rancho State Park: Stonewall
  Peak Trail
Elfin Forest Recreational Reserve: Way Up
  Trail
Hellhole Canyon Open Space Preserve Trail
Iron Mountain Peak Trail

Lake Poway to Mount Woodson Peak
Lake Poway to Mount Woodson Trail
  (through Warren Canyon)
Mission Trails Regional Park: Combined
  Trails Loop
Monserate Mountain Trail
Mount Woodson East Trail
William Heise County Park: Combined Trails

▶ COASTAL HIKES

Bayside Trail
La Jolla: Coast Walk
La Jolla: Tide Pools Walk
San Elijo Lagoon Trail

Sunset Cliffs Park Trail
Torrey Pines State Reserve: Combined Trails
  and Points Loop

▶ HIKES WITH VIEWS

Bayside Trail
Clevenger Canyon South: East Trail
Clevenger Canyon North: East Trail
Cowles Mountain Loop
Cuyamaca Rancho State Park: Stonewall
  Peak Trail

Mission Trails Regional Park: Combined
  Trails Loop
Torrey Pines State Reserve: Combined Trails
  and Points Loop

▶ FAMILY HIKES

Batiquitos Lagoon Trail
Blue Sky Trail to Lake Ramona
Crest Canyon Open Space Preserve Loop
Cuyamaca Rancho State Park: Stonewall
  Peak Trail
Famosa Slough Trail

Guajome Regional Park Trail
Highland Valley Trail
Laguna Mountains: Sunset Trail
La Jolla:Tide Pools Walk
Lake Dixon Shore View Trail
Lake Hodges: North Shore Trail

HIKING RECOMMENDATIONS

▶ FAMILY HIKES *(continued)*

Los Jilgueros Preserve Trail

Los Penasquitos Canyon Preserve: East End to Waterfall Loop

Palomar Mountain: Fry Creek Campground Loop

Palomar Mountain Overview Loop

Piedras Pintadas Interpretive Trail

Santa Margarita River Trail

Sycamore Canyon: Goodan Ranch Open Space Preserve Loop

Stelzer Park Loop

Wilderness Gardens Preserve: Combined Trails Loop

William Heise County Park: Combined Trails

▶ HIKES FOR BIRDING

Batiquitos Lagoon Trail

Famosa Slough Trail

La Jolla: Coast Walk

Lake Dixon Shore View Trail

Lake Hodges: North Shore Trail

Lake Wohlford: South Trails

San Elijo Lagoon Trail

Tijuana Estuary Trail

▶ HIGH-TRAFFIC HIKES

Crest Canyon Open Space Preserve Loop

Cuyamaca Rancho State Park: Stonewall Peak Trail

Elfin Forest Recreational Reserve: Way Up Trail

Hosp Grove Loop

Iron Mountain Peak Trail

Laguna Mountains: Sunset Trail

La Jolla: Coast Walk

La Jolla: Tide Pools Walk

Lake Dixon Shore View Trail

Lake Hodges: West Trail

Lake Hodges: North Shore Trail

Lake Poway Loop

Los Penasquitos Canyon Preserve: East End to Waterfall Loop

Mount Woodson East Trail

Piedras Pintadas Interpretive Trail

San Elijo Lagoon Trail

▶ LOW-TRAFFIC HIKES

Lake Poway to Mount Woodson Trail (through Warren Canyon)

Lake Wohlford: North, Kumeyaay Trail

Three Sisters Waterfall Trail

Wilderness Gardens Preserve: Combined Trails Loop

▶ WILDLIFE HIKES

Agua Caliente Creek Trail

La Jolla: Tide Pools Walk

Los Penasquitos Canyon Preserve: East End to Waterfall Loop

Palomar Mountain Overview Loop

HIKING RECOMMENDATIONS

▶ HIKES WITH STRENUOUS CLIMBS

Clevenger Canyon North: East Trail
Cowles Mountain Loop
Hellhole Canyon Open Space Preserve Trail
Iron Mountain Peak Trail
Lake Poway to Mount Woodson Peak

Mission Trails Regional Park: Combined
  Trails Loop
Monserate Mountain Trail
Mount Woodson East Trail
William Heise County Park: Combined Trails

▶ SPRING HIKES FOR WILDFLOWERS

Anza Borrego State Park: California Riding
  and Hiking Trail
Clevenger Canyon South: West Trail

Laguna Mountains: Sunset Trail
San Pasqual Valley: Mule Hill Trail

▶ FALL HIKES FOR AUTUMN COLORS

Hellhole Canyon Open Space Preserve Trail
Palomar Mountain: Fry Creek Campground
  Loop

Palomar Mountain Overview Loop
William Heise County Park: Canyon
  Oak/Desert View/Nature Trail Loop

▶ LAKE HIKES

Discovery Lake and Hills Loop
Guajome Regional Park Trail
Lake Dixon Shore View Trail
Lake Hodges North Shore Trail
Lake Hodges: West Trail

Lake Morena Trail
Lake Poway Loop
Lake Wohlford: North, Kumeyaay Trail
Lake Wohlford: South Trails
Sweetwater Reservoir: Riding and Hiking Trail

▶ DIVERSE HIKES

Agua Caliente Creek Trail
Laguna Mountains: Penny Pines to Pioneer
  Mail
Lake Morena Trail
Lake Poway to Mount Woodson Trail
  (through Warren Canyon)

Mission Trails Regional Park: Combined
  Trails Loop
Mission Trails Regional Park: Combined
  Trails Loop
San Pasqual Valley: Mule Hill Trail
William Heise County Park: Combined Trails

▶ HIKES FOR VERY YOUNG CHILDREN

Discovery Lake and Hills Loop
Elfin Forest Recreational Reserve: Botanical
  Loop

Heller's Bend Preserve Trail
La Jolla: Tide Pools Walk
Lake Morena Trail

HIKING RECOMMENDATIONS

▶ HIKES FOR DOGS

Blue Sky Trail to Lake Ramona
Iron Mountain Peak Trail
Lake Hodges: West Trail

Los Penasquitos Canyon Preserve: East End
  to Waterfall Loop
Monserate Mountain Trail
San Elijo Lagoon Trail

▶ FLAT HIKES

Batiquitos Lagoon Trail
Famosa Slough Trail
Guajome Regional Park Trail
La Jolla: Tide Pools Walk
Lake Hodges North Shore Trail

Los Jilgueros Preserve Trail
Los Penasquitos Canyon Preserve: East End
  to Waterfall Loop
Tijuana Estuary Trail

▶ HIKES FOR SOLITUDE

Hellhole Canyon Open Space Preserve Trail
Iron Mountain to Ramona Overlook and Pond
Lake Poway to Mount Woodson Trail
  (through Warren Canyon)

Volcan Mountain Preserve Trail
William Heise County Park: Combined Trails

▶ HIKES ALONG WATER

Agua Caliente Creek Trail
Elfin Forest Recreational Reserve: Botanical
  Loop
Guajome Regional Park Trail
La Jolla: Tide Pools Walk
Lake Hodges North Shore Trail
Lake Hodges: West Trail

Los Penasquitos Canyon Preserve: East End
  to Waterfall Loop
Los Penasquitos Canyon Preserve: West End
  to Waterfall Loop
Santa Margarita River Trail
Tijuana Estuary Trail

▶ TRAILS FOR RUNNERS

Batiquitos Lagoon Trail
Daley Ranch: Combined Trails
Daley Ranch: Engelmann Oak Loop
Elfin Forest Recreational Reserve: Way Up
  Trail
Guajome Regional Park Trail
Iron Mountain Peak Trail

Lake Hodges North Shore Trail
Lake Hodges: West Trail
Los Penasquitos Canyon Preserve: East End
  to Waterfall Loop
Mount Woodson East Trail
Piedras Pintadas Interpretive Trail
San Elijo Lagoon Trail

HIKING RECOMMENDATIONS

▶ MULTIUSE TRAILS

Daley Ranch: Combined Trails

Daley Ranch: Engelmann Oak Loop

Elfin Forest Recreational Reserve: Way Up
Trail

Hellhole Canyon Open Space Preserve Trail

Iron Mountain to Ramona Overlook and
Pond

Lake Hodges North Shore Trail

Lake Hodges: West Trail

Los Penasquitos Canyon Preserve: East End
to Waterfall Loop

Los Penasquitos Canyon Preserve: West End
to Waterfall Loop

Piedras Pintadas Interpretive Trail

San Pasqual Valley: Mule Hill Trail

Sycamore Canyon: Goodan Ranch Open
Space Preserve Loop

Sweetwater Reservoir: Riding and Hiking Trail

▶ HIKES WITH HISTORICAL INTEREST

Bayside Trail

Daley Ranch: Combined Trails

La Jolla: Coast Walk

Los Penasquitos Canyon Preserve: East End
to Waterfall Loop

Rancho Carrillo Loop

San Pasqual Valley: Mule Hill Trail

INTRODUCTION

Welcome to *60 Hikes within 60 Miles: San Diego*. If you're new to hiking or even if you're a seasoned trail-smith, take a few minutes to read the following introduction. We'll explain how this book is organized and how to get the best use of it.

▶ HIKE DESCRIPTIONS

Each hike is numbered and contains six key items: a locator map, a brief description of the trail, an information box, directions to the trail, a trail map, and a hike narrative. Combined, the maps and information provide a clear method to assess each trail from the comfort of your favorite chair.

LOCATOR MAP

After narrowing down the general area of the hike on the overview map (see front insde cover), the locator map, along with driving directions given in the narrative, enables you to find the trailhead. Once at the trailhead, park only in designated areas.

IN BRIEF

Think of this section as a snapshot focused on the historical landmarks, beautiful vistas, and other interesting sights you may encounter on the trail.

KEY AT-A-GLANCE INFORMATION

This information box gives you a quick idea of the specifics of the hike. There are up to 12 basic elements covered.

LENGTH This refers to distance traveled within the hike. There may be options to shorten or extend the hikes, but the mileage corresponds to the described hike. Consult the hike description to customize the hike for your ability or time constraints.

CONFIGURATION A description of what the trail might look like from overhead. Trails can be a loop, out-and-back (that is, to and from), figure eight, or balloon with a string (meaning a loop with an entry or exit trail).

DIFFICULTY The degree of effort an "average" hiker should expect on a given hike. For simplicity, difficulty is described as "easy," "moderate," or "strenuous." Moderate or strenuous hikes may have received those ratings due to a particularly steep segment of sustained duration within a generally easy whole. Hikes longer than 5 miles may have been rated more difficult due to length alone. Altitude also affected the rating, since thinner air makes hiking more difficult. As with any physical activity, you're advised to check with your doctor before beginning a program. If you are not physically fit, stick to hikes noted easy. Build up your health and agility before trying moderate or strenuous hikes.

SCENERY Gives the overall environs of the hike and what to expect in terms of vegetation, wildlife, streams, and historic buildings.

INTRODUCTION

EXPOSURE A quick check of how much sun you can expect during the hike. Descriptors used are self-explanatory and include terms such as shady, exposed, and sunny.

TRAFFIC Indicates how busy the trail might be on an average day. In general, weekdays are best for solitude, but trail traffic varies from day to day and season to season.

TRAIL SURFACE Indicates whether the trail is paved, gravel, slippery, rocky, smooth, or a mixture of elements.

HIKING TIME How long it took the author to hike the trail. She reports that on average she gauges about 2 mph, with additional time needed for strenuous terrain. If you hike slowly because you stop to take a lot of photos, rest, or enjoy the scenery, adjust the time for your own use.

ACCESS Notes fees or permits needed to access the trail. Parking or entry fees range from $1 to $6. In the Laguna Mountains, you'll need to purchase an "Adventure Pass." In most cases no fees or permits are required.

MAPS In addition to the maps in this guide, this indicates additional maps that are the best (in the author's opinion) for the hikes and where to find them.

FACILITIES What to expect in terms of rest rooms, phones, water, and other details available at the trailhead or nearby. If there are no facilities, this category is eliminated.

SPECIAL COMMENTS Provides you with those little extra details that don't fit into any of the above categories. Here you'll find information on trail-hiking options and facts such as whether the hike includes cliffs unsuitable for young children.

DIRECTIONS
Used with the locator map, the directions will help you find the trailhead.

DESCRIPTION
The trail description is the heart of each hike profile. Here, the author provides a summary of the trail's essence as well as highlighting any special traits the hike offers. Ultimately, the description will help you choose the hike that is best for you.

NEARBY ACTIVITIES
Not every hike will have this listing. For those that do, look here for information on nearby restaurants or sights of interest.

▶ MAPS

The maps in this book have been produced with great care and, used with the hiking directions, will help you stay on course. But as any experienced hiker knows, things can get tricky off the beaten path.

INTRODUCTION

You will find superior detail and valuable information in the United States Geological Survey's 7.5-minute series topographic maps. Recognizing how indispensable these are to hikers and bikers alike, many outdoor shops and bike shops now carry topos of the local area.

If you're new to hiking you might be wondering, "What's a topographic map?" In short, it indicates not only linear distance but elevation as well. One glance at a topo will show you the difference: contour lines spread across the map like dozens of intricate spiderwebs. Each contour line represents a particular elevation, and at the base of each topo a contour's interval designation is given. It may sound confusing if you're new to the lingo, but it's truly a simple and helpful system. Assume that the 7.5-minute series topo reads "contour interval 40 feet," that the short trail you'll be hiking is two inches in length on the map, and that it crosses five contour lines from its beginning to end. Because the linear scale of this series is 2,000 feet to the inch (roughly two and three-quarters inches representing one mile), the trail is approximately four-fifths of a mile long (two inches are 2,000 feet). You'll also be climbing or descending 200 vertical feet (five contour lines are 40 feet each) over that distance. The elevation designations written on occasional contour lines will tell you if you're heading up or down.

In addition to outdoor shops and bike shops, you'll find topos at major universities and some public libraries, where you might try photocopying the ones you need to avoid the cost of buying them. But if you want your own and can't find them locally, contact USGS Map Sales at Box 25286, Denver, CO 80225; (888) ASK-USGS or 275-8747; or www.mapping.usgs.gov. Ask for an index while you're at it, plus a price list and a copy of the booklet Topographic Maps. In minutes you'll be reading maps like a pro.

▶ LIMITATIONS

At the time of this writing, some closures due to the October 2003 fires remain in effect. Although the Stonewall Peak trail reopened in June and is included herein, much of Cuyamaca Rancho State Park remained devastated. Likewise, William Heise County Park in Julian reopened, but for public safety, some severely damaged trails remained closed—preventing direct observation before the print-date. The Kelly Ditch Trail (see before- and after-fire photos on page 4), a strenuous and magical favorite so dense with trees it's been described as "prehistoric," will likely never quite recover such glory. A drive near the hazy, smoke-laden area several weeks after the fire revealed ashen cinders standing where thick forest once blotted out the sky.

The trio of fires that formed the 2003 firestorm, and caused the President to declare related areas a federal disaster, burned over 25,000 acres of conifer forest. Unlike the area's fairly regenerative oak forest, conifer trees aren't as resilient. Of

Kelly Ditch Trail before the 2003 fires

course, such thick conifer forest—including sugar pines, cedars, and firs—isn't natural phenomenon. A century ago, lightning regularly sparked fires that thinned out the smaller trees. The Kumeyaay Indians used fire to encourage the growth of edible plants and to improve game ranges.

Non-forest areas also suffered devastation. Poway's Sycamore Canyon/Goodan Ranch region (included herein) suffered much damage. Ramona's 10-mile hike at Mount Gower Open Space Preserve was still closed at printing—a trail I can't wait to get back out on.

Kelly Ditch Trail after the 2003 fires

Burned areas provide a good opportunity to learn about nature's resilience. Check with the county's Parks and Recreation departments for guided trail hikes that will educate the public on fire ecology.

San Diego with its diverse landscape has much to be explored. I've outlined hiking trails ranging from mountain terrain, to desert, to coastal shores and open space areas close to the city. Even 60 hikes can't cover all the spirit-lifting nature opportunities in the county. A well-rounded mix has been attempted here, more than enough hikes to allow one per week.

▶ SAFETY MEASURES

No hiking guide would be complete without a word about dangers. Mother Nature in all her wonder can be unforgiving. So while enjoying the outdoors, take a few precautions. Although this is by no means an all-encompassing safety guide, some dangers and how to avoid them are highlighted below.

No valuables should be left in an unattended car. If you must leave something behind, don't invite trouble. Conceal items rather than placing them in plain view.

Please don't hike alone. If you were to become injured or fall ill, vital hours could pass in some remote areas before another hiker happens by. If you insist on going solo, let a trusted friend or family member know where you'll be and you're expected time of return. Consider using two-way radios, and assigning a trail leader and someone to pull up the rear. This is especially important in large groups, to coral older children who may run off ahead of you.

Also, be wary of strangers. Although you're likely to encounter other hikers out to enjoy a brisk workout in the great outdoors rather than harmful criminals, the possibility does exist.

▶ PERSONAL PROTECTION

Sunscreen is recommended to protect your skin everyday, but especially when you are outdoors for extended periods. Overcast days don't provide protection against the sun's penetrating rays. And even in shady areas, sunlight filters through a leafy canopy, or may reflect off surroundings.

Long pants and sleeves can keep plants and insects at bay. Also consider insect repellent—you'll find notations about particularly buggy areas on individual hike stats here in the book.

I recommend traditional hiking footgear. High-top style leather hiking boots with lug soles offer some protection against snake bite and/or bramble or branches that kick up as you walk. You may wish to consult the individual locations for notes on terrain. Slippery, loose soil or rocky ground may require a boot to feel secure, whereas running shoes may be appropriate for a flat, wide open area.

INTRODUCTION

Weather in San Diego is considered mild. The following chart* offers a snapshot of averages for the city.

MONTH	HIGH	LOW	HUMIDITY	RAINFALL	SUNSHINE
January	65	48	63%	2.11 in.	72%
February	66	50	66%	1.43 in.	72%
March	66	52	67%	1.60 in.	70%
April	68	55	67%	0.78 in.	67%
May	69	58	70%	0.24 in.	59%
June	71	61	74%	0.06 in.	58%
July	76	65	74%	0.01 in.	68%
August	78	67	74%	0.11 in.	70%
September	77	65	72%	0.19 in.	69%
October	75	60	70%	0.33 in.	68%
November	70	54	65%	1.10 in.	75%
December	66	49	64%	1.36 in.	73%

Taken from the San Diego Convention and Visitor's Center Bureau Web site

Around the county, you'll find some extreme weather, such as snow at the higher elevations and thunderstorms and flash floods in some of the areas. When hiking in the mountains and/or desert regions, be sure to consult weather reports and be prepared for abrupt changes.

Temperatures in inland regions and mountainous areas can change drastically from day to night. Mild or even hot daytime temps, in the 70s or 80s, say, may dip below freezing at night. If hiking in these areas, you'll want to make sure you have layers of clothing you can peel away during the day and pile on as the air cools.

▶ WILDLIFE

One of the best things about hiking is the possibility of seeing wildlife. Lakeshores allow up-close encounters with cormorants, and you may see a long-necked heron or egret fishing for frogs in a stream. But in addition to the magic of encountering a mule deer grazing in the forest, or seeing the dusky coat of a coyote as it wanders into the early morning brush, you'll need to be alert for dangers as well.

Whether I've noted the possibility of snakes on an individual hike or not, always be wary of them. Rattlesnakes are common nearly year-round in hiking areas, and are especially active in spring. Although rattlesnakes won't seek out contact with humans, they will strike if cornered. Watch carefully where you step, sit, or place your hands. A walking stick, repeatedly tamped against the ground as you hike, is a noise-making method that warns snakes you're headed in their direction. With that advance notice, they're likely to slide off into the brush, or rattle in warning, which puts you on alert.

In the case of a bite, the California Department of Fish and Game recommends removing jewelry near the bite site (for instance, bracelets from near a bite on the arm) to prevent constricted circulation as swelling occurs. Remain calm, and get to a doctor as soon as possible. Consult a first-aid guide or check other reputable resources for specific information about what to do in the case of a bite. There is some controversy over the safe use of snake bite kits.

Also native to the area are mountain lions. In a University of California–Davis report researchers speculate about the lions' use of brush cover since the fires of 2003. Fire fighting was focused around structures, thus saving vegetation close to those structures. Surrounding areas were burned clear. Until vegetation regenerates, wildlife of all sorts may be found closer to structures used by humans, due to the lack of remaining cover elsewhere in which to hide.

Give these majestic 150-pound animals a healthy dose of respect while you tread through their habitat. You'll usually find signs posted in areas where mountain lions live. Make noise as you head through the area (pounding the ground with a stick or speaking loudly), giving the cats warning of your presence so they can move out of your way.

If you do encounter a mountain lion, here are a few helpful guidelines:

▶ **Keep your children close to you, or hold your child. Observed in captivity, mountain lions seem especially drawn to small children.**

▶ **Do not run from a mountain lion. Running may stimulate the animal's instinct to chase.**

▶ **Do not approach a mountain lion. Instead, give him room to get away.**

▶ **Try to make yourself look larger by raising your arms and/or opening your jacket.**

▶ **Do not crouch, kneel down, or bend over. These movements could make you look smaller and more like the lion's prey.**

▶ **Try to convince the lion you are dangerous—not its prey. Without bending or crouching down, gather nearby stones or branches, and toss them at the animal. Slowly wave your arms above your head and speak in a firm voice.**

▶ **If all fails, and you are attacked, fight back. Hikers have successfully fought off an attacking lion with rocks and sticks. Try to remain facing the animal, and fend off attempts to bite at your head or neck—a lion's typical aim.**

INTRODUCTION

▶ INSECTS

Vivid butterflies add color along dusty trails. Nature's geometric perfection is high-lighted on dewy mornings when spiders' webs glisten. Beetles scuttle along as if they own the path. With an attitude of wonder, the tiniest of insects can inspire a sense of awe.

But there are bothersome insects, too. Pesky flies or mosquitoes have been noted on individual hike write ups when they are a common occurrence.

Ticks can also be a problem. Most active between April and October, you may find them clinging to your clothing, looking for a way to reach your skin to access their food source—blood. If you decide to use a tick repellent, the U.S. Environmental Protection Agency (EPA) recommends one designed for use on clothing rather than on skin.

A quick post-hike check in your hair, on the back of the neck, in your armpits, or under the waistbands or socks, is a good idea. According to the EPA, quick removal can aid against Lyme Disease since studies indicate the disease isn't often transmitted during the first 24 hours of a tick's bite. If one has burrowed in, grasp the body firmly (with fingertips or tweezers), and pull straight out. Use disinfectant solution on the wound.

▶ PLANTS

Throughout the book, I describe individual flowers and native plants found on trails and even mention non-native plants that thrive in some areas. Plant communities such as chaparral are also discussed on some hikes. Other beauties, such as wild roses or mulefat bushes that release white tufts to drift through the air in a cottony blizzard are also noted. Hopefully, the descriptions will allow you to identify some of the vegetation. You may want to obtain a book on native plants for even more detail.

You'll also see potentially harmful plants while hiking. Be wary of cactus with its prickly needles that can lodge in your skin. Once in, the needles have a tendency to break off if tugged upon, making removal difficult. A fall into a large stand of cactus near a hiking trail could prove to be a very painful experience. Cactus blooms tempt you to get close, but prevention is the best solution.

Poison oak is the biggest threat to your comfort. Growing in moist areas all over the county (in the shade of trees or near water sources), a close encounter can result in the plant's oil coming into contact with your skin. The oil causes irritation, which can be severe for some individuals.

Identify the plant by its three-leaf structure, with two leaves on opposite sides of the stem, and one extending from the center. (See photo on facing page.) The leaves can grow in attractive boughs twining up around trees. Poison oak can be rosy red and/or yellow-gold, beautiful fall colors that may lure you to touch. Sometimes, the plants grow artfully up over branches, forming lovely arches above the paths. In winter, the leaves fall off, but some oil still remains in the stems. Learn to recognize all parts of the plant.

If you know you've brushed against poison oak, immediately rinsing the contact area with water helps. Although it's a myth that scratching a rash from poison oak releases fluid from the blisters and causes the rash to spread, scratching can cause infection. Also, you might inadvertently spread the offending oil from one site to another. If oil has gotten onto your clothing, the fabric could also spread oil to new areas. Launder contaminated clothing promptly. In some hiking areas, it's easiest to avoid contact by wearing long pants and sleeves. In the hike text, I've tried to notate poison ivy where I've encountered it on individual trails.

Poison oak

▶ TRAIL ETIQUETTE

Whether you're on a city, county, state, or national park trail, always remember that great care and resources (from Nature as well as from your tax dollars) have gone into creating these trails. Treat the trail, wildlife, and fellow hikers with respect. Here are a few general ideas to keep in mind while on the trail.

1. Hike on open trails only. Respect trail and road closures (ask if not sure), avoid possible trespass on private land, obtain all permits and authorization as required. Also, leave gates as you found them or as marked.

2. Leave no trace of your visit other than footprints. Be sensitive to the dirt beneath you. This also means staying on the trail and not creating any new ones. Be sure to pack out what you pack in. No one likes to see the trash someone else has left behind.

3. Never spook animals. An unannounced approach, a sudden movement, or a loud noise startles most animals. A surprised snake or skunk can be dangerous for you, for others, and to themselves. Give animals extra room and time to adjust to your presence.

4. Plan ahead. Know your equipment, your ability, and the area in which you are hiking—and prepare accordingly. Be self-sufficient at all times; carry necessary supplies for changes in weather or other conditions. A well-executed trip is a satisfaction to you and to others.

5. Be courteous to others you meet on the trails.

INTRODUCTION

▶ WATER

"How many bottles are enough? One? Two? Three?! But think of all that extra weight!" Well, one simple physiological fact should convince you to err on the side of excess when it comes to deciding how much water to pack: A human working hard in 90° F heat needs approximately ten quarts of fluid every day. That's two and a half gallons—12 large water bottles or 16 small ones. In other words, pack along one or two bottles even for short hikes.

Bring plenty of water. Your rate of perspiration will vary based on climate, altitude, and individual body chemistry. The higher the altitude, the more water you will need—ditto for hotter weather. Losing between one-half and one quart of water and electrolytes per hour is common when hiking on hot days. Plan ahead by bringing more than you think you'll need. You'll find estimated hiking times per individual location in the book. Drink water even if you don't feel thirsty. Preventing dehydration is better than trying to re-hydrate after the fact.

Some backpackers hit the trail prepared to purify water found along the route. This method, while less dangerous than drinking water untreated, comes with risks. Many hikers pack along the slightly distasteful tetraglycine hydroperiodide tablets (sold under the names Potable Aqua, Coghlan's, and others). Some invest in portable lightweight purifiers that filter out the crud. Unfortunately, both iodine and filtering are now required to be absolutely sure you've killed all the nasties you can't see. *Giardia,* for example, may show symptoms one to four weeks after ingestion. It will have you bloated, vomiting, shivering with chills, and living in the bathroom. But there are other parasites to worry about, including *E. coli* and *cryptosporidium* (affectionately known as "Crypto," and even harder to kill than *Giardia*).

For most people, the pleasures of hiking make carrying water a relatively minor price to pay to remain healthy. If you're tempted to drink "found water," do so only once you thoroughly understand the method, and the risks involved.

▶ HIKING KIT

Here are a few basics for the typical kit:

Ace® bandages or Spenco® joint wraps
Antibiotic ointment (Neosporin® or the generic equivalent)
Aspirin or acetaminophen
Band-Aids®
Butterfy-closure bandages

Compass
Gauze (one roll)
Gauze compress pads (a half-dozen 4 in. x 4 in.)
Benadryl® or the generic equivalent—diphenhydramine (an antihistamine, in case of allergic reactions)

A prefilled syringe of epinephrine (for those known to have severe allergic reactions to such things as bee stings)

Water purification tablets or water filter (see note above)

Moleskin®/Spenco® "Second Skin"

Hydrogen peroxide or iodine

Matches or pocket lighter

Sunscreen

Whistle (more effective in signaling rescuers than your voice)

Pack the items in a waterproof bag such as a Ziploc® bag or a similar product. You will also want to include a snack for hikes longer than a couple of miles. A bag full of GORP (Good Ol' Raisins and Peanuts) will kick up your energy level fast.

▶ LET NATURE TRANSFORM YOU

During the writing of this guide, my family endured many troubles. Getting out among the trees, letting the tangy scents of sage and the sweet songs of native birds fill my senses was a healing salve.

The fall 2003 fires required the book's postponement. Some of my work literally went up in smoke. But closed trails began to reopen, allowing treks onto charred paths for the book's accuracy. And in the spring of 2004, after my oldest son nearly died in a car crash caused by a drunk driver, seeing Mother Nature's regenerative powers helped me scrape past the gloom of uncertainty and stress, and begin a cheerful new season. As charred oak trees formed leafy green wreaths of new growth at their bases, I was inspired to smile again, renewed and invigorated to move past a time of trouble.

Just as prickly caterpillars steal away into darkness and emerge as brilliant butterflies to delight the eye, the earth too emerges brilliant after a season of darkness . . . or simply from winter to spring to summer to fall. And you can, too.

In this book, I've attempted to call attention to tiny, sometimes overlooked details, eager to inspire a child's sense of marvel. Hopefully, the guide not only gives the necessary concrete logistics of directions and maps, but will assist you to continue a joyful relationship with the natural world.

AGUA CALIENTE CREEK TRAIL

▶ IN BRIEF

Around the world in 80,000 steps? Not quite, but the environment ranges from arid to oasis as it travels through dry, sun-drenched country into shady woods along and across the creek—demonstrating the diversity of San Diego's land in one hike.

▶ DESCRIPTION

The trail starts on a rutted, rocky dirt road past an old gate, where the sky is dotted with gliders from nearby Warner Springs Airport. Head up a gradual slope that glitters with mica fragments. After about half a mile, there is a marker for the Pacific Coast Trail on the right. Turn here (it's almost a U-turn) and move southeast; you will begin to descend after a short distance. A view of Lake Henshaw sparkles in the distance, and a rippling wind crosses the vast silence of this desolate area. On hot days, the dappled shade of lemonadeberry and other small trees is a welcome gift. In spring and summer, Indian paintbrush blooms in clusters—the splotches like dollops of red paint on an artist's canvas. Mohave yucca also grows along this stretch. The blooms hang in bunches like jingling bells—but without the merry tinkle.

Approximately a mile from the trailhead, you'll enter a zigzagging section that descends to

▶ DIRECTIONS

Take I-15 North to the CA 76/Pala exit and turn right, heading east for about 34 miles to CA 79, then turn left (toward Warner Springs). Drive about 9 miles to mile marker 37 and park in the turnout on the right. In the second car, continue on CA 79 for a short distance (about 0.1 miles). Turn right onto Lost Valley Road where the sign says "Indian Flats Campground." Travel 4.6 miles on this windy, bumpy road and park at the trailhead kiosk.

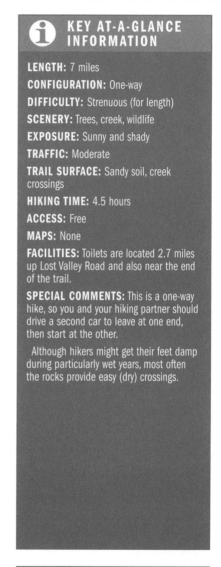

ⓘ KEY AT-A-GLANCE INFORMATION

LENGTH: 7 miles

CONFIGURATION: One-way

DIFFICULTY: Strenuous (for length)

SCENERY: Trees, creek, wildlife

EXPOSURE: Sunny and shady

TRAFFIC: Moderate

TRAIL SURFACE: Sandy soil, creek crossings

HIKING TIME: 4.5 hours

ACCESS: Free

MAPS: None

FACILITIES: Toilets are located 2.7 miles up Lost Valley Road and also near the end of the trail.

SPECIAL COMMENTS: This is a one-way hike, so you and your hiking partner should drive a second car to leave at one end, then start at the other.

Although hikers might get their feet damp during particularly wet years, most often the rocks provide easy (dry) crossings.

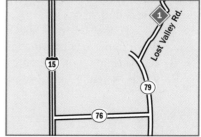

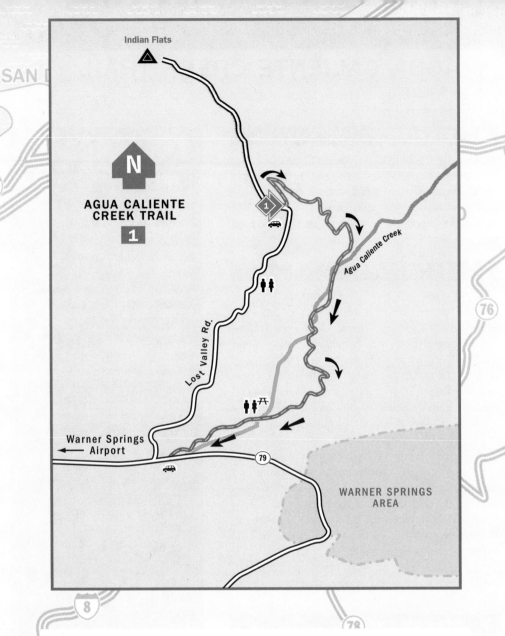

an offshoot trail leading back to Lost Valley Road. Pass this offshoot to continue on a meandering, but generally southward trail. At about 2.5 miles you'll come to oak shade and likely hear the gurgling creek, which soon comes into view.

Follow the trail above the creek, taking any of the small side trails down to the water if you wish. Take a break and listen to the babbling water serenade you—the calming atmosphere makes the relationship between the words "serenity" and "serenade" apparent.

At about 2.7 miles, the creek crosses the trail; there are plenty of flat-topped boulders to make it fairly easy for hikers to get to the other side. Be careful, of course; the wet rocks can be slippery.

Three hundred yards ahead, a group of craggy, lichen-covered boulders on the left mark another creek crossing. Continue a quarter of a mile and cross the stream again.

As on any hike, watch for snakes, particularly around the water and in springtime. You may notice small, crisscrossed tracks made by snakes on the earthen bars in the stream, or spot a hatchling or adult skimming across the water. If you sit still for a few moments you'll hear an amphibious chorus among the chatter of birds, the rustle of leaves in the breeze, and the trickling of water.

Continue in the shade of the oak trees that grow close to the creek, walk through the open meadow, bear right, and continue for another 0.2 miles, then cross the creek again. The trail cuts away from the stream, climbing then leveling, as it heads east on a well-graded, now much wider, route. The route becomes dry, with cholla and prickly pear among the spiny cactus varieties that thrive here. On hot days, even hardy hikers grow a bit weary along this section that is open to the sun and devoid of oaks and the sound of water. You'll begin to descend at about 4.6 miles. Start to bear west to reach the creek for yet another crossing at about 6 miles.

Here, in the shade of oaks, there are picnic tables and a rest room. Look for tiny, funnel-shaped pits in the sandy soil—traps set by antlion larvae to catch passing insects that fall in and become trapped so the antlions can satisfy their voracious appetite for live food. As adults, the nocturnal antlions emerge from their cocoons with transparent, veined wings like a dragonfly's.

The now flat path follows along the right bank of the creek for about a mile, and the sounds of traffic on California 79 grow increasingly louder. Although the dappled shade provides camouflage for them, you may spot mule deer in the area— the noise from the highway can distract them from the sound of your approach. Visitors can get quite close before the beautiful animals turn tail and run.

The trail veers more westward for the last third of a mile and brings you back— tuckered out—to the car you left alongside CA 79.

▶ NEARBY ACTIVITIES

Consider taking a right onto CA 79 from Lost Valley Road. Open from 9 a.m. to 5 p.m., the Warner Springs Airport at 31930 CA 79 is less than a mile away and welcomes visitors. Glider rides are available for a fee, and no reservations are needed on weekends. Call (760) 728-0404 for more information.

ANZA BORREGO STATE PARK:
CALIFORNIA RIDING AND HIKING TRAIL

KEY AT-A-GLANCE INFORMATION

LENGTH: 5 miles

CONFIGURATION: Out-and-back

DIFFICULTY: Moderate

SCENERY: Spring wildflowers, desert vegetation, views of the desert valley

EXPOSURE: Sunny

TRAFFIC: Moderate

TRAIL SURFACE: Sandy soil, some rocky area

HIKING TIME: 3.5 hours

ACCESS: Free

MAPS: At the visitor center, about 8 miles north of the trailhead

SPECIAL COMMENTS: Desert temperatures can be extreme, so dress in layers and bring lots of water. Consider a spring hike (mid-March through mid-April is best) to see the colorful palette of desert wildflowers.

▶ IN BRIEF

The vast desert swallows the sound of the human voice, making encounters with other hikers a surprise. Walking through this arid, yet remarkably vibrant, desert on single-track corridors that aren't easily spotted from the distance, one has the sense of being little more than a dot on the infinite canvas of time.

▶ DESCRIPTION

The California Riding and Hiking Trail moves northeast on flat, sandy soil through chaparral and desert plants such as the prevalent cholla cactus, which reaches with spiny arms toward (and sometimes onto) the trail—a good reason to wear long pants. Be careful of beavertail and hedgehog cactus, as well as pointy Mohave yucca.

In the springtime, the wildflowers are a much-anticipated treat. Peak bloom times vary year to year. If you want to visit during the optimal bloom period, take advantage of the postcard-notification system through the Anza Borrego Desert State Park by writing to: Wildflowers, A.B.D.S.P., 200 Palm Canyon Drive, Borrego Springs, California 92004, (enclose a stamped,

▶ DIRECTIONS

Take Interstate 15 North to the CA 76/Pala exit and drive east for 33.6 miles to CA 79. Turn left, traveling 4.1 miles to S2, where you'll turn right and drive another 4.6 miles to Montezuma Valley Road (commonly called the "Montezuma Highway"). Turn left. Drive 6.8 miles to the trailhead, marked by a yellow-tipped wooden pole on the left. (It is across the street from the slightly better marked "Jasper Trail" on the right.) You can park in a small turnout area at the Jasper Trail and cross the highway, or in the turnout on the left, which is approximately 0.2 miles past the trailhead.

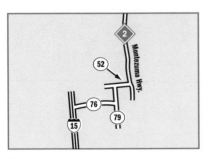

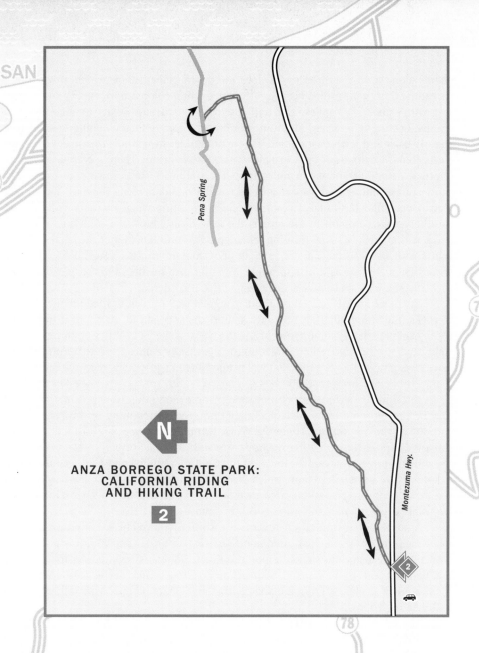

SAN

Pena Spring

N

**ANZA BORREGO STATE PARK:
CALIFORNIA RIDING
AND HIKING TRAIL**

2

Montezuma Hwy.

76

2

78

self-addressed postcard). Cards will be mailed out approximately two weeks before the best prediction of the peak blooming period.

March and April are safe bets for springtime flowers, and you'll find them carpeting the ground in a rainbow of color. Popcorn flower grows close to the ground; the thick groupings look like drifts of snow. Find tiny, yellow desert sunflowers interspersed; the leafless stalks of chia rise several inches and are stacked with balls of tiny blue-violet blooms. Chuparosa with long, leathery green leaves and a dripping spray of tubular lipstick-red flowers often stands alone on the trail edges, as does the desert globemallow, which grows into a spreading bush with ruffled leaves and cupped, coral-colored flowers.

After about 0.3 miles, the trail dips downward and bends to the left, then climbs, bearing right again. The route continues, dipping then climbing, meandering slightly back and forth past an odd variety of boulder formations that make the huge rocks look like dinosaur eggs or stacked sandwich bread. There's even a truck-size "horned lizard" at about 1.5 miles from the trailhead. Rattlesnake weed grows in fluffy clumps, filling in the space around smaller boulders along the trail. You should watch for actual rattlesnakes, too, especially in spring when they are most active. Another snake common to the area is the long, thin whipsnake, which is brown or black with a creamy stripe running its length. If you do encounter this snake, which hunts with its head held up to spot its prey (mostly lizards), you'll likely get little more than a glimpse as it disappears lickety-split into the brush to escape you. However, the shy whipsnake will become aggressive if cornered.

At approximately 1.7 miles, there is a great wall of rock nestled among a "city" of rocks. Encounter another rock city a short distance ahead. At about 2 miles, the route begins to descend more quickly, with a view of the Culp Valley opening on your right, and the Borrego Valley spreading in the distance ahead (north). Puffy clouds leave sweeping shadows on the flat valley floor, the image vaguely reminiscent of photographs of earth from space.

You'll likely begin to encounter more people along this stretch, some of whom may be venturing up from the Culp Valley Primitive Campground or the Pena Spring turnout off the Montezuma Highway. When you reach the bottom, turn left and continue 0.25 miles through a flat washout area toward Pena Spring.

If you prefer, you can continue on the California Riding and Hiking Trail, which extends north for nearly 6 more miles. You could do this entire trail one-way by leaving a car in the large parking area near where the trail comes out on Montezuma Highway, approximately 0.5 miles south of Palm Canyon Drive.

Assuming you turned left toward the spring, you might see running water—most likely in winter or just after rain. Near Pena Spring, flat boulders and sandy banks provide places to sit and enjoy the quiet, boulder-strewn landscape. Here in the flatland, the tissue-papery, white dune evening primrose blooms on prickly, sawtooth-leafed plants. From a distance, the large white blooms with yellow centers look like fried eggs.

The enormous land stretches for miles, the only sounds the wings of a hummingbird hovering curiously close, as if mistaking a colorfully dressed hiker for a nectar-filled flower.

Retrace your steps with a deep appreciation for the desert's unique beauty.

▶ NEARBY ACTIVITIES

On your return trip, be sure to stop for sweet country fruits at Fruits and Gifts, on the corner of CA 76 and Valley Center Road, about 20 miles short of I-15.

BATIQUITOS LAGOON TRAIL

▶ IN BRIEF

Cool ocean breezes and glassy water that laps soothingly at the shore make this a refreshing hike for hotter days, and the trail is easy. Bring your children for an educational experience including a visit to the nature center where friendly guides enjoy sharing information.

▶ DESCRIPTION

Walk southeast on the paved section; you quickly come to the nature center where colorful sea bird cutouts offer still-life clues as to what you're likely to see in full living color ahead—birds, birds, and more birds—grebes, herons, plovers, terns, and more.

Just past the nature center, the dirt trail begins. The lagoon waters gently lap the shore to the right of the path while, beyond it, the freeway incessantly hums. Concentrate on the birds floating along where the ripples take them or ducking their heads beneath the glassy water in search of food. Slow-winged gulls float along on the air. Drawing your attention to the moment, the yellow-beaked gulls seem to carry the traffic noise away on their lazy flight.

Information panels offer facts about surrounding marsh vegetation, like the fleshy pickleweed, rustling cattail, heath, or salt grass. Look closely amid the greenery: a plover rests atop a stick in the mud, and an egret stands so still he seems to be a part of the landscape.

Benches are placed approximately every third of a mile and overlook the lagoon the same

▶ DIRECTIONS

Take I-5 to the Poinsettia Lane exit and drive 0.3 miles east to Batiquitos Drive. Turn right and continue 0.4 miles to where the road curves southwest. Turn right on Gabbiano Lane and drive 0.3 miles to the parking lot at the trailhead.

ⓘ KEY AT-A-GLANCE INFORMATION

LENGTH: 3 miles

CONFIGURATION: Out-and-back

DIFFICULTY: Easy

SCENERY: Native sage scrub; birds and their nesting sites

EXPOSURE: Sunny and shady

TRAFFIC: Heavy

TRAIL SURFACE: Sandy soil

HIKING TIME: 1 hour

ACCESS: Free

MAPS: At the Batiquitos Lagoon Foundation Web site, www.batiquitosfoundation.org

SPECIAL COMMENTS: The nature center offers guided walks and lots of opportunities for learning. The trail does not allow bikes or horses. For more information, see the Web site, or call (760) 931-0800.

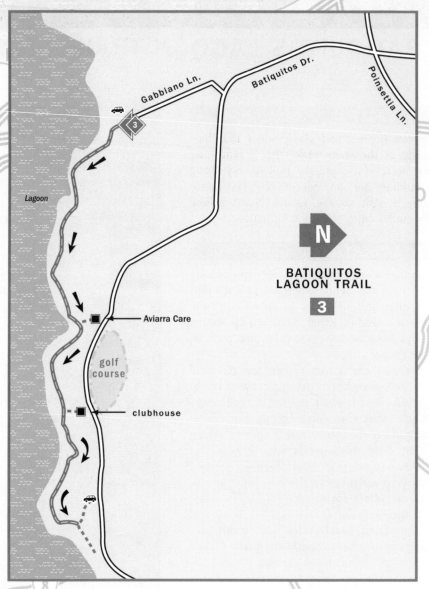

Lagoon

Gabbiano Ln.

Batiquitos Dr.

Poinsettia Ln.

N

**BATIQUITOS
LAGOON TRAIL**

3

Aviarra Care

golf
course

clubhouse

way several houses on the left do, poised to enjoy the rippling water through south-facing windows shaded against the afternoon sun—or perhaps thrown open to allow the musky scent of thriving coastal sage scrub in.

The route bears left through eucalyptus trees with trunks that creak and squeak as the wind pushes them against each other. Note Aviarra Cove on the left (another entrance to the lagoon) and continue east. A golf course appears, with its manicured grass looking almost artificial against this natural setting. Two worlds usually so far apart collide here where golfers in collared shirts

Abundant feathered wonders are a
delight at Batiquitos Lagoon.

wave at hikers in boots or running shoes. Look up into the trees as you head through
this section. Guides tell of great blue herons nesting overhead year after year.

Another quarter of a mile or so brings you past the golf clubhouse and then to
the eastern entrance, which is a good place to turn around. You'll notice a protected
nesting area for the threatened snowy plover and endangered least tern. Be sure to
visit during nesting season, generally May to August.

Enjoy the fresh coastal air and absorb the ever-changing palette of nature's canvas as you retrace your steps. The late afternoon sun forms stripes on the lagoon
waters as though filtered through blinds.

BAYSIDE TRAIL

KEY AT-A-GLANCE INFORMATION

LENGTH: 3 miles

CONFIGURATION: Out-and-back

DIFFICULTY: Easy

SCENERY: View of San Diego bay, coastal sage scrub, wildflowers

EXPOSURE: Mostly sunny

TRAFFIC: Moderate

TRAIL SURFACE: Gravel

HIKING TIME: 1.5 hours

ACCESS: $5 car parking fee; open 9 a.m.–4 p.m. daily

MAPS: Distributed with parking fee at ranger booth

FACILITIES: Rest rooms at nearby Cabrillo National Monument visitor center and also near the lighthouse; for more information call (619) 557-5450 or visit the Web site edweb.sdsu.edu/cab.

SPECIAL COMMENTS: Stay close to children on this trail where cliffs drop to rocky bay shores several hundred feet below in some sections.

IN BRIEF

Cool coastal breezes and sweeping views of San Diego's bay make the Bayside Trail a top choice for warm spring and summer days. Taking in the nearby historic lighthouse and museum lend a historical perspective to this hike.

DESCRIPTION

Its close proximity to the historic Point Loma Lighthouse and the Juan Rodriguez Cabrillo museum make the Bayside Trail a favorite among energetic tourists. Locals come for the pleasant hike with breathtaking bay views.

From the parking area, proceed south across the road (there's a crosswalk) and head up the sidewalk toward the lighthouse. A sign to the west of the lighthouse indicates the route to the Bayside Trail. Follow this asphalt route down to the southwest for approximately 0.3 miles to the marked trailhead where there is a bench from which you can see the bay. Foghorns warn sailboats and military vessels to slow down at regular intervals.

The gravel trail, once used as a military patrol road, gradually descends to the southeast. The valley to your right is furred with thick coastal sage scrub and a grove of mature silver dollar trees stretching up from the cleft base. On the left, the sandstone cliff rises as the trail descends. Numerous whiptail and Western fence lizards scuttle from open sunning spots into the scrub at the side of the trail. Some will dash across the trail then pause to look up with curiosity, as if assessing your reaction to their presence.

DIRECTIONS

From I-5 North or I-8 East, exit at Rosecrans and turn right on Canon, then left on Catalina Boulevard. Follow Catalina Boulevard past Fort Rosecrans Cemetery and drive into the park. Turn left into the well-marked parking area.

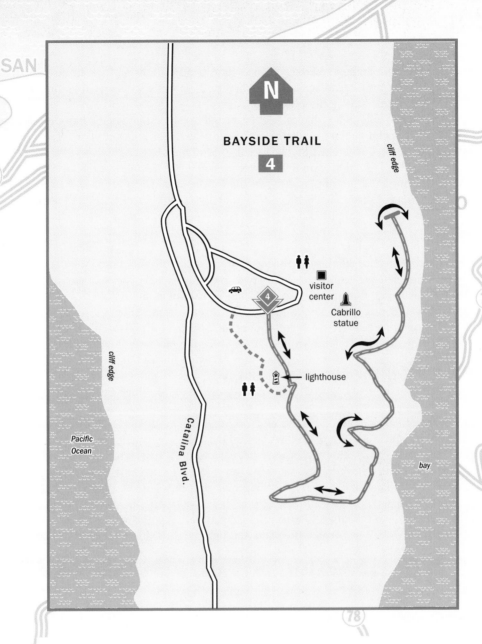

On warm days in the late winter, one can see signs of spring. Like flaming match heads, bright, coral-red Indian paintbrush blooms peep from the ground. The daisy-like flowers of the low-growing *encelia* shrub bloom in yellow profusion all along the trail, while California buckwheat grows in thick, cottony tufts alongside last year's dried brown leftovers.

This eastbound path stretches down about 0.3 miles then bends to the right (north) where the trail levels out for a while. You may hear sea lions barking and catch a glimpse of them frolicking in the water or sunning themselves on the rocks far below. Meanwhile, the blue-green water forever undulates, and sailboats of varying sizes bob peacefully or tilt precariously in the wind. It's not unusual to see a Navy submarine, partially submerged, gliding south like a gray whale among the pleasure boats.

The trail follows a V-shaped inlet in the cliff westward for several hundred yards, past locked metal military bunkers from World War II. There is a drinking fountain at the point of the V where the trail bears left to head back east to the bay view. The trail swings further left, taking you north for approximately 0.25 miles and affording views of rocky shore, the bright blue curve of the Coronado Bay Bridge far to the east, and the buildings of downtown San Diego looking like a child's model in the foreground. Don't let children run ahead or get too close to the edge. The sandstone cliffs can be dangerous.

Another, slightly shorter, inlet takes you into a shaded V where toyon and lemonadeberry bushes thrive, growing in thick, man-tall groupings. Wild cucumber vines with delicate white blossoms creep over the smaller shrubs, and tiny hummingbirds hover, moving this way and that. Be careful as the trail heads east toward the bay—the inlet valley isn't as guarded by shrubs on this side.

Along this last stretch of northbound trail, watch for the succulent tubes of the plant, ladyfingers, along the ground. Also notice the tall, spindly bladderpod and its narrow, pale green leaves and yellow flowers with protruding stamens. The sweet smell of black sage fills the air. You may also note the tangy-sweet smell of wild licorice. Watch for its pale, fernlike leaves growing on foot-high bushes with vanilla-white blooms.

A sign announces the trail's end, and a chain-link fence several yards past the sign blocks further passage. Follow the trail back the way you came, this time uphill. On hot days, you'll enjoy the shady V inlets as you make the gradual 300-foot climb. Slow down and count the succulent agaves growing on the cliff, or spot the creamy white of a cluster of milkmaids peeking out from beneath the cascading ferns that thrive in the cooler nooks of the inlet trail. If you've taken this hike in the afternoon, look at the silver dollar trees in the valley to your left as you head west and up toward the trailhead. The trees catch the wind and light, and the leaves sparkle like coins.

▶ NEARBY ACTIVITIES

Tour the historic Old Point Loma Lighthouse with its spiraling staircase and glassed-in rooms furnished with artifacts and notations that chronicle the lives of the keeper, Robert Israel, and his family. The visitor center offers a museum describing the expeditions of Juan Rodriguez Cabrillo, the first European to set foot on the West coast of the United States. There is also a gift shop, vending machines, and pay-per-view telescopes for viewing the bay.

BLUE SKY TRAIL TO LAKE RAMONA

▶ IN BRIEF

Oak woodland, riparian habitat, coastal sage scrub, and chaparral lend variety to this oasis near the suburbs of Poway. The first 1.5-mile stretch is a flat walk through woodland shade, making the Lake Ramona trail fork a logical turnaround point for anyone not wanting an uphill hike.

▶ DESCRIPTION

Very close to the trailhead, old oaks leave only small patches for a view of the sky, which may make you wonder about the reserve's name. Just enjoy the shaded oak woodland for now. There's plenty of sunlight and blue sky further along the route to Lake Ramona.

At approximately 0.25 miles, you'll notice the "Oak Grove" marker sign for a narrow trail descending on the left side of the wide main trail. Take the side trail down toward the creek that runs along the north side of the trail. You will see an ancient grove of oaks to the left. Sunlight filters through the canopy in glints of gold, producing a hazy, enchanted atmosphere. Baby oaks stand like spindly weeds, while their towering parent trees reach with outstretched limbs as if gathering the seedlings under protective wings. Be careful to stay on the trail to avoid trampling the young oaks.

Listen to the frogs' chorus rising from the water's edge. Their croaking may halt at the sound of intruders. Stand still for a moment and let the sounds of the creek water lull you. There is

▶ KEY AT-A-GLANCE INFORMATION

LENGTH: 5.8 miles

CONFIGURATION: Out-and-back

DIFFICULTY: Easy

SCENERY: Views of Lake Ramona, distant Lake Poway, birds, creek lined with sycamores, oak forest, and a variety of flowering plants along the upper trail

EXPOSURE: Shady with some dappled sunlight on entry trail; full sun on trail to lake

TRAFFIC: Heavy

TRAIL SURFACE: Packed dirt, leaf litter on creekside trail

HIKING TIME: 2.5 hours

ACCESS: Free

MAPS: Free, at kiosk beyond trailhead

FACILITIES: Portable toilets near entry, in picnic area, and above Lake Ramona

SPECIAL COMMENTS: Leashed dogs are permitted. No bicycles or motor vehicles are allowed. Horses permitted on the main trail only—not on the streamside trail. For recorded information, phone (858) 679-5469.

▶ DIRECTIONS

From I-15, exit at Rancho Bernardo Road, and travel east for 3.5 miles. Note that the road becomes Espola Road at the Summerfield intersection. Watch for the "Blue Sky Ecological Reserve" sign on the left, and turn into the nearby parking lot. The trailhead is to the right.

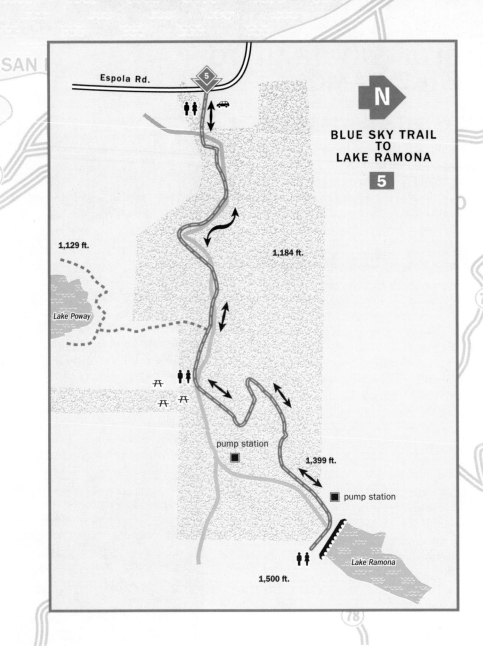

almost always some water in the creek; its depth and the speed of its flow depend on the weather.

Moving back to where the narrower path led down from the main trail, turn right and follow the creekside trail along the streambed, rather than going back up to the main trail. Listen for the rustling of quail running in the thick under-layer of fallen leaves and limbs tangled with the vines of wild roses and poison oak. Alongside the narrow trail strewn with acorns and decaying oak leaves, clusters of fat toadstools sprout from a fluffy orange carpet of leaves, dropped in the fall by the Western sycamores growing immediately adjacent to the stream. Look for toadstools on the other side of the trail, too. There is a variety of them growing here in the cool forest shade. Flattened and having fluted edges, or round as buttons, or shaped like a beanie cap, they burst from the ground, making the moist dirt clump form a tiny earthen fence around the fleshy stems.

The approximately 0.3-mile streamside trail reconnects with the broader main route, where horses are allowed. Pass the side trail, marked Lake Poway, off to the right. Another 0.2 miles brings you to a seldom-used picnic area, also on the right. You've come 0.9 miles from the trailhead. When you reach the sign pointing left to Lake Ramona, take that left turn. The main trail only leads up to a water tower and pump station, and beyond that to the Fish and Game warden's residence, which is not a public area.

Turn left at the Lake Ramona fork in the trail, and emerge into sunlight. Bring drinking water, even in moderate spring and fall weather. You'll hear the roar of the pump station, which comes into view as the trail begins its gradual, 400- to 500-foot ascent to Lake Ramona to the northeast. The trail gets steeper for a short distance, switching back to the west. Don't let the somewhat barren, wide dirt trail fool you into thinking this will be a dull hike. As the path switches back, climbing steadily and gradually to the east, surprisingly delightful foliage awaits. Blooming with tiny white flowers well into autumn, wild cucumber twines up into the branches of laurel sumac growing along the trail. Bright orange clumps of parasitic California dodder, more commonly called "witch's hair," winds around both the cucumber and the laurel sumac. The knotty orange tangles thrive at lower elevations, disappearing as the trail climbs higher. Lupine and a variety of mint begin to appear in bushy tufts along the inner edge of the trail, resting against the rocky face where the road has been cut into the mountain. This hiking route is actually the old Green Valley Truck Trail but is no longer open to motor traffic.

Getting closer to the lake, a wall of rock rises ahead to the east. Here, closer to the water, tobacco tree grows. Its narrow yellow flowers seem to drip from the ends of its spindly stalks. The road becomes asphalt where Blue Sky Ecological Reserve land ends and the Ramona Water District begins. Pause and look to the southwest where the trail etches down the mountain. Lake Poway, about 2 miles away, sparkles in the sunlight. Turkey vultures circle overhead, giving parents an opportunity to tease any children who are tuckered out from the hike—maybe those vultures are circling above a weary hiker who collapsed! You will pass another pump station on the left, then a few yards ahead the asphalt road bends to the south. Avocado groves growing above the road come into view and, as you reach the top, the plumed branches of commercially grown palms line the hillsides to the southeast.

To work out a different set of muscles, or just for fun, walk backward on this last, smooth stretch of asphalt. Once at the top, enjoy a view over the vast blue waters of Lake Ramona from the guardrail. The dense quietude is interrupted only by the quack and flutter of ducks gathered near the lake's shore, or by an occasional small airplane heading east to the airstrip in Ramona.

The trip back down feels entirely different than the climb, which can be tiring, especially in warmer weather. But passing breezes will cool your damp shirt as you make your way back down with the help of gravity. My family likes to stop at the picnic area on the way out of the Reserve, eating the lunch we pack for the trip.

▶ NEARBY ACTIVITIES

A treat for both the eyes and the taste buds can be found at the Hamburger Factory Restaurant. Old-fashioned memorabilia, a friendly neighborhood atmosphere, and an inexpensive menu that includes barbecue chicken, ribs, and much more than the name implies offers diners an experience sure to satisfy. From Blue Sky Ecological Reserve, turn left onto Espola Road. Drive for approximately 3 miles and turn right on Twin Peaks. At about 0.8 miles, turn left on Midland. The restaurant is about a half mile down on the right at 14122 Midland Road, Poway. Call (858) 486-4575.

CLEVENGER CANYON NORTH:
EAST TRAIL

▶ IN BRIEF

This tasking hike includes 3 straight miles of up-hill walking on a sometimes narrow trail. Experienced hikers will enjoy the challenge, with its rewarding views.

▶ DESCRIPTION

In autumn one can see the bright yellow-orange leaves of the Western sycamore trees stretching out in the valley below CA 78 like a ribbon, marking the Santa Ysabel Creek, which runs through Clevenger Canyon. Fall and spring are the best times to visit because of the moderate weather, but foot traffic can be heavy even in the heat of summer.

The trail begins by descending west between two large boulders, then continues down well-placed natural rock steps. Walk west a few yards and the trail bears to the northeast. The leisurely descent, with two short footbridges, lulls unknowing visitors into believing that this will be an easy hike—and easy it is on this 0.3-mile section down to the creek, which flows year round. There is no bridge to cross the creek, and the area can be dangerous after heavy rainfall. Water rushes around the granite rocks, and towering oak, cottonwood, and sycamore trees, becoming almost stagnant in summer. This shady respite at the valley's bottom is a good sack-lunch spot, with huge, lichen-covered granite rocks for sitting. Be careful of poison oak, which is plentiful here. Rattlesnakes are also common.

The real workout begins where the trail picks up on the other side of the shaded creek.

▶ DIRECTIONS

Take CA 78 east to the staging area, which is on the left, 5.3 miles east of the San Diego Wild Animal Park. Turn left (north) into the lot and park. The trailhead is located at the northeast corner of the parking area.

ℹ KEY AT-A-GLANCE INFORMATION

LENGTH: 8 miles

CONFIGURATION: Out-and-back

DIFFICULTY: Strenuous

SCENERY: Views of the San Pasqual Valley and the canyon; large boulders

EXPOSURE: Sunny, with a small section of shade at creek

TRAFFIC: Moderately heavy

TRAIL SURFACE: Packed soil, often loose and slippery

HIKING TIME: 4 hours

ACCESS: Free

MAPS: Available free, call (858) 674-2270

SPECIAL COMMENTS: Tote in lots of water, especially on hot days. Not suitable for children under ten, and even then, use your best judgment as to a child's ability. For that matter, this route is unsuitable for anyone who isn't used to uphill hiking.

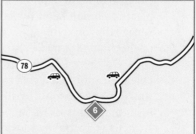

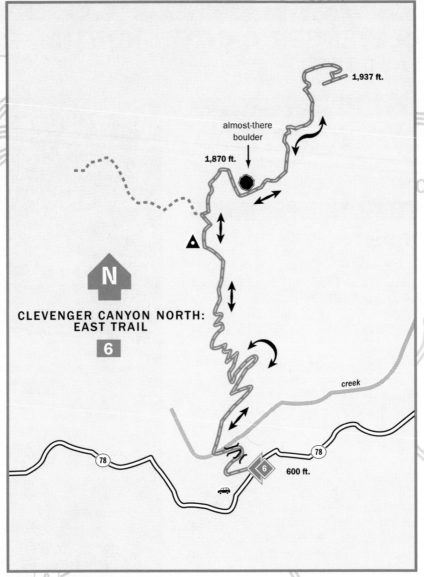

SAN

1,937 ft.

almost-there
boulder

1,870 ft.

N

**CLEVENGER CANYON NORTH:
EAST TRAIL**

6

creek

78

78

6

600 ft.

The narrow footpath stretches in a zigzag pattern up the mountain, with only a few, tiny shade spots provided by a curved boulder or an overgrown chamise or scrub oak, prominent members of the southern mixed chaparral plants common here. While resting for a moment in the shade, listen for the squawking of scrub jays, or for the repetitive chirp of the small brown towhee that also makes its home here among the chaparral.

On these unprotected trails winding up the canyon, cautious parents may be fearful that a gust of wind will blow small children right off the trail, which is one reason why I don't recommend bringing young children along. Also, the trail narrows in areas to less than a foot in width and is framed by scratchy chaparral and foxtail and drops to a semi-sheer edge in this steeply sloped canyon. The trail also winds through bush and rock, which makes getting separated from exuberant children who may run ahead an issue. If you do bring children, use two-way radios and establish rules beforehand about one adult staying at the front of the pack and one at the rear. Mountain lions and bobcats use this canyon to travel, and, although hikers aren't likely to see these shy animals, safety is never a wasted effort.

At approximately 2.5 miles up the canyon trail, the path edges around the west side of the mountain to a small plateau that overlooks a beautiful patchwork display of the Escondido orange groves far below.

Continue north on the trail for 0.2 miles where another trail that heads west intersects the main trail. Pass this by and continue for approximately 0.3 miles. Here, a huge, precariously positioned outcropping of granite boulders marks an "almost-there" point—only one more mile to the end. Many turn back here, though, because the trail all but disappears. A sign pointing straight up through a tunnel in the shed-size

A rock doorway to the west begins the descent into Clevenger Canyon.

boulders seems a practical joke. Agile climbers can clamber up through the stone tunnel and over the rock formations. But for the less adventurous, retracing one's steps a few yards reveals an overlooked side path that runs a slippery and steep, but more logical, route up to the continuing trail. Take this slippery section of loose dirt north up around the boulders then head east. Another 15 to 20 minutes of flatter trail brings you to a cluster of huge, house-size sitting rocks marked "viewpoint."

From this 1,937-foot vantage point, CA 78 twists by like a narrow snake in the distance. Listen closely for the barely discernible hum of cars, a reminder that civilization is nearby. High on the north side of the canyon, the environment can feel desolate. Because of its narrowness and poor condition, the Northeast Clevenger Canyon Trail—especially here at the very end—isn't as heavily trafficked as some other trails that are also close to the urban inland. Before reaching this stretch, many hikers will have grown weary of the climb and turned around. One can rest here on a granite rock warmed by the sun and feel all alone, with only the scuttling sound of curious Western fence lizards to distract you from your thoughts. Enjoy the solitude—and catch your breath—before retracing your steps.

▶ **NEARBY ACTIVITIES**

The San Diego Wild Animal Park is 5.3 miles west on CA 78. Twenty times larger than the San Diego Zoo, the 1,800-acre facility offers visitors a chance to see animals in herds, living as if in their natural habitat. For more information, call (760) 747-8702, or visit the Web site at www.sandiegozoo.org/wap/visitorinfo.

CLEVENGER CANYON SOUTH:
EAST TRAIL

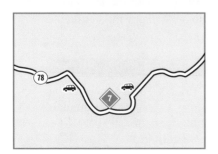

IN BRIEF

This moderately steep ascent makes for a vigorous aerobic workout on well-defined trails beside which chaparral, manzanita, and aromatic sage grow. The view from the top is sprawling, but it's the serene atmosphere and easy return that make this somewhat taxing hike a favorite.

DESCRIPTION

If you hike mid-afternoon, the sunlight will be over the crest of the canyon, leaving the trail a cool, shady path that begins to work its relaxing magic just a few yards from the parking lot. That's not to say that this hike is a breeze. Gentler than the steeper slopes on the northern trails of Clevenger Canyon (see page 29), the path is, however, an uphill one, ascending 1,000 feet. But as you head up into the canyon along a southbound trail edged with sagebrush, toyon, and manzanita, the sweet smells of nature drift back to you on light gusts of wind. Birds such as the towhee and scrub jay call for you to join them far away from the stresses of your busy life. Even adults may find themselves responding to a wrentit hidden in the bush, then waiting to hear a return call from this tiny bird you're more likely to hear than see.

Unlike the open trails accessible via the north staging area, the south trail is framed closely by the chaparral that covers the hillsides with an almost impenetrable thicket. You'll see coyote droppings on the trail, proving that even animals use the easier man-made route upon emerging from the dense shrubs to hunt in the cover of darkness.

DIRECTIONS

Take CA 78 east to the staging area, which is on the right side of the road, a little more than 5 miles east of the San Diego Wild Animal Park. Turn right (south) into the paved lot and park.

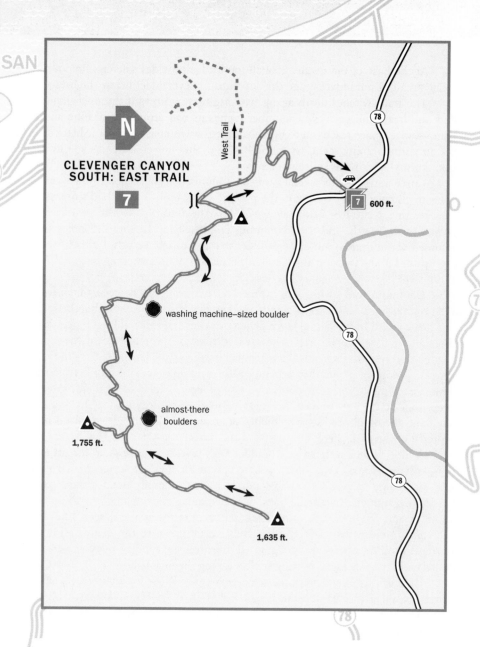

CLEVENGER CANYON
SOUTH: EAST TRAIL

7

N

West Trail

7 600 ft.

78

78

78

78

washing machine–sized boulder

almost-there
boulders

1,755 ft.

1,635 ft.

SAN

5

5

76

From the start, the southeast trail switchbacks up to the 0.5-mile
point, where a marker signals the beginning of the west trail—one you may
choose to hike another day. Continue moving on a stretch of south trail
descending into a wooded ravine shaded by live oak. A fallen tree blocks the
path, but an arch in the trunk fits neatly over the trail for small children to
walk under. Adults can stoop or shimmy over one leg at a time. On hotter
days, this is a wonderful place to stop and rest in the cool shade. Though
you've come only about 0.7 miles, the steady ascent plays tricks on your
sense of distance, making it seem you've hiked twice as far.

At the base of the ravine, a small footbridge provides safe crossing over a seasonal stream. Even in wet years, the stream runs several feet below the bridge.

The trail switches north again, working its way upward through granite boulders and heavy foliage. Wild cucumber twines its way around manzanita and bushy laurel sumac. Vines reach out to brush your legs as you pass. Aromatic black sage fills the air with its minty scent. In spring, its light blue flowers extend like tiny orchids from knotty outgrowths on slender stems.

Curve northeast for several yards on a more open trail. Look to the west, where you can glimpse your car back in the parking lot. It looks like a child's toy, as do the cars buzzing 1,200-feet below along CA 78. The trail dips to the southeast again, curves to the north, and then continues southeast for another 0.5 miles or so. A rounded washing machine–sized boulder marks a sharp westward switchback, leading upward a few yards to the 1-mile trail marker, then switching back again to the southeast.

Continuing on, a wide, flat, exposed stretch overlooks Ramona to the southeast then narrows again near the 1.5-mile marker, heads south uphill, then bends to the northeast again. In the fall, look for lichen growing atop tufts of bright green moss on the slanted edges of the trail. The moss thrives in the moisture of the chaparral-shaded trail edge and spreads like a blanket on the earth. The paler caps of lichen are actually groups of plants that depend on the symbiotic relationship between fungus and algae. Fungus fibers surround a section of algae, which needs their protection to keep from drying out. In turn, the algae carries out photosynthesis, making food for itself and the fungi. You'll see splotches of lichen, looking like dried bird droppings, on most of the rocks here, not just atop the moss.

A little farther, a trailer-size boulder with several smaller, good-for-sitting boulders at its base marks the "almost-there" point for the first scenic view. Follow the trail several yards to a marker that points right to identify the 150-yard path to a 1,755-foot summit. Catch the view of the sycamores—bright green in spring and summer, and yellow in fall—stretching like a colorful Chinese dragon's tail through the canyon and across CA 78, then amble back down to the main trail and head north. A meadow opens up on a gradual downhill slope where the yucca plant's tall stalks mark the way like flowering staffs, earning the nickname, "Our Lord's Candle."

Here, in the open space, the wind gets gusty. Pause for a moment where manzanita grows near a boulder, its small leaves rustling. Listen closely. The smooth branches make a faint whistling sound, similar to a harmonica, when they rub together in the breeze.

The 2.2-mile marker comes as a surprise. At the base of a large boulder— where those who have run ahead will be perched to beckon slower hikers—you can look back across the canyon to the parking lot below and marvel at how this is the longest 2.2 miles you've ever hiked. Trail fatigue gives way to playful exuberance as the setting sun reveals a brilliant red-orange palette in the Western sky.

If you've begun the trail in mid-afternoon to avoid the direct sunlight, any dalliances now pose a threat. As the sun begins to set on the ocean's horizon, coyotes yip. But don't worry too much. Although it could easily have taken over two hours to reach the trail's endpoint, little more than an hour is needed for the return hike.

However, to be on the safe side, allow an hour and a half. Although swift steps and gravity carry you downhill almost like flowing water, the fun ends if an attendant starts honking his car horn from the parking lot below. I know, because my family has raced down the mountain with darkness closing in, bats flitting about in the twilight, and the fresh dung of coyotes awakened from their day naps marking the trail.

▶ NEARBY ACTIVITIES

The San Pasqual Battlefield State Historic Park, about 3 miles west on CA 78, honors soldiers from the Mexican-American War of 1846. The site is meant as a reminder of the human ideals, passions, and actions that can lead to bloodshed. The 50-acre park features a visitor center with video and interpretive displays and a 0.5-mile nature trail and picnic tables. In December, volunteers reenact the battle; the performances are complete with costumes and cannon firing. Open weekends from 10 a.m. to 5 p.m. For more information, visit www.ci.escondido.ca.us/visitors/uniquely/battle.

CLEVENGER CANYON SOUTH:
WEST TRAIL

LENGTH: 2.8 miles

CONFIGURATION: Out-and-back

DIFFICULTY: Moderate

SCENERY: Views to the east and west; views of nearby orange groves, chaparral, and birds

EXPOSURE: Mostly sunny

TRAFFIC: Moderate; less traffic than trails accessed via the northern trailhead

TRAIL SURFACE: Packed soil

HIKING TIME: 2 hours

ACCESS: Free

MAPS: Free, call (858) 674-2270

SPECIAL COMMENTS: Parking lot at staging area is open sunrise to sunset. Use caution when bringing children because the single-track trail moves along some steep open slopes.

IN BRIEF

A steady, though fairly gradual, ascent makes this a brisk workout on well-defined trails where chaparral and aromatic sage provide a thick habitat for birds. The birdsong-filled atmosphere makes this hike seem farther into wilderness than it actually is.

DESCRIPTION

A small trail leads off the east edge of the parking lot then south past a gate before heading up a steep hill. The first half mile is shared by hikers taking the southeast trail (for details, see Clevenger Canyon South: East Trail, page 32). The trail splits near a cluster of flattish boulders with an eastern view, offering a good place to pause.

Once you've had your fill of the view and have caught your breath from the initial 350-foot ascent, head right. The westward trail affords a view of the parking lot and your tiny car. The route will continue to climb steadily but gradually, zigzagging upward for an additional 550-foot gain in elevation.

After you've walked a short distance on the first westward stretch, the path turns sharply left and levels for an easy southward stroll, then heads right again, moving gradually uphill. The narrow trail is angled, slanting downhill in spots, as if the mountain wants to throw you off. Watch your step, but enjoy the scenery and the sage-scented air. You'll continue on this westward stretch for about 0.25 miles then will head left again, toward the southeast. A 1-mile marker pole

DIRECTIONS

From southeastern Escondido, take CA 78 east to the staging area, which is on the south side of the road, just a little more than 5 miles east of the San Diego Wild Animal Park. Turn right (south) into the paved lot and park.

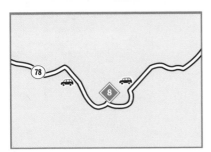

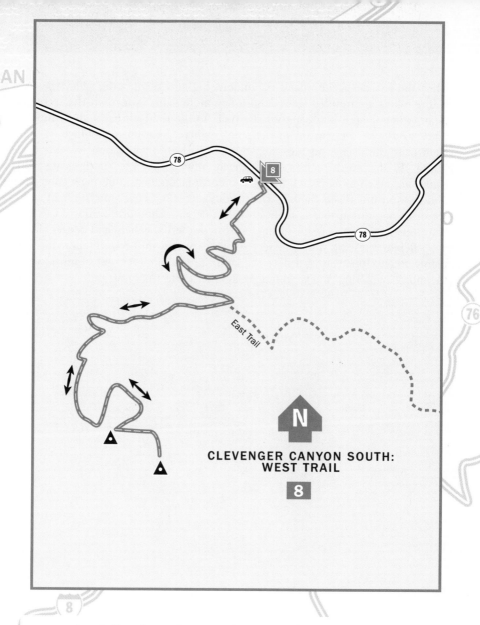

CLEVENGER CANYON SOUTH:
WEST TRAIL

8

appears just before the trail turns right again to head west for only a short distance before bending southeast.

The slopes along this section of the hike are grassy, with less chaparral, leaving open spaces where spring flowers paint the landscape in splashes of color. Blooms start to appear as early as February, continuing well into summer when the hike seems more difficult because of the inland San Diego County heat. Yucca grows here, too. Amid the round clustered boulders, a single, smooth-skinned rod rises from the center of the spiky-stemmed plant. In late summer, the stalk matures, shooting upward two to three feet and erupting into purple-tinged bloom.

The trail continues to zigzag for a bit, then turns west toward a view-point where a large flat boulder beckons picnickers. On winter mornings when the sun heats the inland mountains, fog may blanket the valleys below, providing hikers a shrouded view. After a few more yards you reach the second viewpoint, where a split boulder ends the trail. To the right of the boulder, the vantage point overlooks the canyon to the south, where great-lobed boulder resembles a giant bear, rhinoceros, or pig—depending on whose imagination is doing the conjuring. To the north, across the highway, notice that the south-facing canyon's slopes are much more barren than these north-facing ones, offering a good example of how exposure affects habitat. The south-facing slopes get more sunlight and heat, requiring vegetation that is more drought-tolerant. The north-facing slopes get less sun, thus retaining more life-giving moisture for ferns, lichen, and denser chaparral.

Before retracing your footsteps for an easy downhill return, allow the quiet of nature to envelope you as it does the land. Birds share their gift of music and send the mind wandering. You've found yet another perfect natural spot.

COWLES MOUNTAIN LOOP

▶ IN BRIEF

A pleasant trek through chaparral and streamside, punctuated by an *exhalation peak*. Cowles Mountain is a favorite of locals seeking an aerobic workout with a view.

▶ DESCRIPTION

From the trailhead kiosk, head up the wide trail running southwest past houses on the right, and crossing a narrow section of Big Rock Creek. The trail bears left through chaparral. A rainbow of wildflowers blooms in spring. Even the wild grasses seem to bloom, their dusky mauve broom-heads swaying in the wind.

The route switchbacks to climb, and the sounds from nearby homes and the park begin to fade. But evidence of people still lingers. An aluminum can cast haphazardly into the bush makes a shady home for beetles; the shiny shell of a deflated Mylar balloon hangs from a tree that snagged it.

At approximately 0.8 miles, the chaparral becomes denser, and partially buried boulders jaggedly line the trail. You may see quail running in the brush or hear the fluttering hum of their wings as they fly off, spooked by your presence. A short distance further, Mother Nature offers you a seat on a stone.

At about a mile, you'll come to a trail junction where the Mesa Road Trail leads off to the left. Pass this by for now, and continue climbing. After another half a mile, you'll reach a T where the trail meets a wide, gravel service road. Turn

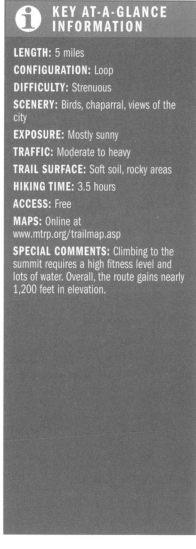

▶ KEY AT-A-GLANCE INFORMATION

LENGTH: 5 miles

CONFIGURATION: Loop

DIFFICULTY: Strenuous

SCENERY: Birds, chaparral, views of the city

EXPOSURE: Mostly sunny

TRAFFIC: Moderate to heavy

TRAIL SURFACE: Soft soil, rocky areas

HIKING TIME: 3.5 hours

ACCESS: Free

MAPS: Online at www.mtrp.org/trailmap.asp

SPECIAL COMMENTS: Climbing to the summit requires a high fitness level and lots of water. Overall, the route gains nearly 1,200 feet in elevation.

▶ DIRECTIONS

Take CA 52 east to the Mission Gorge exit and turn right, heading west approximately 0.3 miles to Mesa Road. Turn left (south), and travel 0.4 miles to a point just past Big Rock Park and find a space on the right, along the street.

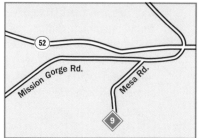

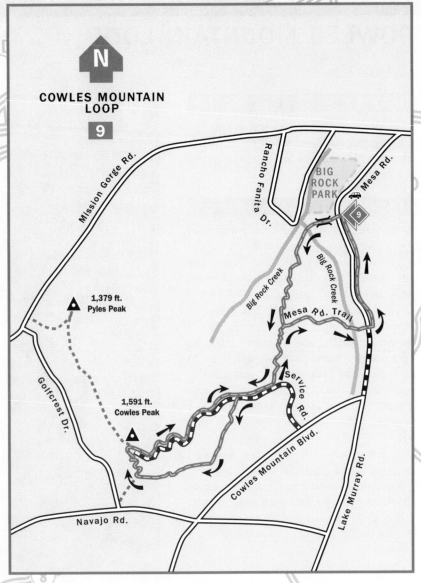

COWLES MOUNTAIN LOOP

9

N

Mission Gorge Rd.

Rancho Fanita Dr.

BIG ROCK PARK

Mesa Rd.

9

15

76

Big Rock Creek

Big Rock Creek

Mesa Rd. Trail

1,379 ft. Pyles Peak

Service Rd.

Golfcrest Dr.

1,591 ft. Cowles Peak

Cowles Mountain Blvd.

Lake Murray Rd.

Navajo Rd.

8

78

right here. On hot days, the breeze will cool you as you make the 0.2-mile walk up the road. When you see a sign for "Barker Way Cowles Mountain Trail," veer left onto this narrow downward-sloping path. After gently descending the trail, bordered by thick chaparral, take the right-hand trail that begins climbing toward the west. Lake Murray comes into view in the southwest while a sea of roofs stretches out to the southeast. The path climbs through a few very steep sections alternating with long, level sections.

Lake Murray sparkles beyond the rooftops of San Diego.

Another 0.3 miles brings you to an intersection where you'll turn right and climb steep switchbacks to the peak of Cowles Mountain. Here's where you are likely to encounter lots of other hikers accessing a shorter route to the summit from Golfcrest Drive.

At the 1,591-foot summit, there are lovely views in all directions—clear to the Santa Rosa Mountains in the northeast and the Catalina and Coronado Islands in the west. Information panels provide details.

When you're ready, either go back the way you came or take the service road on the northeast side of the summit. Watch for cyclists pushing their mountain bikes up the steep ascent—then be wary of them coasting back down. It's approximately 0.8 miles back to the T where you originally turned onto the service road. Make a left here, back into the chaparral. Retrace your steps half a mile to the marked "Mesa Road" route that you passed on the way up. Hang a right here, traveling through the thickets of tall chaparral that shade the path. Cross the stream and turn left onto Mesa Road. Follow the road, with the stream to your right, for approximately 0.7 miles back to the trailhead kiosk where you parked your car.

CREST CANYON OPEN SPACE PRESERVE LOOP

KEY AT-A-GLANCE INFORMATION

LENGTH: 1.5 miles

CONFIGURATION: Loop

DIFFICULTY: Easy

SCENERY: Trees, wetlands

EXPOSURE: Mostly sunny

TRAFFIC: Moderately heavy

TRAIL SURFACE: Sandy soil

HIKING TIME: 1 hour

ACCESS: Free

MAPS: None

IN BRIEF

Scarcely more than a stone's throw from the beaches of Del Mar, Crest Canyon is a pleasant walk through coastal sage scrub that can seem a world away from the hustle and bustle of a busy life.

DESCRIPTION

The trail opens through scrub brush to the right of the sign, continues west for several yards, then makes a rather abrupt drop off a wide earthen step. If making a two- to three-foot drop seems ungainly, there is a narrow path to the right that will lead you more gradually past this point.

Past the drop, continue west, descending rapidly on semi-slippery dirt surface. At the bottom, about 0.1 mile from the start, turn right onto the well-defined flat canyon path. You'll hear the roar of traffic on busy Del Mar Heights Road and perhaps the sounds of people going about their day in and around the houses along the bluff on the right. An airplane may buzz by. . . . Tune your ears to the life within this small canyon strip instead, letting the sounds of civilization drift away as you attend the gentle sound of chaparral rippling in the breeze.

A few large pines dot the area, mingling with some much smaller trees. You'll see lots of lemonadeberry with its leathery green leaves, along with bushy coyote brush—covered in tiny white flowers in the fall. California buckwheat is also prevalent,

DIRECTIONS

Take I-5 to Del Mar Heights Road and head west. Drive approximately 0.4 miles to Durango Drive and turn right. Houses line the right side of the street. The canyon is hidden on the left, dropping beyond the scrub growing close to the road. Follow Durango Drive 0.2 miles and park at the end, near the Crest Canyon Open Space sign.

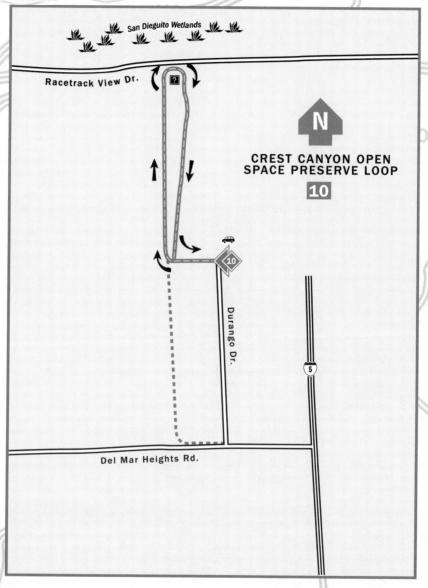

San Dieguito Wetlands

Racetrack View Dr.

N

CREST CANYON OPEN SPACE PRESERVE LOOP

10

Durango Dr.

5

Del Mar Heights Rd.

bursting with snowy bloom-tufts that turn pink and rust as summer ends and fall settles.

The canyon is a haven for bird life. Mockingbirds run through their mimicking repertoire, sounding colorful compared to the repetitive, bouncing call of the wrentit, and the heckling of common ravens that soar overhead, their black bodies stark against the sky.

At approximately 0.5 miles, the trail creeps along near homes on the left, their back fences made of chain link and other open-weave materials for a view of the canyon. Dogs in these yards sound the alarm, the barking message traveling along the canine alert team. Late in the day, you're likely to encounter nearby residents who exercise their dogs here—big and little, bushy and smooth—their looks as varied as those of the owners who walk them.

It's about 0.75 miles to the north end of the canyon, which runs up against Racetrack View Drive. You can see San Dieguito Wetlands just across the narrow road. If you have the time and inclination, you can cross the pavement for an even better look at the water, stretching like a curvy snake over the land. Fishing is allowed from the shoreline, but the most prevalent fishers are huge groups of waterfowl near the shore. Startled by visitors, the birds pad from the muddy banks down into the water in a flapping, splashing riot to the relative safety beyond the water's edge. There, they float effortlessly along in the shallows, with reflected clouds and the blue of sky brushing the surface like a Monet painting.

An information panel tells more about the wetlands and area restoration efforts. From here, either return the way you came, or turn right past the sign. You'll find the narrower path that heads south and closes the canyon loop. This narrow trail briefly heads uphill, adding a little more exertion to this easy hike. The chaparral grows closer along this single-trek route, lending a more desolate feel despite the closeness of the city.

Return to the sloping entry path and make your way back up to the road. Or, if you want to walk another half a mile, continue south on the main path all the way to Del Mar Heights Road. Turn east on the dirt path, then make a left at Durango Drive and head back to your car.

On your return hike, be sure to stop periodically and look to the north. Views of the sky above the canyon bluffs can be awe-inspiring. Often, hot-air balloons launched from nearby Encinitas will drift lazily by. The scenery is especially pretty in fall or early spring, when the sun shines but the air is crisp, with puffy clouds holding moisture. Consider coming here at the end of the day, when the setting sun washes the sky in pink, and the clouds to the west glow yellow.

▶ NEARBY ACTIVITIES

Consider turning right on Del Mar Heights Road and continuing the short distance to the coastline in Del Mar. You'll be able to see the ocean almost immediately after turning. In fall and winter, it isn't too difficult to find a parking spot with access to the beach where Del Mar Heights Road hits the coast.

CUYAMACA RANCHO STATE PARK:
STONEWALL PEAK TRAIL

▶ IN BRIEF

This easy, well-graded path leads to a panoramic view and many perching spots on sun-warmed rocks. This is the most popular hike in Cuyamaca Rancho State Park and was one of the first trails to reopen after the 2003 wildfires. Except for the last two-tenths of a mile to the final peak, the trail is safe and easy even for smaller children. But it's mostly couples you'll see here—out for a romantic stroll through nature.

▶ DESCRIPTION

This 4.4-mile hike starts with a wide upward grade through oak forest. Prior to the fire, autumn leaves covered the trailside ground like a foot-thick fluffy golden blanket. Trees here are regenerating growth, and leaves will eventually carpet the ground again.

Heading up this steep section, which has the most rapid elevation gain of this hike, you'll come to the first viewpoint at approximately 0.15 miles—a good spot to catch your breath. Look out over the gaping valley where thick tree forest used to be. You can now see clear to the top of the mountain, the bald rock top a craggy, exposed target for the hike.

The trail leads around to the northwest and

▶ DIRECTIONS

Take I-8 East past Alpine; exit onto CA 79 and proceed north for approximately 13 miles to the Paso Picacho campground on the left. You will pass the Green Valley campsite and the park headquarters before reaching Paso Picacho. Turn left and pay the day-use fee at the ranger station. Park in the lot on the right and proceed on foot across CA 79 to the trailhead, which is at the edge of the road, directly across from the ranger station. If you prefer free parking, there is designated roadside space 1 mile south of the trailhead.

ⓘ KEY AT-A-GLANCE INFORMATION

LENGTH: 4.4 miles

CONFIGURATION: Out-and-back

DIFFICULTY: Moderate

SCENERY: Regrowth from fire devastation; interesting rock formations and panoramic views; spring and summer wildflowers; woodpeckers, crows, and other birds year-round

EXPOSURE: Mostly sunny

TRAFFIC: Moderate to heavy

TRAIL SURFACE: Packed, sooty dirt with a couple of short rocky stretches

HIKING TIME: 1.5 hours

SEASON: Year-round, with rare closings in winter if snowfall is heavy

ACCESS: $6 day-use fee

MAPS: Available at ranger stations

FACILITIES: Toilets at the parking area in Paso Picacho and on the south side of the ranger station

SPECIAL COMMENTS: For more information call the park at (760) 765-0755, or visit their Web site at www.cuyamaca.statepark.org.

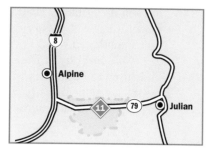

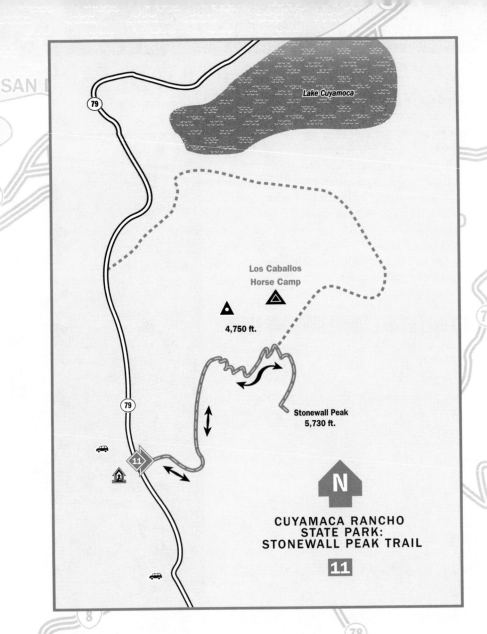

Lake Cuyamoca

Los Caballos
Horse Camp

4,750 ft.

Stonewall Peak
5,730 ft.

N

CUYAMACA RANCHO
STATE PARK:
STONEWALL PEAK TRAIL

11

opens to a view of the sparkling, blue-gray waters of the 110-acre Lake Cuya-maca in the distance. Manzanita is beginning to regenerate along this stretch, though years will pass before they are large enough for hikers to run a palm over smooth, red wood.

Woodpeckers call out like Woody the cartoon character. The resilient birds used to flutter, nearly hidden among the towering incense cedar growing thickly along this stretch. Flying jerkily overhead, they land in clear view now, upon charred branches.

The trail begins to switchback here as it approaches the peak. Each zigzagged section gains elevation at a barely discernible rate, making this an easy stroll for inexperienced hikers or families. Replaced after the fire, split-rail fencing at various junctures encloses the path on this well-maintained trail. Some areas are a little rocky, making for a good lower-leg workout as you pick your way across the rounded, bowling ball–sized rocks.

Halfway to the top, a wall of granite comes into view, explaining the trail's name. Quartz and granite boulders jut out toward the path, providing a rich landscape to excite visitors' imaginations. You might see a smiling seal's face or a dinosaur nestled in the next corner of the switchback trail.

Nature has provided flat-rock seats for hikers to rest at various junctures, but most hikers won't need to stop for anything other than chatting or enjoying the view. If you do take a break, the absolute quiet will astound you. Voices are lost on the wind. Another group of hikers may startle you as they round a bend, but even on busy weekends in spring when the flowers carpet the ground in purples, yellows, oranges, and reds, long stretches of golden silence are only occasionally broken by fellow hikers who disappear from earshot quickly on the winding trail. Although no markers are posted for 2 miles past the trailhead, it would be difficult to get lost on this well-defined path. You may be surprised to encounter the marker telling you Stonewall Peak is just 0.2 miles to the right. You won't feel as if you've traveled 2 miles on this climbing hike designed for ease.

At the marker, it may be unclear as to which way to go. After following the trail to the right, you will scale a few feet of rock before coming to solid footing. Where trees once blocked the edge, the expanse gapes off to the left, so be careful. If you have younger children along, consider stopping at the base of the peak.

The final section of the peak trail is a few steps up the rock ahead and slightly to the left around a bend in the stony surface. Man-made stone steps lead upward along the edge. A steel handrail offers security as you pick your way up to the small viewing platform at the top. The 5,730-foot elevation features a panoramic view. To the east, the Salton Sea extends like a vaporous blue stripe on the horizon. On clear days, you can see the ocean stretching out into the distant west. Lake Cuyamaca looks more like a thimble of water than a well-stocked fishing spot from here.

Once other state park trails have opened, you can choose to veer right back at the trail marker for a much rougher descent alongside Los Caballos horse camp, then head west on California Riding and Hiking Trail to hike a total of 2.5 miles from the peak back to the parking lot. Descend the way you came to enjoy the easy switchback route, and you'll coast down quickly.

▶ NEARBY ATTRACTIONS

For a quiet getaway in rustic cabins with Jacuzzi tubs and fireplaces, drive 25 miles east on I-8 to the Live Oak Springs exit. Live Oak Springs Resort is a favorite of honeymooners and couples celebrating their wedding anniversaries. Various packages offer hearty meals at the resort restaurant, which is well worth the trip even without a cabin stay. Call (619) 766-4288 or visit www.liveoaksprings.com.

DALEY RANCH:
COMBINED TRAILS

KEY AT-A-GLANCE INFORMATION

LENGTH: 6.2 miles

CONFIGURATION: Loose figure 8

DIFFICULTY: Easy

SCENERY: Chaparral, ranch house, rock formations, ponds

EXPOSURE: Sunny

TRAFFIC: Moderate to heavy

TRAIL SURFACE: 1.1-mile asphalt entry, then silt; some rutted areas

HIKING TIME: 3 hours

ACCESS: Free

MAPS: Available in kiosk boxes at trailhead

FACILITIES: A portable toilet is located near the ranch house.

SPECIAL COMMENTS: Open daily from dawn to dusk. Hikers must yield to bikers and horseback riders. On Sundays, a free shuttle runs from the parking lot to the ranch house every half hour from 8 a.m. to 4 p.m. (trimming off the 1.1-mile asphalt entry walk). Guided hikes can be scheduled; phone (760) 839-4680 for details.

IN BRIEF

This easy combined-trails loop offers the best of Daley Ranch, with its wide-open spaces, rustling grasses, and ponds. The description below takes you back to a central point, allowing you to leave out sections for a shorter hike if you prefer.

DESCRIPTION

Start by heading north under the arching "Daley Ranch" sign and begin walking up the paved road. On Sundays, be careful of the shuttle, which uses the 1.1-mile "Ranch House" entry road to deliver visitors to the picnic area. On foot, you'll encounter signs identifying native plants such as Ramona lilac and Mohave yucca on this uphill stretch of asphalt. As the city sounds fade, listen for the piercing cry of a hawk soaring overhead, the repeating *chip-chip* call of the California towhee as it forages in the bushes, and the high-pitched buzz of masses of cicadas. The insects' whirring sound is similar to the ominous warning of rattlesnakes—also found at Daley Ranch and most often seen in spring and summer. Keep your eyes open for them. On a recent visit, one large snake didn't bother to rattle a warning at all as it cautiously slithered past.

A bench sits in the shade on the right at about a third of a mile, after which the road begins sloping downhill. You'll spot a side route on the right leading to Middle Pond. This short path goes past the water to another trail that you will take on your way out. If you can't wait, take a side trip to the pond now. The connection of

DIRECTIONS

Take I-15 to the El Norte Parkway exit. Travel east on El Norte for about 4 miles to La Honda Drive and turn left. Follow La Honda Drive to the top and turn left into the dirt parking area directly across from the entrance gate to Dixon Lake.

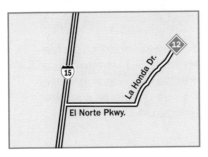

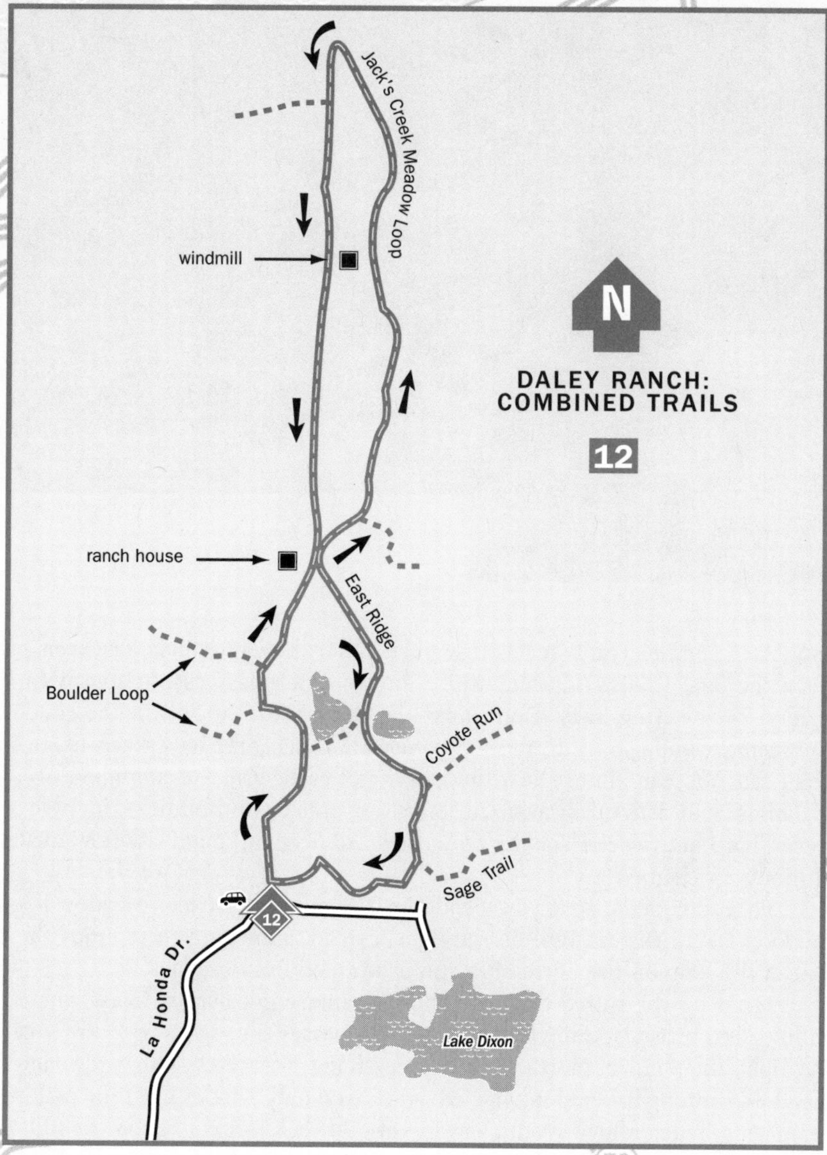

many trails that cross one another within Daley Ranch make this an easy area to explore. Consult the official trail guide, available at the parking lot kiosk, for a complete map.

Assuming you've stayed on the asphalt road, you'll pass Engelmann and live oaks and large laurel sumac bushes closely enough to enjoy their spotty, welcome shade. The road continues north, bending to the west where it meets the entry and exit for the Boulder Loop, which you might want to explore another day. Also growing along the road is the light-purple flowered fleabane, coastal sagebrush, black sage, and even some wild roses.

Perhaps Jim Henson found his inspiration for the Muppets at Daley Ranch.

At 1.1 mile, you'll reach the green ranch house, which has been preserved since the late 1800s. Adjacent to the house is a grassy picnic area with benches shaded by towering oaks. Don't miss the opportunity to loll in the shade, letting your mind wander back to what this historic ranch may have been like a hundred years ago. You can almost hear the mooing of cattle and the pounding of hoofbeats as hands rounded up strays. Close to the house, outbuildings include a metal-roofed barn and several smaller structures. All original, many are now unstable and off-limits to visitors.

From the picnic area, you'll spot the 3.4-mile Jack's Creek Meadow Loop. Enter the loop via an eastern trail on the right instead, allowing you to enjoy the breezier part of the loop on the north after you're warmed from exercise.

Head up the rutted dirt path through sparse eucalyptus forest where swaying willows and oaks also mingle. The wide trail passes the entrance to the Sage Trail on the right then moves north. Spotty tree shade alternates with wide views of the meadow, running lower along the left. Approximately 2 miles from the parking lot, an east-facing bench allows restful viewing of odd rock formations on the hill. Look for one easily recognized boulder nicknamed "Muppet Rock." Its stony profile looks like the late Jim Henson's creations.

Turn the corner of the Jack's Creek Meadow Loop at approximately 2.7 miles, near the chain-link boundary, and head in the opposite direction (south) along the straightaway. The wide trail undulates over hills and dales for a short while. You'll pass a rusting windmill on the left and see the Hidden Springs route on the right—another of the many Daley Ranch trails you may wish to eventually explore. Continuing south, notice the hushed whisper of the grasses murmuring nature's secrets in the breeze, and see the road stretch out before you, seemingly endless before the restful-looking ranch house finally comes into view again.

Jack's Creek Meadow Loop closes back at the picnic area, marking 4.5 miles of hiking so far. Head south past the ranch house and take a trail on the left marked "East Ridge," which will take you gradually uphill toward the southeast.

In creative imaginations, boulders on the hillside to the left of the trail take on the shape of giant frogs or other creatures. The path begins sloping downward again. After walking about half a mile on the East Ridge route, you'll likely notice water out to the right. This is Middle Pond. A side trail leads past and hooks up with the asphalt "Ranch House" road you entered on. You'll remember seeing the entry to this short connector path on your way in. Skip the side route and continue southeast on East Ridge. A short distance ahead, you'll see water on the left, closer to the trail. As the water recedes seasonally, you'll notice single-trek side trails to the water's edge, forged by other hikers.

Past the water lies a steep hill, but the 0.1-mile distance up makes grip-soled shoes and a willful burst of speed and energy all that's necessary to reach the top, where the path levels. You'll spot the secondary trail, Coyote Run, on the left, and also see Lake Wohlford Dam in the southeastern distance. When the trail begins heading downhill again, watch for a rutted side trail on the right. This is the Creek Crossing Trail and your way out. Unmarked as of this writing, there is, however, a botanical sign that reads "Giant Needle Grass" where the trail begins. Head right. You'll soon see Lake Dixon on the left. Eventually, the dirt parking area where you left your car also comes into view. On weekends, the sounds of merrymakers picnicking at adjacent Dixon Lake will serenade (or perhaps annoy) you as you head toward the parking lot and end your hike.

▶ NEARBY ACTIVITIES

Who can resist a trip to Escondido's nearby Mayflower Dog Park to watch man's best friends interact? The new canine-friendly park is located at 3420 Valley Center Road, Escondido. Call (760) 839-4691 for more information.

DALEY RANCH:
ENGELMANN OAK LOOP

KEY AT-A-GLANCE INFORMATION

LENGTH: 3.5 miles

CONFIGURATION: Loop

DIFFICULTY: Easy to moderate

SCENERY: Scenic views to the north, east, and southwest; Engelmann and coast live oaks; and a variety of wildlife

EXPOSURE: Half sunny and half shady

TRAFFIC: Light on weekdays; heavy weekend use

TRAIL SURFACE: Packed earth with some rocky and rutted areas

HIKING TIME: 3 hours

ACCESS: Free

MAPS: Free in well-stocked map box at Cougar Pass Road entrance

SPECIAL COMMENTS: Open daily from dawn till dusk. Hikers must yield to bikers and horseback riders. Volunteer naturalists also plan guided educational tours. Tour schedules vary, and reservations are required; call (760) 839-4680 for details.

IN BRIEF

This truck-width trail is well graded and offers views to the north, east, and southwest. With only a few steep areas and the promise of quails, a variety of other birds, and even the glimpse of a coyote, Engelmann Oak Loop is an easy-to-get-to choice for a family day hike.

DESCRIPTION

To reach the Engelmann Oak Loop, start by heading east on the Cougar Ridge Trail, which begins at the Cougar Pass Road entrance. Follow this wide, flat trail shared by mountain bikes, horse riders, and hikers through a meadow dotted with young coast live oak trees. Stands of laurel sumac, with its unique red-tinged leaves, add color to this flat section of Cougar Ridge.

At approximately 0.6 miles, the trail dips and heads toward the southeast, continuing through a stretch of mature oaks with branches reaching across the path, nearly blocking the sunlight. Except on the hottest summer days, hikers wear sweaters on this chilly, shaded section where runoff water crosses the path after rainfall. One hears the steady hum of honeybees, hinting at hives hidden in the branches towering over the path. Curiosity sometimes causes hikers to stand here with their necks bent, straining to locate an elusive hive above.

At just under half a mile from the entrance, the first trail marker comes into view, identifying

DIRECTIONS

Take I-15 to CA 78 east. Follow CA 78 east to the traffic signal, which intersects Broadway, and turn left. Travel north on Broadway for approximately 4 miles and go right on Cougar Pass Road. One mile up this twisting dirt road, you will see the Daley Ranch entrance gate on the right. Park in the turnout on the left.

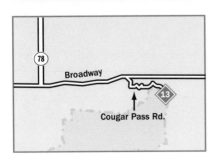

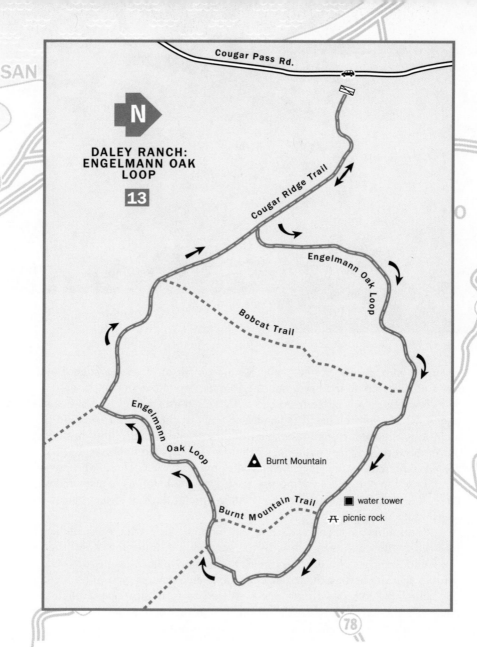

DALEY RANCH: ENGELMANN OAK LOOP

13

Cougar Pass Rd.

Cougar Ridge Trail

Engelmann Oak Loop

Bobcat Trail

Engelmann Oak Loop

▲ Burnt Mountain

Burnt Mountain Trail

■ water tower

⊓ picnic rock

76

78

the Engelmann Oak Loop intersection. Bear left and take this path to the north, through steep sections littered with fist-size rocks. These uphill sections get the heart pounding and are interspersed with short plateaus that allow a moment's cool-down as hikers pace forward. Yucca is prevalent here, blooming in white profusion during spring and summer, then receding to spiky green skeletons in fall and winter.

The trail bends to the east, opening into meadows sprinkled with tall oak trees. Closer to the trail, small oaks offer cover for the Western scrub jays that flutter by, giving hikers a glimpse of vibrant blue wings before they

Stretching oak branches form a canopy of shade over the trail.

disappear into the larger trees. Stop for a moment to enjoy the silence and clear views of Fallbrook to the north and the Palomar Mountain area to the east.

Few hikers will be seen on the trail. This northern end of 3,500-acre Daley Ranch, which was purchased for multiuse trails by the City of Escondido in 1996, often feels desolate. Horses leave behind their fertile evidence, but most riders are out in the very early morning hours. Mountain bikers yield to horses, but few bikers are encountered on the Engelmann Oak loop trail itself. Those who are on foot should yield to both bikes and horses. Posted signs ask visitors to stay on designated trails, but many bikers are off-trail, pedaling up and down the steep bike tire–wide illegal trails beyond the loop.

Continuing the hike, Engelmann Oak loop intersects with the secondary 1-mile trail called "Bobcat," then curves to the southeast. A water tower and the twisted trunk and branches of a dead oak mark the halfway point. Coyotes are common in the hills that rise beyond the trail to the east. Even at midday, you will sometimes see the contrasting gold tint of their sandy-colored coats as they lope through the dark green yucca and rosy laurel sumac on the hillside. Coyotes are more often spotted in the early morning, though, or during the dusky hours near sunset.

Just beyond the water tower, a flat grouping of rocks that visitors call "Picnic Rock" offers a partially shaded respite. Don't relax too long, though. Hikers, who recline like lizards, are often lulled by the sun-warmed rocks. The spot's nickname changes to "Nap Rock," at a snore's notice. Nodding off means you miss out on the twittering of wild finches often seen among the velvety gray-green sage that grows thick across the western meadow.

A few yards ahead, a trail marker identifies the northern end of Burnt Mountain Trail, which is 0.4 miles of trail you won't want to miss. Use this cutoff to shave about 0.5 miles off the hike and reconnect with the Engelmann Oak Loop on the other end. Or, if you're feeling energetic, pass up this northern entrance, continue around the loop past the intersecting Hidden Springs Trail, and enter Burnt Mountain Trail from the southern end. From this entrance, a slight ascent on this path that is little more than a ditch takes you up into the chaparral where quails run into the bushes and cottontails hop for cover. Iridescent green and red hummingbirds rest in groups on the branches of an Engelmann oak that stands out among the shrubs beyond the path. Some hover close, curious about the visitors. After the short upward slope, Burnt Mountain Trail is downhill in this direction, making it an easier hike than the northern entrance. Pick up the Engelmann Oak loop trail near Picnic Rock and retrace your steps around to the southwest, or trek back up over the shorter 0.4-mile Burnt Mountain Trail.

Continuing on the Engelmann Oak Loop, ancient coast live oak trees are prevalent and they reach out with twisting branches to block the sunlight, keeping this area moist into summer. The trail will be muddy in fall, winter, and spring. Beyond the trail, the song of crickets echoes among the cottage-size boulders that form stony villages among the trees.

At the southwestern tip of the Engelmann Oak Loop, a marker signals the intersection with Cougar Ridge, which will complete the loop for this hike. Go right to make your way back to the entrance and the parking area. This rutted downhill ridge trail travels above an untouched valley and its lush green view. Beyond that, the city of Escondido stretches out in the southwest. Pass the southern entrance to Bobcat Trail and continue down through the shady trees. After heavy rainfall, water runs along the east side of Cougar Ridge for a short stretch, leading up to the marker that led you off onto the Engelmann Oak Trail earlier, to make the loop. Continue past it this time, retracing your steps along the path that now leads northwest, back to the heralding buzz of the beehives still hidden in the trees, and up across the flat meadow to the gate.

▶ NEARBY ACTIVITIES

If your legs are still craving a workout, try some family fun at the Ups and Downs Roller Rink. Drive south on Broadway a half a block past the CA 78 intersection and turn left into the parking lot at 862 North Broadway in Escondido. Call (760) 745-5966 for more information.

DISCOVERY LAKE AND HILLS LOOP

KEY AT-A-GLANCE INFORMATION

LENGTH: 2.5 miles

CONFIGURATION: Loop

DIFFICULTY: Moderately easy

SCENERY: Waterfowl, lake, surrounding homes

EXPOSURE: Sunny

TRAFFIC: Moderate

TRAIL SURFACE: Asphalt and soft soil

HIKING TIME: 1 hour

ACCESS: Free

MAPS: Online at www.ci.san-marcos.ca.us/departments.asp?id=2825

SPECIAL COMMENTS: It can be quite hot on these trails that are mainly surrounded by blacktop streets in a new neighborhood where vegetation isn't well-established (at this writing). Bring water and be prepared for lots of kids, joggers, and dog walkers around the lake itself—especially on weekends.

IN BRIEF

An urban trek, varying in appearance from park to greenbelt to open chaparral, this loop is used by locals as an exercise route. The small lake holds a bevy of coots and ducks that gather at a dock for those who feed them.

DESCRIPTION

Follow the asphalt to the right of the parking lot for just a few steps to reach the lake. From the bridge watch a heron or egret fishing, their long legs and necks the perfect tools for wading and dipping their beaks into the water, seemingly effortless in their habits.

Alive with ducks, coots, fish, and frogs, the small lake glistens brightly in the sun. Despite the nearby houses and human activity, the animals appear at ease in an environment surrounded by tall reeds where they can easily retreat into hiding. According to City of San Marcos information, bobcats and deer have also been spotted. Early morning hours are probably best if you hope to see these more elusive creatures.

Across the bridge, you'll come to a downward sloping dirt trail that curves left toward nearby houses. Oak trees offer some shade on this section. A side trail leads off to the left, but you'll pass this by and continue along with the creek on the right; off-season, the creek may be dry.

At about 0.75 miles, you'll come to a paved road that heads into the housing complex. Be careful of cars as you cross a street then hook up

DIRECTIONS

Take CA 78 to San Marcos Boulevard and drive west for 0.5 miles to Bent Avenue, then turn left. Almost immediately, Bent becomes Craven. Drive 0.3 miles and turn right on Foxhall. Proceed another 0.2 miles and you'll run right into the parking area for Lakeview Park.

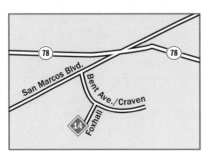

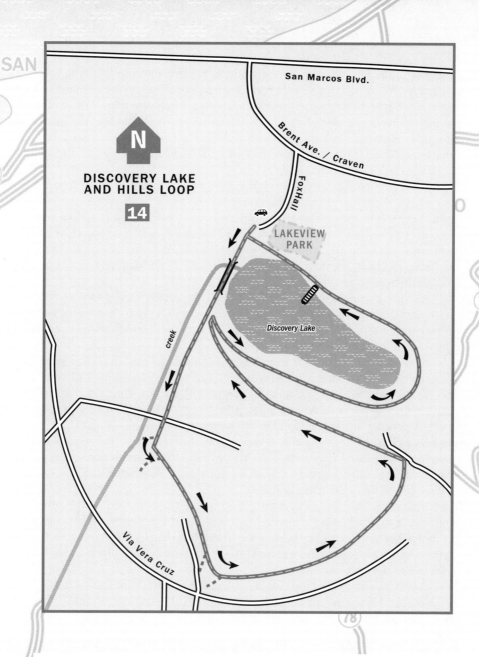

San Marcos Blvd.

Brent Ave. / Craven

Foxhall

LAKEVIEW PARK

Discovery Lake

creek

Via Vera Cruz

with a dirt path on the opposite side. Ignore that right fork that crosses the creek, and instead go uphill. Bushy chamise grows abundantly. Also notice straggly tree tobacco, with its smooth bluish-green leaves and cylindrical yellow-green blooms that may appear year-round. Its spindly limbs sway in even the gentlest of breezes—which may be all you get inland on hot days.

At a little over a mile, the trail splits off into the housing tract on the right. Take the left path uphill; do the same when the path splits again. These plentiful side routes make the paths convenient for nearby residents.

Continue to the left, heading up the moderately steep hill that curves to follow the route of Via Vera Cruz, the vehicle road down below. Here, on the chaparral-covered hillside, the hike begins to feel more rural. After little more than a third of a mile, the path delivers you along the ridge with views to the east, beyond the quarry, and into the mountains. On clear days, you really can see forever—or close to it. Unfortunately, clear skies mean a view of brown smog as well, hanging like a dismal tent above the earth in the distance.

You'll pass houses very close on the right. Continue east, moving downhill with the view on the left and fenced backyards on the right. When you reach pavement again, head left to go back down the hill toward the lake. If you're feeling adventurous, you can choose to hook up with the Double Peak Trail to the right. Leading about one mile to an elevation of 1,644 feet, Double Peak affords panoramic views of the Pacific Ocean to the west and of the mountains to the north and east. A park and an equestrian area for Double Peak are being planned.

Assuming you've turned left, Discovery Lake comes back into view. The blue-green oasis contrasts sharply with the barren quarry's ugly rock-crushing machines hulking in the distance. When the quarry is silent, the tooting calls of coots squabbling on the water grow louder.

At the bottom, head right for a 0.8-mile trip around the lake before going back. The pleasant loop is lined with berry bushes and native plants (marked with signs), and the calls of the coots splashing on the lake fill the air. The ashen-colored birds splash noisily about, quarreling endlessly among themselves—but they're also very smart. According to a recent study by a University of California, Santa Cruz biologist that was published in the journal *Nature,* the birds can count and keep track of how many eggs they lay. Coots who don't win prime nesting spots don't give up their chance to have offspring either. They lay their eggs in other birds' nests—maybe that's what all the squabbling is about!

Where the lake loop bears left, making the curve around to the other side, you'll see a rickety-looking conveyer track and metal machinery sticking up against the open sky on the right (behind the chain-link fence). This is part of a rock quarry—quiet on weekends, the hulking stillness of the machinery adds a ghost-town feel to the environment.

Just before the lake loop completes itself, a pathway leads down to the dock. Perhaps spend a few moments there, peering into the sparkling depths, then head back to your car with the coots calling ever more quietly as you depart.

▶ NEARBY ACTIVITIES

If you're hungry after your hike, turn left on San Marcos Boulevard and drive for about a mile to San Marcos's restaurant row. Cuisine runs the gamut from Thai to Mexican to seafood.

ELFIN FOREST RECREATIONAL RESERVE: BOTANICAL LOOP

▶ IN BRIEF

This well-maintained trail offers a quiet, easy loop that makes it perfect for any age. The Botanical Trail Guide published by reserve staff lends an educational element that makes this foray into nature even richer.

▶ DESCRIPTION

To access the Botanical Loop Trail, head south across the cement creek bridge as if to hike the Way Up Trail, which is marked by a sign near the reserve's entrance. Once across the cement, turn right and walk uphill for about 200 feet. The trail bends east, connecting with the Botanical Loop Trail after about a half a mile.

Take a Botanical Trail Guide from the box on the left and head down the hill onto the loop trail. Numbered marker poles correspond with informative paragraphs in the guide. From this direction, begin with number 27, hollyleaf cherry, a bushy plant with holly-like leaves. Have you ever wondered about the reddish-brown fruit often seen hanging from small oak trees? No, they're not oak apples, oak oranges, or any other oak fruit. Number 22 identifies the ping-pong–sized balls as

▶ KEY AT-A-GLANCE INFORMATION

LENGTH: 1.5 miles

CONFIGURATION: Loop (balloon with string)

DIFFICULTY: Easy

SCENERY: Native plants, described with interesting facts in the Botanical Trail Guide, available in box at the trail's start

EXPOSURE: Sunny and shady

TRAFFIC: Moderate

TRAIL SURFACE: Earthen path, leaf litter

HIKING TIME: 30 minutes

ACCESS: Free

MAPS: Available at kiosk near parking area

FACILITIES: Rest rooms near parking area

SPECIAL COMMENTS: The reserve is open from 8 a.m. to 45 minutes before sunset every day except Christmas. The Botanical Loop is designated hiking only and includes a creek crossing. For more information about the reserve, call (760) 753-6466, ext. 147.

▶ DIRECTIONS

From I-15, take the Auto Parkway exit and head west (left if coming from the south on I-15), then turn left on Ninth Avenue, at the traffic signal. Proceed on Ninth, across the Valley Parkway intersection; the road bends sharply left. Ninth Avenue becomes Hale here. Continue on Hale to Harmony Grove Road. To stay on Harmony Grove you must make the first two left turns, otherwise, you'll end up on Enterprise or Kauana Loa. Past the second left turn, proceed on Harmony Grove Road to Elfin Forest Recreational Reserve, which appears on the left 1.5 miles past Country Club Drive. Turn left into the parking lot.

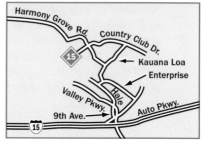

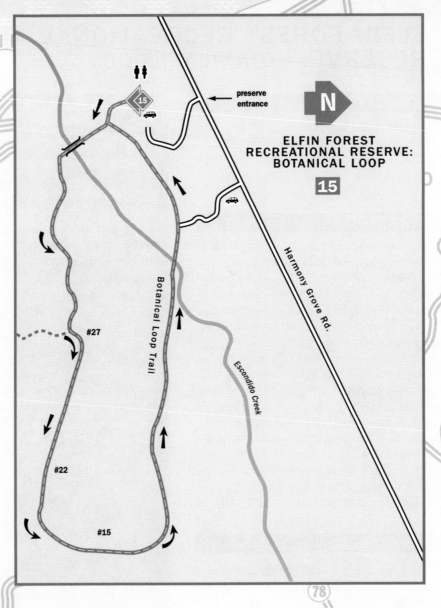

preserve
entrance

N

**ELFIN FOREST
RECREATIONAL RESERVE:
BOTANICAL LOOP**

15

Botanical Loop Trail

Harmony Grove Rd.

Escondido Creek

#27

#22

#15

76

78

"galls" made when the California gall wasp lays its eggs in the stem. When the larvae emerge from their eggs, they release a chemical that causes the stem to swell into a gall. The gall provides food and protection for the tiny wasps.

Some plants aren't included in the guide, like the clumps of thistle, with their "milk"-splattered leaves, that grow on the right of the trail almost from the start of the loop. The tangy, herbaceous scent of black sage wafts up as the trail levels and heads east through the partial shade of oak trees growing along the path.

Continuing, the route turns left (north), beginning the loop formation, and gradually descends at an easy grade. The ground is rocky through this section but not dangerously so. There is a bench in the shade at number 15. Mountain mahogany is the featured plant here. The tree or shrub is found on the dry hillsides of San Diego County and provides shade for a variety of other plants.

Make the curve to the left and head west, moving into the denser shade of thicker oak forest. You'll hear the creek running, and within a few more steps, will spot the water gurgling over the large, flat rocks you'll use to cross. Heed the posted warnings. The creek crossing is a natural one and can be dangerous when the water is high. Use common sense and caution.

Once across, notice the arroyo willow, with its feathery blooms that turn to cottony fuzz. You'll see a road on the right that leads to a second parking lot. Pass this and continue west to the reserve's entrance. The path ahead is framed by placed rocks and pole-and-cable fencing, leading the way back to the marker for the Way Up Trail, the entrance, and your car.

ELFIN FOREST RECREATIONAL RESERVE: WAY UP TRAIL

IN BRIEF

Delicate spring flowers in this rugged terrain may surprise you. The "Way Up" Trail earned its name because of its uphill tread.

DESCRIPTION

Immediately past the information kiosk, you are likely to hear the water rushing down Escondido Creek. It flows year-round from nearby Lake Wohlford all the way to the Pacific Ocean. It is fitting that water is an element here in the 750-acre Elfin Forest Recreational Reserve since the reserve was developed by the Olivenhain Municipal Water District as part of the Olivenhain Water Storage Project currently underway.

At the sign marked "Way Up Trail" head south across a cement creek bridge, then turn right and head uphill for about 200 feet. The trail curves left (east). Miner's lettuce grows all around. The leaves are edible and supposedly taste good raw, or boiled and salted. Don't try eating the fleshy succulent that grows here. There is no collecting allowed on reserve land, but the plants were easy picking for Native Americans and others traveling through the area in days gone by.

DIRECTIONS

From I-15, take the Auto Parkway exit and head west (left if coming from the south on I-15), then turn left on Ninth Avenue, at the traffic signal. Proceed on Ninth across the Valley Parkway intersection; the road bends sharply left. Ninth Avenue becomes Hale here. Continue on Hale to Harmony Grove Road. To stay on Harmony Grove you must make the first two left turns, otherwise, you'll end up on Enterprise on Kauana Loa. After the second left turn, proceed on Harmony Grove Road to Elfin Forest Recreational Reserve, which appears on the left 1.5 miles past Country Club Drive. Turn left into the parking lot.

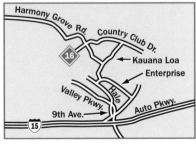

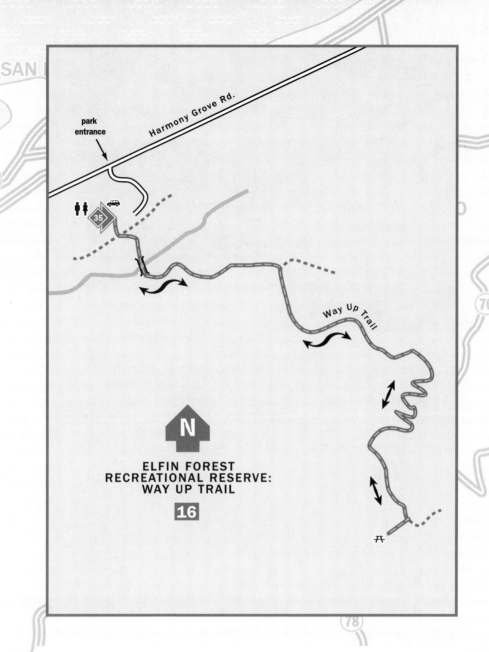

park
entrance

Harmony Grove Rd.

Way Up Trail

N

**ELFIN FOREST
RECREATIONAL RESERVE:
WAY UP TRAIL**

16

Thick and green in early spring, with a tiny white flower blooming in the center of the leaf bowl, the succulent's color turns a rusty red as spring's moisture evaporates in the summer heat.

Also prevalent here are the pearly purple-white blooms of morning glories. The trailing herb that is common to Southern California's chaparral twines over rocks and bushes, forming a lacy backdrop for the monkey flowers' bright splashes of red and orange. Another bright, orange-red flower found here is fringed Indian pink, with its slashed ("fringed") petals and sticky, hairy stems that discourage ants and other small crawling insects.

You'll share the Way Up route with lizards that dart away from their rocky sun spots as you pass.

At approximately 0.5 miles, the route bends to the right (south) again and meets with the Botanical Loop Trail. Pass this by, climbing steadily south for about 0.3 miles. The route bears left for a short distance, then back to the right, then left again. These long curves soon tighten into short, steep switchbacks with views of chaparral and interesting rock formations. Lizards dart about as you pass them where they sun themselves on solar-heated rocks along the trail.

Once out of the tight-switchback section, the ground levels for a welcome, but short, stretch. Hikers don't quite catch their breath here before the trail curves southeast (bearing left), moving uphill again for approximately 0.3 miles. The trail curves to the right again and levels off. There's no shade in sight, but a short side trail on the right leads to a picnic table and several benches. This is the turnaround spot, although there are other designated trails to the southwest and overlooking the water storage reservoir, which at press time was still under construction. Consult the reserve's map for guidance, or head back down the path and out.

▶ NEARBY ACTIVITIES

If you're heading back to the freeway, there are several drive-thru and traditional restaurants near the Valley Parkway and Auto Parkway intersection.

FAMOSA SLOUGH TRAIL

▶ IN BRIEF

City dwellers in their rush-a-day life drive right by this tiny (30-acre) wetland ensconced in urban development, but for those who pause to ponder the way of water, Famosa Slough holds wonder and wildlife.

▶ DESCRIPTION

From the parking area head north for a few feet onto a dirt path that continues left beyond a chain-link fence. Walk along outside the fence for 0.1 mile. You'll come to the end of Mentone Street. Cross this asphalt dead end and pick up the narrow trail again, with the backyards of houses on the hill to your left.

After another 0.1 mile, a path on the right leads toward the water and a small viewing area with a shaded bench. This is a comfortable spot for bird-watching. Year-round, graceful egrets and striking avocets wade along the shore, dipping hungry beaks into rippling water in search of fish. Terns and herons are also common, as are a variety of ducks.

Benches are spaced at intervals that allow convenient views of the water and wildlife without trudging close and damaging delicate shore plants. Remember, the slough is a preserve. Over the years the slough suffered much destruction during the area's development, which included the creation of a landfill for nearby construction

ⓘ KEY AT-A-GLANCE INFORMATION

LENGTH: 1.5 miles

CONFIGURATION: Out-and-back

DIFFICULTY: Easy

SCENERY: Sea birds, horn snails, marsh

EXPOSURE: Mostly sunny

TRAFFIC: Moderate

TRAIL SURFACE: Sandy soil, can be muddy in wet months

HIKING TIME: 45 minutes

ACCESS: Free

MAPS: Online at the Friends of Famosa Slough Web site: www.geocities.com/famosa_slough

FACILITIES: Portable toilet in parking area

SPECIAL COMMENTS: Leashed dogs only. Please respect this natural habitat and consider learning more about local birds at a guided bird walk. For more information, check the Web site: www.geocities.com/famosa_slough.

▶ DIRECTIONS

Take I-8 west to the Sports Arena Boulevard exit and turn left (west). Drive less than 0.2 miles, turn right on West Point Loma Boulevard and travel 0.5 miles to Famosa Boulevard. Turn left. The road becomes Camalos Street after 0.2 miles. After driving another 0.2 miles, turn left on Valeta Street. After 0.1 mile, Famosa Boulevard begins again. Head left and park in the dirt parking area.

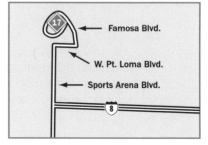

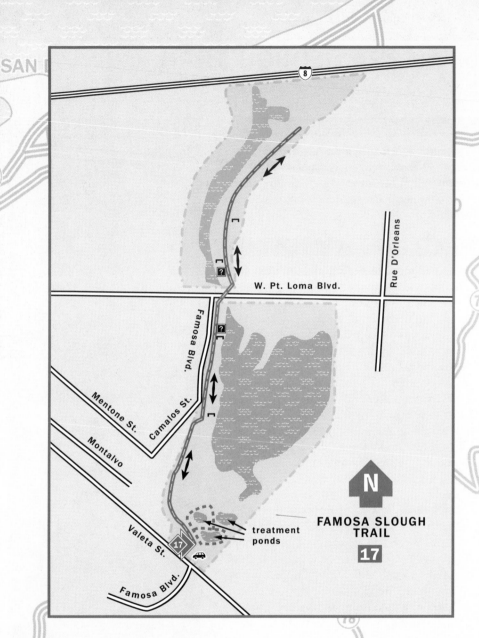

FAMOSA SLOUGH
TRAIL
17

treatment
ponds

projects (landfills not permitted). Volunteers continue to work hard to protect and restore the slough, including removing invasive plants and revege-
tating native ones.

The trail moves closer to Famosa Boulevard for a stretch and opens to
the shore beyond a kiosk offering wetland information and a birding chart.
At the shore you'll notice zillions of conical, inch-long shells in the mud.
Watch for a moment and you'll see that the mottled shells are alive and

moving—they're California horn snails. Feeding off the organic matter that is plentiful in the shoreline mud, these little snails are part of a slough's bigger purpose: to work as a filter, removing chemicals, pollutants, and sediments from urban runoff.

The trail continues past the kiosk for about 200 yards and meets West Point Loma Boulevard. You'll see people crossing here, but the street is often busy. I prefer to turn right and walk up the sidewalk about half a mile to Rue D'Orleans and cross at the traffic light, then make my way back to the slough. You could also turn back here and call it a hike.

Across the street, another kiosk and a bench are located right at the opening to the slough. The dilapidated remnants of a wooden bridge provide a perch for egrets, the wind ruffling their snowy feathers. Gulls fly overhead, sometimes in groups of 50 or more, caught in circular eddies of wind high above. The trail on this side of West Point Loma Boulevard heads north for approximately 0.1 mile but ends short of I-8. Find a soft spot to sit on the ground and watch the birds wade for fish. Surface ripples widen where fish come up. Witness their scattering at the shadow of a bird soaring overhead.

A statuesque egret poses by the water's edge.

After a soul-regenerating time among the birds, lulled by the gently flowing water and the whooshing music of the wind rushing through the reeds, retrace your steps back to your car. Near the parking lot, you'll discover three reedy ponds. These are treatment ponds, created and planted with vegetation to trap sediment and filter runoff from nearby storm drains. The pond areas, with their thick vegetation, provide good hiding spots for birds, mollusks, and crabs. Walk the looping path around them before climbing back into your car and returning to your busy life—your outlook "filtered" by the Famosa Slough.

▶ NEARBY ACTIVITIES

For hearty deli sandwiches, try longstanding Chris' Liquor and Deli on the corner of Sunset Cliffs and West Point Loma Boulevard (head west on West Point Loma Boulevard for about 1.5 miles). For more information, call (619) 222-0518.

GUAJOME REGIONAL PARK TRAIL

KEY AT-A-GLANCE INFORMATION

LENGTH: 4 miles

CONFIGURATION: Out-and-back with loop

DIFFICULTY: Easy

SCENERY: Lake and riparian woodland

EXPOSURE: Sunny and shady

TRAFFIC: Moderate to heavy

TRAIL SURFACE: Sandy soil

HIKING TIME: 2.5 hours

ACCESS: $2 parking fee

MAPS: Available at park, or online at www.sdcounty.ca.gov/parks/camping/guajo_map.html

FACILITIES: Public rest rooms near parking area

SPECIAL COMMENTS: As is the rule for all San Diego wilderness hikes, be wary of rattlesnakes. Visit weekdays during school sessions for the least traffic, and bring drinking water—this park can be very hot in warmer months.

IN BRIEF

These easy trails close to the city of Oceanside provide a convenient exercise route with a wilderness feel. The peaceful backdrop of the lake attracts wildlife and overnighters to the campsites.

DESCRIPTION

From the parking area, head past the rest rooms and a small playground behind them. You'll see the lake to the north, down the hill, where you'll find the trail.

Near the shore, ducks rest in the shade of small pine trees. In fall and winter, there will be geese spending the cool season in San Diego's moderate climate. Although feeding wild animals is never a good idea, these geese are conditioned for food from visitors to the park. Therefore, the fowl immediately begin quacking, honking, and mewling as they waddle excitedly toward you. A loud flock of geese as big as medium-size dogs can be frightening, and geese can be aggressive. If you don't offer food, the flock will likely lose interest and quickly return to their shoreline resting spot.

The trail begins moving southwest past some small pine trees. Look closely. You may see a dragonfly at rest, its transparent gold-veined wings nearly disappearing among the low-hanging boughs.

Along this first quarter mile, the lakeshore is mostly hidden by reeds but opens to occasional

DIRECTIONS

Take I-15 north to CA 76 west. Travel just under 10 miles and turn left on Guajome Lake Road. From I-5 north, take CA 76 east, travel about 7 miles, and turn right on Guajome Lake Road. Turn right into the park entrance 0.1 mile south, pay at the self-pay device, and park in the spaces in front of the first rest room building on your right.

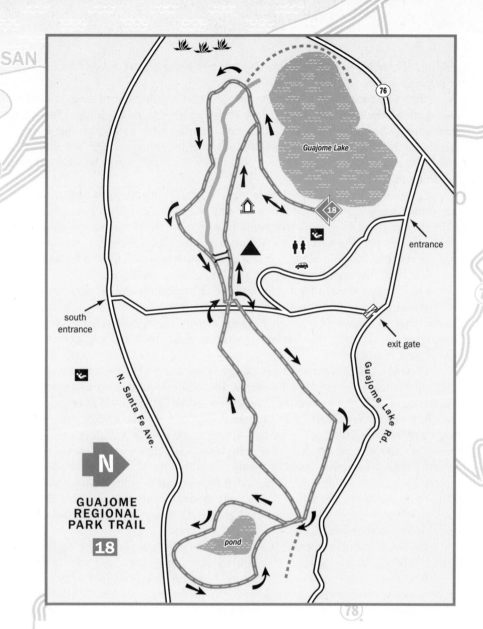

GUAJOME REGIONAL PARK TRAIL

18

Guajome Lake

76

18

entrance

south entrance

exit gate

N. Santa Fe Ave.

Guajome Lake Rd.

pond

SAN

5

76

views of the glassy water. Small inlets shaded by twisting trees provide shallow waters where tiny fish ripple the surface, jetting about in schools.

When the path bends right, you'll spot a wooden footbridge on the left. Continue around the lake for another quarter mile if you choose, then backtrack to this spot and head across the bridge. Perhaps pause for a few moments in the shade, listening to the pleasant gurgle of water under the bridge. Crawdads move about in the shallows beneath. Once over the bridge, immediately turn left onto the narrow, single-trek trail that runs along the marsh.

Reeds grow thickly along this stretch, allowing only brief glimpses of water. Willows and other trees provide shade, creating a "Sleepy Hollow" feel. In a few areas, the path widens and low tree branches act as benches for hikers to stop and reflect.

After approximately a quarter mile on the southeastward and sometimes swampy trail, the path curves northeast across another short footbridge. Fan palms grow among the trailside bramble, and yerba mansa—with its spinach-like leaves—carpets the marshy ground. In spring and summer the perennial herb's white flower with a spiked, elongated middle gives off a tangy, medicinal scent. Watch for poison oak along this section.

Coast goldenbush, with its bright yellow flower clusters, grows here, too. You may notice foamy globs of what looks like spit clinging to its stems. Don't worry; the white masses aren't from an ill-mannered hiker but are the protective covering of the spittlebug nymph. The nymphs suck juice from the plants then secrete body fluids into the mixture, blowing bubbles into a frothy mass in which they hide. Adult spittlebugs instead hop about with amazing agility to avoid their predators.

Pass another wooden footbridge and the campgrounds and picnic areas it leads to, continuing to a wide dirt path stretching north from the lower picnic entrance off North Santa Fe Avenue. You'll notice a sign recognizing middle school students for helping restore the trail. Turn left here, then turn right about 200 yards north, where a wide path heads east.

There are tall cottonwood trees on the right. The wind whispers through their heart-shaped leaves in spring and summer. The hushed sound turns to a crackle that mimics fire as fall sets in and the leaves grow brittle. Milk thistle grows along this stretch, too. The flowers dry into fuzzy clumps that look like golden suns by summer's end, releasing their seeds for next spring's new growth.

After about a quarter mile, Guajome Lake Road comes into view on your left several hundred feet away, running parallel for a quarter of a mile. When the route dips to the right away from the road, watch for the trail to split. You can take either route up to the pond. The left path is a more gradual climb. If you choose the right-hand split, you'll go about three hundred yards west then access the pond via a steep uphill route on your left.

The loop around the pond itself is about a mile long. Start out on the right, bearing left all the way around. Reeds block the shore almost the whole way, but you'll hear the splish-splash of startled frogs hopping into the murky depths beyond the vegetation. Midway around the pond loop, the trail reaches North Santa Fe Avenue, continuing adjacent to the road beyond a chain-link fence for a short distance then turning left to complete the loop.

Once back to the pond loop's start, retrace your steps or take the opposite access trail back to the main one, this time heading west. When you come to the wide dirt road leading up from the lower entrance, continue across, entering the path marked "wildlife area." This path runs behind the campsites. A short distance ahead on the right, you'll see a red-roofed gazebo atop a grassy knoll. Stop for a few moments if you'd like. There are no seats inside the structure, but there are benches nearby. A big tree stump has even been carved into comfortable kitty-corner bench seats, perfect for conversing with a hiking mate.

These grazing geese are near Guajome Lake.

Watch closely for rattlers. Although we've never spotted any out on the rural stretches in this park, we have spotted a snake camouflaged by the grass here near the gazebo. Signs are posted at the rest rooms reporting rattler sightings in and around the buildings.

From here, head back down to the path, which meets up with the lake trail. Turn right and retrace your steps back toward the playground and parking area—perhaps with ducks and geese flocking noisily behind.

HELLER'S BEND PRESERVE TRAIL

ⓘ KEY AT-A-GLANCE INFORMATION

LENGTH: 1 mile

CONFIGURATION: Out-and-back with side trails

DIFFICULTY: Moderately easy

SCENERY: Birds, stream, trees, view of the city of Fallbrook

EXPOSURE: Mostly shady, but some sunny

TRAFFIC: Light

TRAIL SURFACE: Asphalt; optional side trails are sandy soil

HIKING TIME: 30 minutes

ACCESS: Free

MAPS: None

SPECIAL COMMENTS: Although not a traditional horse park where riders can trailer in their horses, the preserve is used by equestrian enthusiasts living nearby.

▶ IN BRIEF

This peaceful 27-acre preserve offers a short jaunt into natural surroundings where the cares of the day are easily forgotten. It's a lovely spot for families looking for a short, easy foray into nature.

▶ DESCRIPTION

Just on the other side of the white fence that runs along Heller's Bend Road, the sounds of city life are drowned out by the croaky refrain of frogs and toads making their homes around Ostrich Farms Creek. The year-round creek runs east to west and is visible just a few yards down the hill from the entrance, whose path runs east before quickly bending southward. On the right is a bench nestled in the shade of oaks near some boulders. If you care to pause a while and let the preserve's serenity calm you, this is a convenient spot.

On the other side of the cement bridge, the path begins ascending, bending east then south again through a jungle of oak forest tangled in wild grapes and guarded by a variety of spiky-leafed thistle. Sunlight filters in through the stretching branches of the mature live oaks as you make your way up the trail. At approximately 0.3 miles, the oak forest thins, letting in sunlight. The passage levels a bit, leading you through the remnants of old orange and avocado groves full of mostly non-producing trees. In early spring, the orange trees bloom, releasing a gentle, tangy scent.

At approximately 0.4 miles, a short offshoot on the left takes you to an eastern lookout point,

▶ DIRECTIONS

Take I-15 north to the Pala/CA 76 exit and go left (west) 4.9 miles to Mission Road, then turn right. After 1.4 miles, make a left on Heller's Bend. The preserve sign and entrance are on the left, at 0.3 miles. Turn around where safe and park on the shoulder of the road, outside the gate.

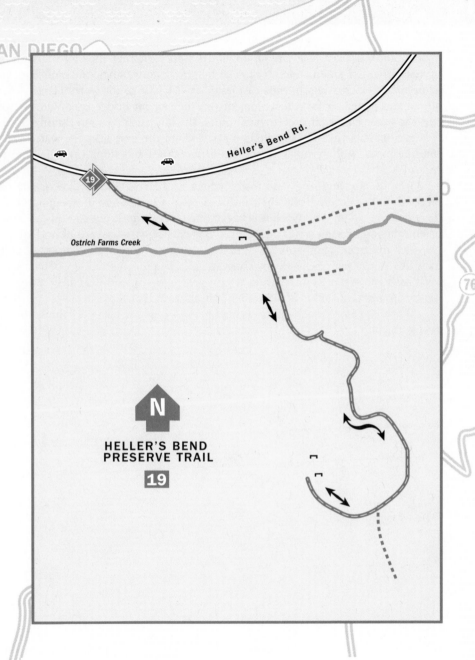

HELLER'S BEND
PRESERVE TRAIL

19

which is only about 50 yards off the path. The main trail continues steeply uphill for a short distance then levels abruptly. At the top, which is half a mile from the gate, benches overlook the rolling hills of Fallbrook to the northeast. This is the end of the trail, offering an eagle's nest view.

Descending is quicker than climbing the half mile, but take time to enjoy the scenery. Both the laurel sumac, with its red-tinged leaves, and a variety of sage bushes grow all along the route, giving off a spicy scent.

On the way back, if you're up for a little more exploring, look for trails stretching east on either side of the creek. The first is a sandy, single-track offshoot just before the creek crossing. It leads east less than 0.1 mile to the water's edge.

If you prefer, sit for a few moments on the cement bridge itself. On the west side, the water enters large corrugated pipes, the low, rushing sound similar to that of a train moving rhythmically along its tracks. On the east side, the water gushes from the pipes, spilling out into the creek that slows and ripples its way into the trees.

Wait quietly, and frogs and toads hidden in the vegetation will serenade you. Triggered by one leading call, their music rises to a symphony of mingling croaks. Then, just as suddenly as the chorus began, the song abruptly ends—you can almost imagine an amphibious bandleader demanding silence with a sweep of his baton.

Past the creek, another offshoot trail stretches east for approximately 0.2 miles. Walk this sandy path beneath towering sycamores. From its treetop perch, a red-tailed hawk may utter its displeasure at your presence—especially at dusk, when he's hungry for a rodent that may hide when it hears your footsteps.

When you amble back up the asphalt path to your car, take the calm of the preserve with you.

HELLHOLE CANYON OPEN SPACE PRESERVE TRAIL

▶ IN BRIEF

Members of the Friends of Hellhole Canyon organization have T-shirts that say "Hellhole Canyon Is Heavenly." If you like wide-open spaces and don't mind the heat, you will agree that this 1,712-acre preserve is an earthly paradise.

▶ DESCRIPTION

Though not far, the lovely country scenery on the two-lane road to Hellhole Canyon gets nature-loving hikers into a relaxed mood before they step foot onto the trail.

A kiosk at the trailhead holds maps and information about Hellhole Canyon. From here, walk north on the easy path, which quickly changes to a steep descent through manzanita forest that is in a pattern of regrowth after the firestorms of fall 2003. After about 0.1 mile, find a topographical map molded from metal sitting atop a stone pillar. Placed in 2001, the map shows preserve trails and elevations.

As of this writing, only the remains of a wooden bench stand at approximately 0.3 miles. The bench will likely be replaced in this shady spot—appreciated more on the trek out of the park when you're moving uphill than descending on the way in. Past the bench, yucca plants sprout

▶ DIRECTIONS

From I-15 take the Valley Parkway exit and travel east toward Valley Center for about 9 miles. From Valley Parkway, turn right on Woods Valley Road, which becomes Paradise Mountain Road at Lake Wohlford Road. From the start of Woods Valley Road, travel about 7 miles to a 5-way intersection. Make a right on Los Hormanos Roach Road then an immediate left on Kiavo Drive. Travel north for 0.5 miles. Turn left where you see the Hellhole Canyon sign, and park in the gravel lot at the top of the hill.

ⓘ KEY AT-A-GLANCE INFORMATION

LENGTH: 5.5 miles

CONFIGURATION: Balloon

DIFFICULTY: Easy to moderate

SCENERY: Trees, chaparral, wide open space

EXPOSURE: Mostly sunny

TRAFFIC: Heavy on first mile

TRAIL SURFACE: Packed dirt, some rocky areas

HIKING TIME: 3.5 hours

ACCESS: Free

MAPS: Free from the box at the trailhead kiosk

FACILITIES: Public rest rooms at trailhead

SPECIAL COMMENTS: Open 8 a.m.–sunset daily. Closed August 1–Labor Day, due to extreme heat. Shared equestrian and pedestrian trail. Bring plenty of water, even in moderate and cool weather. Wear a hat. Pets are not permitted in the preserve, although leashed dogs are common on this trail.

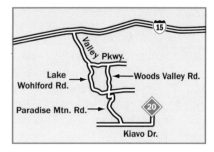

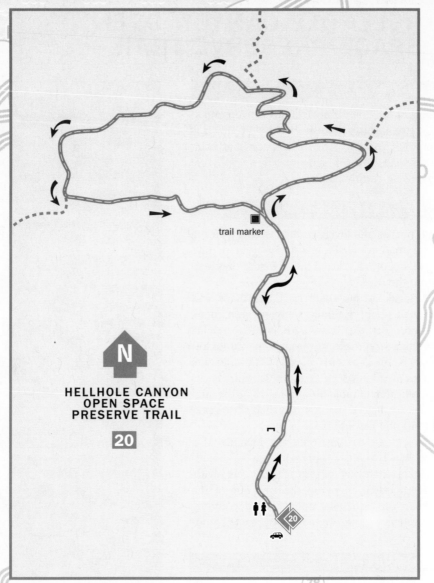

HELLHOLE CANYON
OPEN SPACE
PRESERVE TRAIL

20

trail marker

along the edges of the rutted trail, looking a lot like pineapples in their early efforts at recovering from the fire.

At 0.75 miles, the path flattens and becomes sandy, leading around granite boulders to seasonal Hell Creek. The creek used to run year-round, but lack of adequate rainfall in recent years means water is present only after winter and spring rains. The riparian landscape of Western sycamores and twisting oaks provides welcome shade all along the creek bed. If there is a flow, stop for a few moments and listen to the gurgle of water, or simply

Manzanita and scrub oak show signs of regenerating from the devastating wildfires of 2003.

appreciate the serenity of nature here under the spreading oak canopy. Be careful of poison oak, which grows all along this shady stretch.

Despite poison oak, the creek area is a favorite of picnickers. Many come to Hellhole Canyon Open Space Preserve just for the entry trail. Others hike farther into the canyon, stopping to rest in the shade on their way back to civilization. A stone wall above the creek bed provides adequate seating beneath the trees, although there is quite a drop; watch children carefully. The tree limbs stretch out over the creek, and reach across the trail. Dapples of filtered sunlight glint rainbow-like in the shade.

The route down to the creek and back is the most traveled portion of the canyon. Although no pets are allowed, the influx of new homes and their inhabitants in Valley Center has brought more visitors—and many disregard the rules. Watch your step here where dogs often leave their calling cards, especially on weekends when trail use is heaviest.

Emerging from the shady creek area, the level trail travels in the open for about 0.2 miles, then narrows and bends northeast through the spotty shade of chaparral and oak trees. The hillside rises on the right as well, also providing shade. Wild cucumber grows in a thick net on outstretched manzanita branches, charred by the fire. The route bends northwest again, and reaches a fork leading either left or right, into the loop trail. This is a logical turnaround spot for those ready to go back.

Hardy hikers who are unafraid of dry heat can turn right at the trail marker and begin climbing. The first 0.5-mile section of the loop gains 200 feet in elevation on a rocky, red dirt trail reminiscent of the Red Planet. The only water here is in your toted in bottles, which you'll need even in moderate fall or spring weather here at Hellhole Canyon.

Turn left at the trail marker, and travel 0.7 miles of steep switchbacks over lighter colored, rocky soil to an elevation of 2,475 feet. Watch for locusts. The plentiful insects blend in with the rocky dirt, and often don't move until you're right upon them, at which time they burst from the ground in a buzzing flurry—sometimes right up to your face. The insects may be the only signs of life you spot out here where fewer hikers venture.

On these higher segments of the loop trail, the chaparral grows smaller due to the dryer soil. This becomes even more evident near the end of the next segment of trail, reached by bearing left at the next marker. This third, southwesterly 0.8-mile section of the loop starts out steep, then descends more gradually down to an elevation of 1,820 feet. The surroundings grow greener as you descend. Wild cucumber vines twine onto the path, and aromatic sage springs up near yucca and prickly pear cactus.

At the next trail marker, turn left onto the 0.7-mile closing segment of the loop. This mostly sunny, very gently climbing trail has a couple of sections where trees grow on either side. Pause at these three- and four-yard oases where the wind ruffles the leaves, and birds come to call.

Turn right at the trail marker back onto the entry trail and retrace your steps past the creek and up through the manzanita forest.

▶ NEARBY ACTIVITIES

Back on Woods Valley Road, you'll find Bates Nut Farm and shady picnic areas where you can watch ducks, geese, chicken, goats, and sheep in nearby pens. Inside the store among dried fruits, nuts, and other goodies, a bag of feeding corn costs pennies and keeps the critters coming to the fence for a pat by eager children. Handicrafts are sold here by local artisans on some weekends, and in the fall, there are hayrides and a pumpkin patch. For more information call (760) 749-3333, or visit www.bates nutfarm.biz.

HIGHLAND VALLEY TRAIL

▶ IN BRIEF

This easy trail meanders past a stream and through patches of oak forest that provide welcome shade on hot days. Located just off I-15, it's a quick drive into nature.

▶ DESCRIPTION

The three-foot wide silt path begins at the northeast corner of the gravel parking lot. The chaparral here is heavy with California buckwheat. The tufted blooms in such masses appear almost like snowdrifts in late spring and begin turning a vibrant red as the seasons change.

You may notice harvest ants here. Their holes swarm with activity in spring and summer, riddling the length of the hiking path. The ants can sting but most often seem oblivious to hikers. They gather bits of vegetation and perform the worthwhile job of dispersing plants' seeds. These busy workers are also food for the horned lizard, which San Diego naturalists believe needs protection. The introduction of aggressive Argentine ants has destroyed some of the harvester ant population, making the horned lizard's food scarcer. It's fun to watch these miniscule ants awkwardly navigate the way to their nesting holes carrying things twice their size, but keep in mind their ecological importance and respect their habitat.

For the first 0.2 miles, the sloping land to the left of the trail is lined with pine trees grown commercially for Christmas. Ignore the hum of cars on I-15, squint your eyes to blur the city in the distance, and pretend you're far, far away from asphalt and car exhaust. The fresh pine scent

▶ DIRECTIONS

Take I-15 to the Pomerado Road exit and head inland about 0.5 miles to Highland Valley Road. Turn left. The gravel parking lot is immediately on the right, directly across from the nursery.

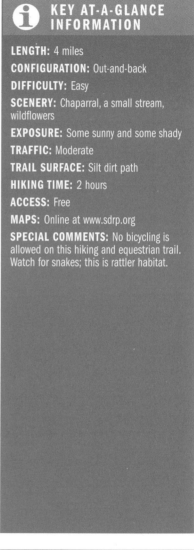

ⓘ KEY AT-A-GLANCE INFORMATION

LENGTH: 4 miles

CONFIGURATION: Out-and-back

DIFFICULTY: Easy

SCENERY: Chaparral, a small stream, wildflowers

EXPOSURE: Some sunny and some shady

TRAFFIC: Moderate

TRAIL SURFACE: Silt dirt path

HIKING TIME: 2 hours

ACCESS: Free

MAPS: Online at www.sdrp.org

SPECIAL COMMENTS: No bicycling is allowed on this hiking and equestrian trail. Watch for snakes; this is rattler habitat.

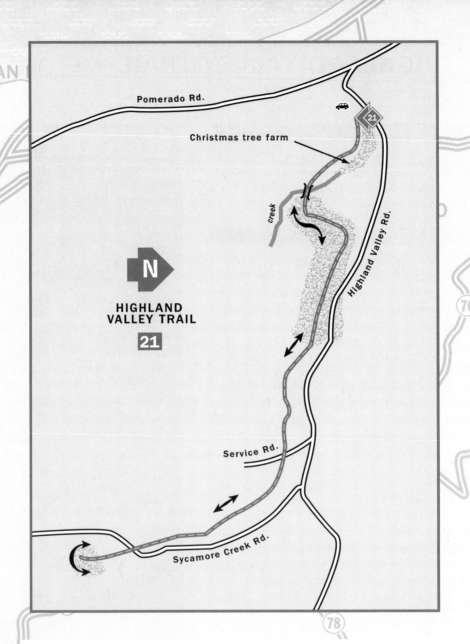

Pomerado Rd.

Christmas tree farm

Creek

Highland Valley Rd.

N

**HIGHLAND
VALLEY TRAIL**

21

Service Rd.

Sycamore Creek Rd.

mingles with the intoxicating fragrance of the abundant white sage that grows here, filtering out the city's smells.

At about 0.25 miles, if you are hiking in early summer, you'll notice clusters of bright pink Canchalagua with a white center and prominent yellow-tipped stamens. Early Spanish settlers collected and dried the annual for use as a fever remedy.

After about 0.3 miles, you'll cross an old dirt road and continue southeast into an oak forest complete with a babbling brook. There are benches here in the cool shade. Concave areas in large boulders allow water to pool—delightful for foot-dipping in hotter months. Be careful of poison oak and

Houses along the trail are forgotten with the rustling wind and sweet scents of nature's bouquet.

slippery wet rocks. A small wooden bridge crosses the stream and the trail turns abruptly left (north) for a short open stretch as it heads very gradually uphill.

The trail continues, leveling and bearing more to the right (northeast). Watch for clumps of jimsonweed, a pretty poison. A member of the nightshade family, the attractive plant has soft green leaves and showy, pale violet or white trumpet-shaped flowers. In ancient times, Indians crushed and brewed the roots for their narcotic properties. Today, the Centers for Disease Control reports sporadic incidents of people intentionally ingesting this plant and being severely poisoned. All parts of this plant that commonly grows along roadsides and in rural habitats in San Diego are poisonous and the Poison Control Center reports that jimsonweed is one of the plants for which callers most often seek first aid.

The route quickly bends southeast through more woodland shade, then heads downhill, making this stretch doubly delightful on hot days. The path soon levels again, continuing southeast through alternating sun and shade. At about a mile, angular, lichen-crusted boulders form interesting shapes along the route. You'll come to a narrow asphalt service road at about 1.25 miles. Pick up the trail on the other side and continue for about another 0.25 miles along Highland Valley Road, which is about 50 yards down the hill on the left. The trail bends more southward where Sycamore Creek Road meets Highland Valley Road, and continues for nearly 0.5 miles in the open.

Keep your eyes open along this stretch. We've seen a small rattler, a king snake, and freshly shed snakeskin. The trail crosses Sycamore Creek Road and heads southeast for a short distance past Western sycamore trees. Patches of stinking gourd, with its triangular leaves, lie along the path. The root of this small native gourd with foul-smelling foliage was pounded into soap by Native Americans and is another plant commonly found along roads throughout the county. The final few steps lead to benches in the shade of Western sycamores and live oaks. When you're ready to return, follow the path 2 miles back to the starting point.

HOSP GROVE LOOP

ℹ️ KEY AT-A-GLANCE INFORMATION

LENGTH: 1 mile

CONFIGURATION: Loop

DIFFICULTY: Easy

SCENERY: Trees, urban view, filtered sunlight

EXPOSURE: Mostly shady

TRAFFIC: Light to moderate

TRAIL SURFACE: Leaf-littered soil

HIKING TIME: 30 minutes

ACCESS: Free

MAPS: Online at the San Diego County Trails Association Web site: www.sdctc.com/carlsbad

▶ IN BRIEF

These easy one-mile loop trails with some uphill sections provide a convenient in-town exercise route. Do the one described here, or add another mile with the paths on the east side of Monroe Street, depending on how much time and energy you have.

▶ DESCRIPTION

From the parking area, take the footpath heading southeast past the playground and cross a narrow wooden bridge. You'll be heading through eucalyptus forest and past a picnic table on the left. The trail bends right, up a gradual slope for a few yards, then heads left, moving more steeply uphill. The trail soon levels for a few steps then heads left again to continue its climb.

The route curves right again and levels for a long southeastward stretch. This high portion of the trail runs above Marron Road, with tree trunks allowing spotty, rooftop views of the shopping mall across the street. Although the mall seems huge from inside, the big buildings look a bit like cubicles from this vantage point, putting man's creations in a different perspective.

Heading gradually downhill now, the trail curves south, angling toward Monroe Street. Among eucalyptus trees that all look alike at first, you'll begin to notice variations. Shaggy trees with leaves running up and down the trunk intermingle with ones that are spindly from top to bottom. Many trees bear carvings of romantic

▶ DIRECTIONS

Take CA 78 to the Jefferson Street exit (about a mile east of I-5), head south 0.3 miles, and turn right to stay on Jefferson Street. Immediately turn left into the parking lot near a playground, where the sign reads "Hosp Grove Park."

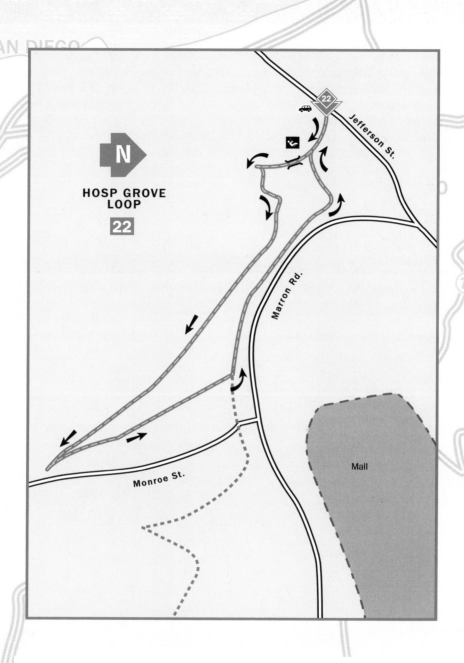

HOSP GROVE
LOOP
22

couples who have etched their names here for the world—or at least other hikers—to see.

As of this writing, many of the trees have grown weak and begun to fall because of the tiny insect "lerp psyllid." Many trees have been removed, and replanting is in progress. The Australian insects, also known as "tree lice," suck juice from the leaves and secrete a waxy protective covering. You might spot the tiny round patches on leaf surfaces. Discovered in Los Angeles

County in the late 1990s, the insects have worked their way into other counties. The secretions of the immature insect nymphs cause mildew, resulting in black mold and leaf loss that weakens the trees and makes them more susceptible to pests such as the wood-boring beetle. Scientists hope that the recent introduction of a tiny wasp, the lerp psyllid's natural predator in Australia, will do its job here, halting further infestation and eventually eradicating the lerp psyllid from California.

As the path approaches Monroe Street, take a sharp left and head northwest on an intersecting trail. This leads to a dusty path running west alongside Marron Road all the way to Jefferson and the parking lot where you started.

The very similar trails on the opposite (east) side of Monroe Street run about the same total distance as the loop described here. You can access the east loop from the corner of Monroe and Marron.

▶ NEARBY ACTIVITIES

The shopping mall directly across the street offers a variety of restaurants and department and specialty stores. Have fun!

IRON MOUNTAIN PEAK TRAIL

The mountain is named for its iron ore content, but the moniker could just as easily refer to the brute strength it takes to get to the top of this winding trail. The 2,696-foot peak allows hikers to touch the sky.

▶ **DESCRIPTION**

From the trailhead where CA 67 meets Poway Road, you'll start out on a very gently up-sloping path that leads east through rows of small oak trees. Although scorched in the fall 2003 firestorm, the trees survived. The cool shade they provide increases with each year of growth. Pass by the side trail you'll spot after about a quarter of a mile; the north-stretching trail leads to the Ellie Lane staging area, which is popular with the equestrian crowd. Continue east on the silt-soil path that grows rockier from here, typical of much of this hike.

After about 1.5 miles, you will come to an intersection; head south (left). The path moves southwest up a rocky but well-maintained path that zigzags through air pleasantly scented by wild sage. Orange, yellow, violet, and peach wildflowers bloom through late spring; yuccas stretch upward, their tall central shaft bursting into bloom-adorned flags. In some areas the ground is an ashen black, reminders of fires that roared through this area—one in 1995, and another in 2003. Logs placed at right angles on the path guard against erosion and help with footing. Small children will need to stoop for handgrips occasionally along the rocky and sometimes steep path.

▶ **DIRECTIONS**

Take I-15 to the Poway Road exit and travel 8.8 miles east to CA 67. Go south (left). The trailhead and parking is located about 200 yards ahead on the left side of the road.

KEY AT-A-GLANCE INFORMATION

LENGTH: 6.5 miles

CONFIGURATION: Out-and-back

DIFFICULTY: Moderately strenuous

SCENERY: Panoramic views

EXPOSURE: Sunny

TRAFFIC: Heavy

TRAIL SURFACE: Rocky soil

HIKING TIME: 3.5 hours

MAPS: Available at trailhead

FACILITIES: None as of this writing. Before the fall 2003 fire, portable toilets were located approximately half a mile in on the entry trail; they may be replaced.

SPECIAL COMMENTS: Climbing to an elevation of 2,696 feet, this trail is not recommended for unconditioned or inexperienced hikers. Consider bringing binoculars to enjoy panoramic vistas from the peak.

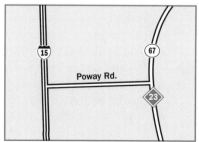

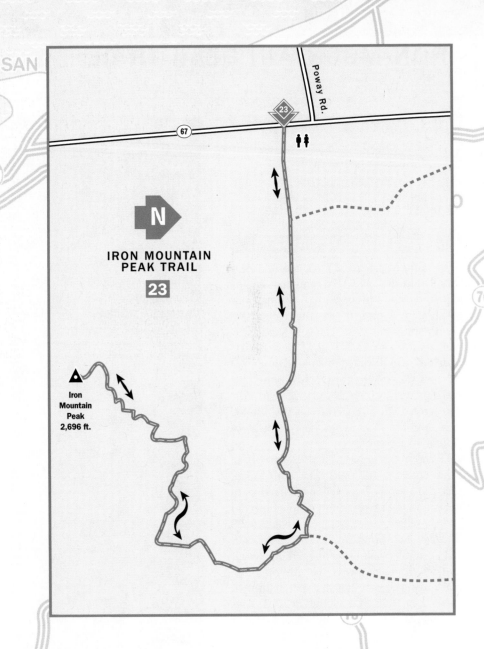

Watch for runners making their way swiftly down the mountain. Others pass with hiking poles—especially useful on the way down. Leashed dogs pass, tongues lolling, with kind owners who dribble bottled water into cupped hands from which their dogs gratefully lap.

About a mile from the intersection you'll spot manzanita, which tends to grow at higher elevations. The path continues for another 0.7 miles to the peak, alternating between steep, rocky sections and soft-soiled plateaus that appear just when hikers run short of breath.

At the peak, a picnic bench and several boulders offer a restful reward in the form of spectacular views. The lookout is especially magnificent near sunset when the sky turns a red-purple hue. Before trekking back down the mountain, watch a crow glide peacefully overhead, and ponder your place in the universe. From this vantage point, the world of limitless possibilities stretches below.

▶ NEARBY ACTIVITIES

Consider stopping in at Mary's Secret Garden at 13414 Poway Road, where a variety of yard and patio goods help make your home a retreat. Call (858) 486-0023 for more information.

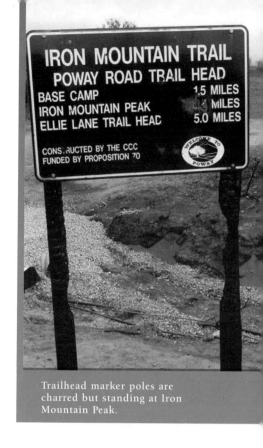

IRON MOUNTAIN TRAIL
POWAY ROAD TRAIL HEAD
BASE CAMP   1.5 MILES
IRON MOUNTAIN PEAK   MILES
ELLIE LANE TRAIL HEAD   5.0 MILES

CONSTRUCTED BY THE CCC
FUNDED BY PROPOSITION 70

Trailhead marker poles are charred but standing at Iron Mountain Peak.

IRON MOUNTAIN TO LAKE RAMONA OVERLOOK AND POND

KEY AT-A-GLANCE INFORMATION

LENGTH: 6 miles

CONFIGURATION: Balloon and string

DIFFICULTY: Moderately strenuous

SCENERY: Interesting rock formations; possibility of wildlife, waterfowl at pond

EXPOSURE: Sunny

TRAFFIC: Light to moderate

TRAIL SURFACE: Rocky soil

HIKING TIME: 3.5 hours

ACCESS: Free

MAPS: Available at trailhead

FACILITIES: None as of this writing. Before their destruction in the fall 2003 fire, portable toilets were located about half a mile in on the entry trail; they may be replaced.

SPECIAL COMMENTS: Open sunrise to sunset. Bring plenty of water and choose mild days; otherwise, it's too hot and dusty to enjoy the trek.

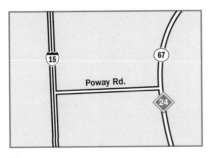

▶ IN BRIEF

About the same length as the trail to the peak, this loop has a wide-open feel; the mountains seem to part, the trail cleaving a path into the wilderness.

▶ DESCRIPTION

From the trailhead where CA 67 meets Poway Road, take the gently up-sloping path heading east, as described for the Iron Mountain Peak Trail. When you reach the intersection at 1.5 miles, go left. The path slopes downhill, curving more northward, with mountains on either side damping the noise from CA 67. You'll note the effects of the recent fires here, but chaparral burnt to ashen sticks has a way of regenerating itself. The new growth evident as of this writing looks like bright green tufts holding up spindly, charred wood.

About a quarter mile past the intersection, switchbacks lead uphill. The trail reaches the overlook point after another quarter mile. A sign directs visitors several yards to the right for a view of Ramona.

Here the path joins the 2.8-mile Ellie Lane Trail and leads west across dry, rocky land. A long southwestward stretch is almost level, zigzagging in spots. After about a mile, the trail turns north again. Side trails stretch west toward the eucalyptus trees and a pond. Continue north. The route becomes steep and slippery, an undulating up-and-down pattern on rocky ground that soon levels and turns west again. Hundreds of huge boulders dwarf passersby. Some of the massive

▶ DIRECTIONS

Take I-15 to the Poway Road exit and travel 8.8 miles east to CA 67. Go south (right). The trailhead and parking are located about 200 yards ahead on the left side of the road.

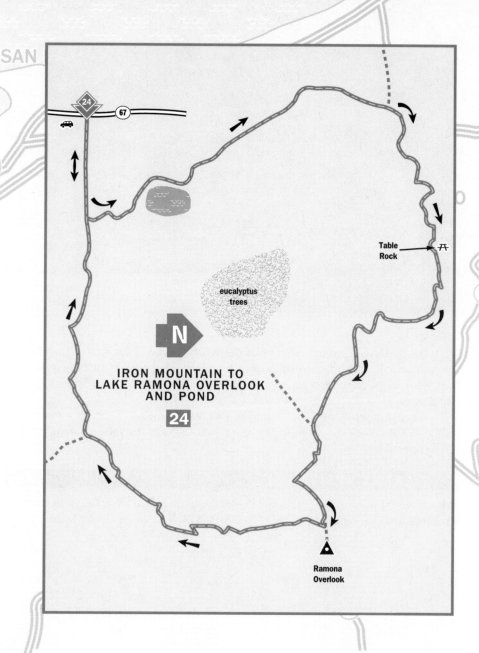

IRON MOUNTAIN TO
LAKE RAMONA OVERLOOK
AND POND

24

Table
Rock

eucalyptus
trees

Ramona
Overlook

rocks sit in piles of flaked stone. When the flames whipped through this area in the fall of 2003, the speed of the stones' natural flaking process was increased because trapped air expanded quickly, causing the boulders' outermost layers to burst and fall to the ground.

You'll notice "Table Rock" on your left. The interesting formation looks as if it were plucked straight from Fred Flintstone's cartoon kitchen. A short distance ahead, there is an oak tree—scorched but showing signs of regrowth and the promise of increasing shade as its leaves regenerate.

Graceful afloat, ducks paddle
lazily along.

The trail will dip southwest to join the 1.2-mile Wild Horse Trail—tiring to contemplate after having hiked so far already. Enjoy the pond with its rustling reeds. Perhaps spot frogs escaping in a splash when you approach, or see a duck or two paddling lazily in the sparkling water.

When you reach the Iron Mountain Trail, turn right and head back toward the trailhead. If you look closely, you may spot rabbit tracks in the soft soil along the oak-lined entry trail.

▶ NEARBY ACTIVITIES

Not that you'd want to go . . . but the Poway Bernardo Mortuary, featured in the A&E channel's Monday night reality show *Family Plots,* is located on Poway Road.

LA JOLLA: COAST WALK

This easy, cliff-side walk offers up close views of resident seabirds. Despite the area's shops and tourism, the habitat of La Jolla's coastline is still a haven for the birds.

▶ DESCRIPTION

To the right and left of the cliff-side parking spaces on Coast Walk, benches overlooking the ocean offer a spectacular view. Depending on the tide, the waves crash with striking force against the cliffs or gently swell and ebb in a rolling rhythm. The area is popular among kayakers. You may spot them paddling their narrow vessels along the coastline, getting a closer look at the series of watery caves carved into the cliffs below.

The path starts to the left of the parking area, where the trail is guarded from the cliff's edge by thick stands of lemonadeberry bushes. You'll quickly come to a plank bridge and head up wooden steps, reaching an earthen path open to the cliffs. Be careful here, especially with children.

▶ DIRECTIONS

Take I-52 West into La Jolla, where it merges onto La Jolla Parkway. Continue northwest on La Jolla Parkway for approximately 1 mile, where it becomes Torrey Pines Road. Continue for approximately 1 more mile and turn right on Coast Walk, a narrow street that holds two cliff-side parking spaces a short distance ahead. Because they are hidden, these spaces are often open. If they're in use, turn right back onto Torrey Pines Road. Travel about a 0.1 mile then turn right again where you see the sign marked "Cave Street." Park curbside wherever you can—the path's opposite end can be accessed about 200 yards from the junction of Torrey Pines Road, at a grove of pine trees near the Cave Store.

ⓘ KEY AT-A-GLANCE INFORMATION

LENGTH: 0.5 miles

CONFIGURATION: Out-and-back or loop

DIFFICULTY: Easy

SCENERY: Ocean views, birds

EXPOSURE: Mostly sunny

TRAFFIC: Moderately heavy

TRAIL SURFACE: Packed cliff-side soil, optional sidewalk add-ons

HIKING TIME: 30 minutes

ACCESS: Free

MAPS: None

SPECIAL COMMENTS: Children enjoy this hike, but watch them carefully or insist on holding hands because sheer cliffs that drop 100 feet to the rocky shoreline can be dangerous. Though this hike is enjoyable anytime, fall and winter promise smaller crowds.

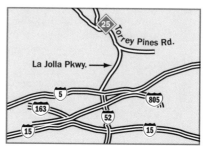

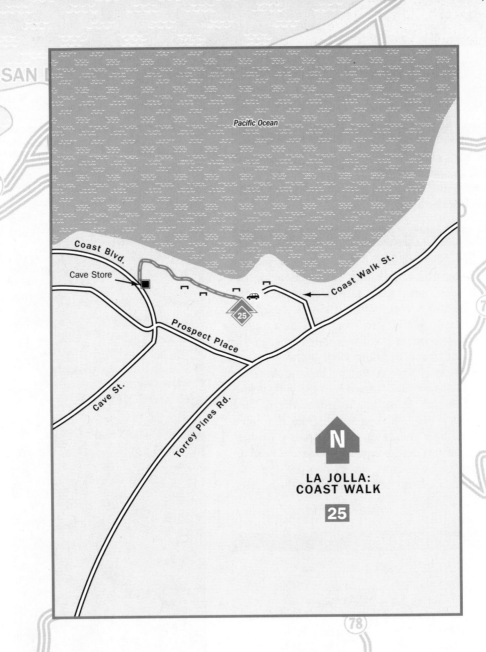

Pacific Ocean

Coast Blvd.

Cave Store

Coast Walk St.

Prospect Place

Cave St.

Torrey Pines Rd.

N

**LA JOLLA:
COAST WALK**

25

A strong ammonia-like smell fills the air here. Birds—cormorants, pelicans, and a variety of gulls—are the culprits. They gather on the rocky cliffs in huge groups, the cormorants clinging to the sides of the steep cliffs, while the gulls and pelicans congregate in groups on the flatter rocks jutting out beyond the path.

Several benches placed along the 0.25-mile-long strip provide opportunities to sit and let the ocean lull you. The strong odor isn't as shocking after a few moments, and it's relaxing to sit here on the brink of the cliffs over-

Let spectacular views and the ebb and flow of the tide lull you on this cliffside trail in paradise.

looking the vast watery expanse. The cliff-side coast walk is a surprising change of pace from the hustle and bustle of tourist activity along La Jolla's shop-lined streets. But there are other surprises here. You will discover that pelicans may look a bit slow and clumsy on land, but they fly with regal elegance. In large flocks, the graceful-in-flight birds soar toward the coast, surveying the cliffs then doubling back to land among the masses.

A viewing platform near the Cave Street end of the path gets visitors closest to the birds, which gather, preening, on the rocks just a few feet beyond the railing. The clustered birds, the sparkling Pacific Ocean, and the spectacular curving San Diego coastline make this is a favorite spot for photos.

From here, you can exit the path and turn right onto Cave Street then continue walking along the sidewalk another 0.25 miles or so with pleasant breezes and ocean views. Or, instead, turn left, heading up the hill and left again onto Torrey Pines Road, meeting Coast Walk and heading around to your car. If you have the time and energy, do both. Everything is in close proximity here.

▶ NEARBY ACTIVITIES

Don't miss an opportunity to visit Sunny Jim's Cave—144 slippery steps stretch down (and back up—whew!) a cliff tunnel accessed inside the La Jolla Cave and Curio Shop. You'll find the shop, which has been here since 1902, just a few short steps to the left of the path's end, at 1325 Cave Street. Open daily 9 a.m. to 5 p.m. Phone (858) 459-0746 for more information.

LA JOLLA: TIDE POOLS WALK

KEY AT-A-GLANCE INFORMATION

LENGTH: 2 miles

CONFIGURATION: Out-and-back

DIFFICULTY: Easy

SCENERY: Ocean waves, tide-pool creatures

EXPOSURE: Sunny

TRAFFIC: Moderate to heavy

TRAIL SURFACE: Sand and surf, rocks

HIKING TIME: 1 hour

ACCESS: Free

MAPS: None needed

FACILITIES: In the parking area near the lifeguard tower

SPECIAL COMMENTS: Wear sturdy rubber-soled shoes that will cling to wet rock surfaces. You'll need protection as you climb among the tide pools. Be sure to visit around low tide. For tide schedules, check www.scilib.ucsd.edu/sio/tide/piertide.

IN BRIEF

The ocean breeze, rolling waves, and sand beneath your feet. Who could ask for more? But that's only the beginning—low tides mean plenty of sea creatures to marvel over.

DESCRIPTION

From the grassy area at the north end of Kellogg Park, where free parking is plentiful in the off-season or early on weekday mornings, head north up the beach toward the pier. You might as well kick off your shoes on this wide sandy beach, and let the surf roll in around your feet.

It's about half a mile to the pier that extends from UCSD's Scripps Institute of Oceanography on the cliff above the beach (the cliff and the institute are not open to the public). Standing beneath the pier between the wide mussel-encrusted supports, one can only marvel at man's ability to build structures strong enough to withstand the ocean's power. A short distance ahead, though, tiny creatures thrive in the ocean's ebb and flow—proving worthy design on a small scale.

As you continue north you'll see more and more large rocks pitted by the sea and sand strewn along the beach. Stuff your feet back into shoes to cross a strip of piled, rounded rocks that form a hobbling path near the base of the cliffs. The larger rocks, roughened into various shapes by wind, water, and sand, clump together, leaving little sand between them.

DIRECTIONS

From CA 52 west, merge onto La Jolla Parkway, drive 1.4 miles, and turn right on Calle de la Plata. Continue 0.2 miles to Avenida de la Playa and turn left. Drive 0.1 mile to Camino del Oro and spot the park. Drive to the north end of the parking area and park near the lifeguard tower and rest rooms.

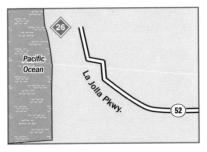

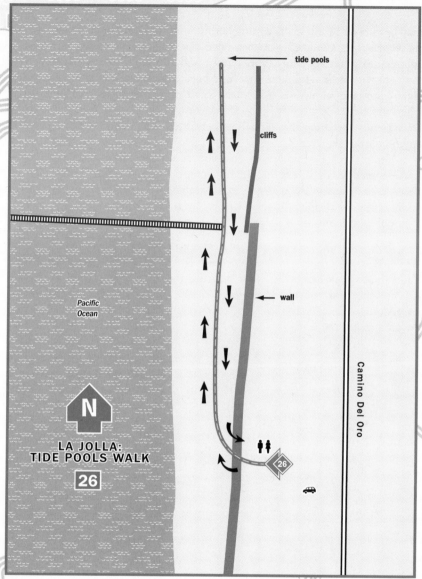

tide pools

cliffs

wall

Pacific
Ocean

N

**LA JOLLA:
TIDE POOLS WALK**

26

Camino Del Oro

As you hop from rock to rock, startled crabs scurry sideways into crevices. Schools of fish trapped in pools left by the receding tide swim to safety among fluttery pink and mauve sea plants. Take the time to stoop and get a closer look at what may seem at first just an empty pool. Often, you'll discover the collected water teems with life.

Squabbling over territory, hermit crabs scuttle about in temporary shell houses that are sometimes smaller than a pea. The bigger crabs carry larger shells. Notice the variety of shapes and sizes they select. Even a broken shell may be chosen by a less discerning hermit crab, as he haltingly makes his way across the waterscape, the shell's uneven edge catching on everything he passes. A rusty-colored sea plant suddenly moves away, and you realize it's a sea slug. Watch for a moment and see several more that have been camouflaged in plain sight advance into view. Clumps of elongated oval mussels adhere to the rocks. Sea anemones contract when touched.

Gently touching the animals is permitted, but you may not collect or remove anything from the area.

From the rocky tide-pool area, you could hike about 3.5 more miles to Flat Rock, named for its shape, and access a climbing route ("Beach Trail") up into Torrey Pines State Reserve. You may spot nude sunbathers along the way: past the rocky tide pools is the area called "Black's Beach," well known as a clothing-optional zone—although public nudity is illegal.

▶ **NEARBY ACTIVITIES**

If the tide pools have whet your appetite for knowledge about the ocean and its wildlife, the nearby Birch Aquarium at 2300 Expedition Way in La Jolla is worth a visit. Consult the facility's Web site at www.aquarium.ucsd.edu or call (858) 534-FISH for more information.

LAGUNA MOUNTAINS:
PENNY PINES TO PIONEER MAIL

▶ IN BRIEF

Beginning along dry, rocky terrain with a desert view and creeping slowly toward forest, this route straddles two worlds, offering a unique perspective on the diverse nature of the San Diego area. Where else can you drive 50 miles from downtown and find lush mountain forest contrasting with arid desert?

▶ DESCRIPTION

If you're at the north end of the parking lot, start out on the narrow trail that begins behind the signs explaining reforestation. The path treks through fragrant sage, often alive with the buzz of bees and the colorful flutter of butterflies. This trail bends to the right and joins the wider main trail. Or access the Pacific Crest Trail directly from the south end of the parking area.

The northeasterly path leads through pine and black oak forest. Watch out for low branches with bony finger-like limbs that droop into the path. Pesky flies and bees are prevalent here, a menace on much of this hike.

After a short distance, the atmosphere abruptly changes from mountain forest to chaparral habitat that soon thins, becoming a rocky ridge trail with sparse vegetation and a breathtaking view of the Anza Borrego Desert. Watch for the showy white blooms of the prickly poppy. From a distance, the crinkly white petals and a bright yellow center look like fried eggs growing on spindly gray-green stems.

KEY AT-A-GLANCE INFORMATION

LENGTH: 7 miles

CONFIGURATION: Out-and-back

DIFFICULTY: Moderate

SCENERY: View of desert valley, possible wildlife

EXPOSURE: Mostly sunny

TRAFFIC: Light to moderate

TRAIL SURFACE: Terrain alternates among rocky, sandy, or leaf-littered

HIKING TIME: 5 hours

ACCESS: Parked vehicles must display an "Adventure Pass," sold at the visitor center or at the Mount Laguna Lodge Store located about 8 miles north of I-8 on the Sunrise Highway. For more information, call (619) 473-8547 or visit www.lmva.org.

MAPS: Purchase at the visitor center, online at www.lmva.org, at the Lodge Store, or at the Blue Jay Restaurant; seewww.lmva.org or www.lagunamountain.com for more information.

FACILITIES: Pubic rest rooms are located at the Pioneer Mail picnic area, 3.5 miles into this hike.

SPECIAL COMMENTS: This hike is unsuitable for young children. The trail sometimes takes one along a sheer, rocky edge. Occasionally, winter snow closes the Sunset Highway (a.k.a. S1) or makes tire chains necessary. For current conditions call the California Highway Patrol at (858) 637-3800 or check the "traffic incidents" section at www.cad.chp.ca.gov.

▶ DIRECTIONS

From I-8, take the Sunset Highway exit, turn left (north), and drive for about 14 miles to the Penny Pines trailhead. Park on the right, where signs describe reforestation efforts and the "Penny Pines" moniker.

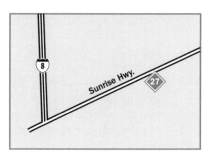

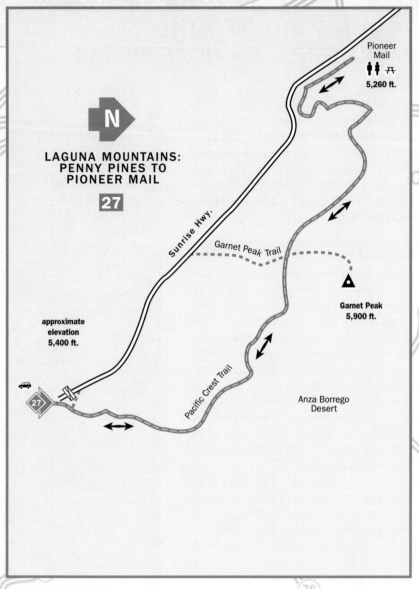

LAGUNA MOUNTAINS:
PENNY PINES TO
PIONEER MAIL

27

Pioneer Mail
5,260 ft.

Garnet Peak Trail

Garnet Peak
5,900 ft.

approximate
elevation
5,400 ft.

Pacific Crest Trail

Anza Borrego
Desert

Sunrise Hwy.

The trail bends to the left, heading generally northwest. Manzanita trees, devastated by recent fires, are regrowing here. You may notice warty red formations, like oblong berries, along the edges of some of the pale green leaves. Insects lay their eggs inside the leaf structure and berry-red galls form to encase the eggs.

At about one mile, the trail appears to dead end at a rocky ledge overlooking the drab, brown desert valley. But look to the left and you'll notice that the route actually turns abruptly to the southwest. Take this fairly short switchback path that soon bends northwest again.

The desert valley stretches out beyond the fragrant forest.

On this downward sloping section, tread carefully. Loose rocks can slide, causing you to fall. After another quarter of a mile, the trail heads upward again, cuttings through two terrains: thick pine forest to the left and arid desert to the right.

At 1.5 miles, the trail intersects with the Garnet Peak Trail, which ascends a few hundred feet in elevation on a path about a half mile long or heads left and southwest to the Sunrise Highway. If you're full of energy and want to add a round-trip mile, the view from Garnet Peak is worth the climb. Otherwise, save the peak for another day and continue northwest on the Pacific Crest Trail.

Watch for horned lizards as you move along this stretch where manzanita is prevalent. The rocks and sandy soil camouflage the rusty brown lizards.

About half a mile past the intersection, the trail bends west, moving gradually along a ridge then leaving desert behind. The trail meanders south from here then doubles back along the highway, through pine and oak forest. You'll notice burned areas here; the raging firestorm of October 2003 ripped through the area.

At 3.5 miles, the shaded tables of Pioneer Mail picnic area beckon you to rest. You might spot quail running in the bush along the edge of the picnic grounds.

At press time, a favorite route was still closed because of fire damage. This trail led one across the Sunrise Highway and 4.5 miles through meadows where the path ripples along like a ribbon and up into thick oak forest and beautiful manzanita becomes monotonous, ending on the opposite side of the road back at the Penney Pines starting point. Cleanup is necessary before the trail is safe again. If you're up for it, check whether the trails have been reopened, and consult the map (available as listed above) for a loop of adventure. Otherwise, head back the way you came.

▶ NEARBY ACTIVITIES

Try the Blue Jay Lodge Restaurant where the mountain cabin atmosphere adds a woodsy feel to the culinary experience. Call (619) 473-8844 for more information.

LAGUNA MOUNTAINS:
SUNSET TRAIL

KEY AT-A-GLANCE INFORMATION

LENGTH: 3 miles

CONFIGURATION: Out-and-back

DIFFICULTY: Easy

SCENERY: Forest, water, birds

EXPOSURE: Filtered and full sun

TRAFFIC: Moderate

TRAIL SURFACE: Earthen path, some rocky areas

HIKING TIME: 1.5 hours

ACCESS: Parked vehicles must display an "Adventure Pass," sold at the visitor center or at the Mount Laguna Lodge Store located about 8 miles north of I-8 on Sunrise Highway. For more information, call (619) 473-8547 or visit www.lmva.org.

MAPS: Available for purchase at the visitor center, online at www.lmva.org, at the Lodge Store, and the Blue Jay Restaurant; see www.lmva.org or www.lagunamountain.com for more information.

SPECIAL COMMENTS: The thin air at nearly 6,000 feet can make this easy hike seem slightly longer than the measured mileage. Occasionally, winter snow closes the Sunset Highway (a.k.a. S1) or makes tire chains necessary; for current conditions, call the California Highway Patrol at (858) 637-3800 or check the "traffic incidents" section at www.cad.chp.ca.gov.

IN BRIEF

This fairly short route to the water in the woods is only a portion of the Sunset Trail but provides a quick, quiet interlude with nature and all its stress-relieving qualities. Squirrels abound on this park-like hike without the pavement, joggers, or city commotion, but there are biting flies (consider an insect repellant).

DESCRIPTION

The narrow trail starts off heading north through meadowland and toward trees, climbing ever so gradually. The path is reserved for foot traffic, but you may notice (thankfully only a few) bicycle tire tracks. After a few steps, you'll come to a trail split; go left toward "water in the woods."

At around 0.4 miles, the trail comes to a ridge overlooking distant, golden meadows. Early mornings mean a view of the clouds settling over the valley meadows. Later, the setting sun's rays spill orange and pink into the dusky sky. There's a rocky area along this section, but nothing difficult. Some large boulders provide resting spots for those who wish to pause and appreciate the views.

Turning right takes you to a meadow dotted with trees, thick in places. Beware of biting flies wanting to make a meal of exposed skin. In the spring you'll see a variety of butterflies flitting from flower to flower—pale purple fleabane with its yellow center, bright scarlet bugler and Indian paintbrush, sunny golden yarrow, and an array of others.

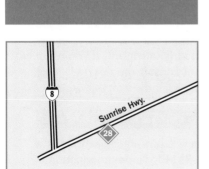

DIRECTIONS

From I-8, take the Sunset Highway exit, turn left (north), and drive 5.1 miles. You'll spot an information kiosk on the right; park on the shoulder (where there is plenty of room). The trailhead is across the street, a few hundred feet north.

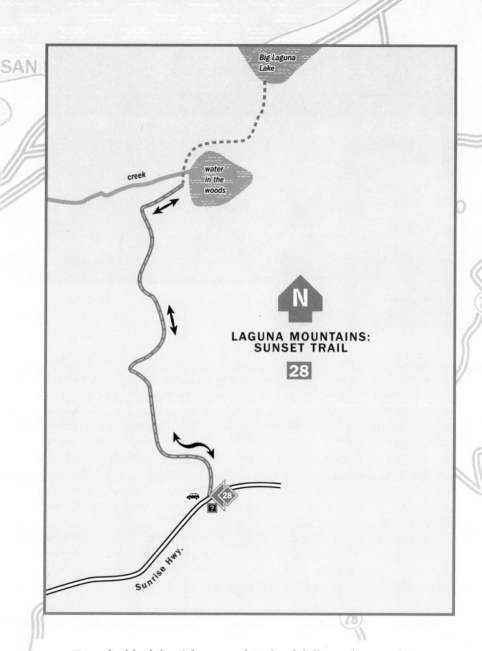

Disturbed by hikers' feet, a multitude of dull grasshoppers lying cam-ouflaged in the dirt open their wings to reveal the vibrant orange. Fluttering away, they sound like shaking maracas.

At about 0.6 miles, the trail moves fairly steeply downhill, into black oak forest. The steep section is short and not so vertical that you must slow down. A more gradual descent stretches about a third of a mile further. The trail then levels for a bit before climbing upward through thicker forest. The shade casts shadows, and rocks sticking up in the path might go unseen: watch your step as you pick your way through the woods.

A curious squirrel shares the log bench overlooking the Water in the Woods.

When you come to an outcropping of rocks on the right and the path crosses the flat edge of a boulder, you'll know you've nearly reached the pond. The trail opens to a wide meadow, revealing a seasonal creek to the left just ahead. The pond teems with life. A variety of algae provides hiding places for aquatic bugs; birds come for a drink and dragonflies buzz about then rest atop the scummy floating pads of algae.

If you want to go farther, an additional half mile or so leads to Big Laguna Lake (but thanks to drought, you can't count on the presence of water). Go left past the pond and head northwest to reach the lake. The Sunset Trail also continues to the north side of the lake, allowing you to connect to other trails for a long loop if you prefer (consult the Mount Laguna area map).

Otherwise, sit on a log overlooking the pond. If you brought lunch, count on squirrels to pay a visit, hoping for a handout. Enjoy the reflection of the trees on the water's blue-green surface, breathe in the fresh scent of the mountain air, and relax before retracing your steps back to the highway and your car.

▶ NEARBY ACTIVITIES

On a cool day, a cup of steaming hot chocolate or coffee can warm your bones. On hot days, you usually crave cold drinks. They're both plentiful at the Mount Laguna Lodge Store. Located several miles north, next to the post office on the Sunrise Highway, the store has a variety of souvenirs and educational items, too.

LAKE DIXON SHORE VIEW TRAIL

▶ IN BRIEF

There's something about ambling along a large body of water that calms the spirit. Unbelievably peaceful on weekdays, Dixon Lake is a slice of inland paradise: sage scrub, wildflowers, birds, and water all combine to make this an easy, rewarding hike.

▶ DESCRIPTION

From the parking area, proceed northeast and find the trail marker near the vehicle road. The rock-edged path heads south, just above the grassy picnic area and continues a short distance past some small pines and acacias where scrub jays flutter. The trail gets a little rocky as it gradually descends, bringing the northwestern edge of the lake into view. A wooden footbridge crosses Jack's Creek, which slows to a trickle in summer and fall.

Past the footbridge, the trail heads around the cattail-filled Jack's Creek Cove and bends to the left toward the pier. A breathtaking view of the entire lake stretches out to the east—making it feel like you've stumbled into paradise. The brilliant blue-green water is alive with squabbling American coots. The duck-like birds hunt for a meal alongside the anglers, who pose like statues in their boats. The lively coots are fun to watch. Tread lightly, though. The ash-dark birds with bright-white bills glide away in a V of gentle breakwater as you near. If you're quiet and catch one unaware, you may see a bird dive through the clear water to the lake bottom, grab a tasty crustacean, and paddle to the surface to eat.

▶ DIRECTIONS

Take I-15 to the El Norte Parkway exit. Travel east on El Norte for about 4 miles to La Honda Drive, then turn left. Follow the road to the top, and turn right into the gate for Lake Dixon. Make an immediate right and park in the lot.

ℹ KEY AT-A-GLANCE INFORMATION

LENGTH: 3 miles

CONFIGURATION: Out-and-back

DIFFICULTY: Easy

SCENERY: Lake, birds, chaparral, wildflowers

EXPOSURE: Mostly sunny

TRAFFIC: Heavy on weekends; light on weekdays

TRAIL SURFACE: Packed dirt

HIKING TIME: 1.5 hours

ACCESS: $1 parking fee on weekends and holidays

MAPS: Free at the ranger station

FACILITIES: Public rest rooms at the parking lot near picnic area; portable toilets along the trail

SPECIAL COMMENTS: Daily, 6 a.m.–sunset; weekends and weekdays are like night and day. For a peaceful commune with nature, hike this easy, family-friendly trail on non-holiday weekdays. As always when near water, be alert and supervise children.

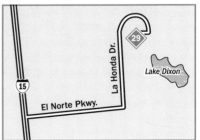

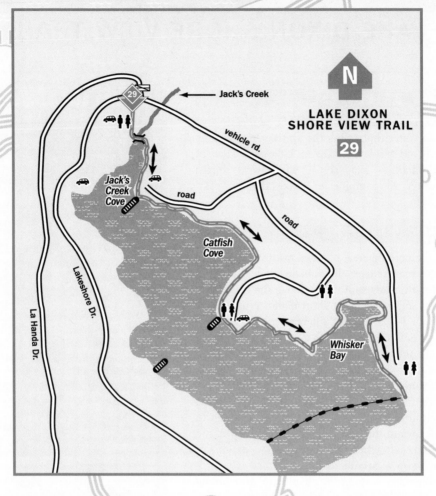

Jack's Creek

N

LAKE DIXON
SHORE VIEW TRAIL

29

vehicle rd.

road

road

Jack's
Creek
Cove

Catfish
Cove

Lakeshore Dr.

La Handa Dr.

Whisker
Bay

You can walk out onto the first pier to see anglers hanging their poles out for a catch. Continuing on the trail, you will find lots of areas where you can easily get closer to the water and sit on large rocks along the shore. A second pier is just past Catfish Cove. There is a portable toilet in the parking area, a few short steps from the trail.

The sage scrub thins and you'll come to a drier section where the trail is higher above the water. The coots like to hang out here, near Bass Cove, where they're hidden from view of the path. You'll hear them, though. With series of short clicks, they warn of your presence; the birds pass the signal from one to the next. These sounds intersperse with longer, higher notes. Close your eyes and the birds' more excited squabbling may conjure the image of a child's bicycle horn.

Head on around to Whisker Bay where people fish from the shore. When you reach the bench at a fork in the path, go right. You'll pass through a cool, shady area where ferns cascade down the decomposing granite alongside the trail, and willows and overgrown laurel sumac are tangled with wild berry and wild cucumber vines. Sage and mint grow in abundance on this stretch as well, pleasantly scenting the air.

The trail widens into an open rock face approaching the buoy line, which is the end of the hike. Dusky brown cormorants balance on the cable line and atop the oblong red buoys, drying their not-quite-waterproof wings in the sun. With their long necks outstretched, they keep a cautious eye on anyone watching them. It's difficult to get a photograph of these ultra-wary birds. They will fly away even as you aim your camera. Enjoy the cormorants for the time you can— they serve as a good reminder to enjoy every moment, a mentality that will serve you well while hiking.

As you head back, focus on the vegetation. Mesmerized by the water, you may have missed it on the way. From early spring through late summer, you will likely see skullcap, with its upright, dark-purple flowers. California fuchsia, sometimes called honeysuckle trumpet, blooms in profusion here. I've seen the narrow, orange-red flowers right into fall here at the lake. California lilac offers delicate clusters of pale blue–lilac flowers that contrast with the dark green leaves of the shrub. When you reach the bench at the trail fork, you can turn right and head west up to the vehicle road. The trail ends here, where there are two portable toilets, and you can walk along the vehicle road if you choose. Returning the way you came is more beautiful, though, and retracing your steps always lends a new perspective to a hike.

LAKE HODGES:
NORTH SHORE TRAIL

KEY AT-A-GLANCE INFORMATION

LENGTH: 4.5 miles

CONFIGURATION: One-way

DIFFICULTY: Easy

SCENERY: Views of the lake, birds, and a creek

EXPOSURE: Mostly sunny

TRAFFIC: Heavy on weekends

TRAIL SURFACE: Sandy dirt

HIKING TIME: 3.5 hours

ACCESS: Free

MAPS: Call (858) 674-2270

FACILITIES: There is a portable toilet across the street from trailhead, rest rooms near the concession stand, and another along the lake.

SPECIAL COMMENTS: During fishing season, a concession stand is open near the picnic area.

IN BRIEF

This easy hike is overrun by bicyclists on the weekends, but weekdays outside fishing season are quiet and serene.

DESCRIPTION

From the parking lot, head south on the paved walkway that makes the first section accessible for people with disabilities. I-15 runs along the right of this paved area for about 0.5 miles. Sage scrub, black sage, and California buckwheat grow close to the trail, scenting the air. On windy days, the rustling of grasses in the meadows to the left sounds like ocean waves and dulls the roar of traffic on the adjacent interstate.

The walkway bends to the right, ducking under the freeway. In the spring, cliff swallows gather by the thousands, swooping to and from their mud nests beneath the freeway. The paved walkway bears right in the cool shade where cyclists speed by (be careful!) and heads north for a short distance until the pavement ends and the dirt trail begins.

Turn left onto the level trail to head southwest. Notice that old cracked asphalt clings to the ground in some places, remnants of Old Highway (US) 395, which served as the main vehicle road until the interstate was built.

DIRECTIONS

To do this as a one-way hike, take cars on I-15 to Via Rancho Parkway and head west for 3 miles. Turn left on Lake Drive and park across from Del Dios Country Store, about 0.9 miles from the Lake Drive turnoff. In the second vehicle, travel back up to Via Rancho Parkway and head east for about 3.5 miles. Turn right on Sunset Drive and follow it less than 0.1 mile to the end, where there is a small parking lot at the trailhead.

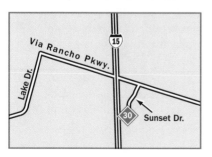

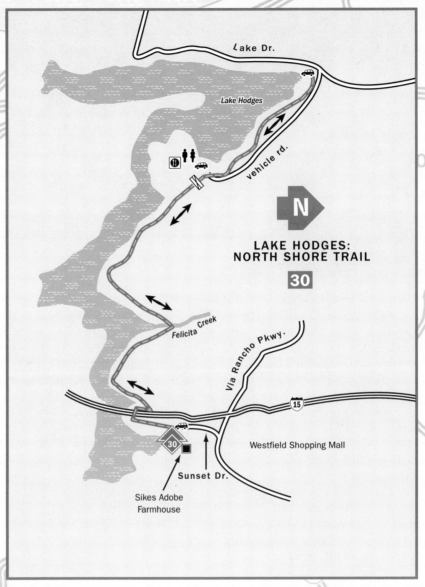

SAN

Lake Dr.

Lake Hodges

vehicle rd.

N

**LAKE HODGES:
NORTH SHORE TRAIL**

30

Felicita Creek

Via Rancho Pkwy.

15

30

Westfield Shopping Mall

Sunset Dr.

Sikes Adobe
Farmhouse

5

76

The route bends to the right, heading northwest, and the freeway sounds begin to fade, leaving the airwaves open to birdsong. Quails, startled from their foraging in the brush, will flutter across the path, and finches twitter in the bush.

Another 0.25 miles bring the trail to an oasis of sorts, with sprawling oaks and palm trees growing near Felicita Creek. Use rocks to cross the creek (bicyclists splash right through) then head uphill about 50 yards. The trail turns left, climbing southwest for a short distance.

The lake stretches out like a shiny ribbon.

Continue southwest on the wide flat trail, which will soon bear to the right (northwest) again. Even in drier years, you will begin to see the lake water along this stretch. Follow the route downhill; a 0.5-mile stretch runs closer to the water. Cottontails may dart out onto the path here, and roadrunners hop out of the prickly pear cactus that grows in massive clumps. Bright orange California dodder and wild cucumber vines top the cactus formations like zany wigs.

A metal gate leads to the parking lot and the concession stand and public rest rooms—facilities are open only during fishing season, which is generally March through October. The hike continues from the northwest corner of the parking lot, but if you like to picnic, this is a logical stopping point. Grassy areas hold tree-shaded picnic tables.

Continuing the hike, you will turn right and follow the asphalt path a short way. Watch for the dirt trail on the left, and follow the path with a view of the lake for about 0.25 miles. There is another parking lot here; this one has a portable toilet and a cement pathway leading down to the lake through stands of mulefat, leather root, and other tall bushes.

Back on the trail, you'll pass another parking area and reach a shady area and the parking lot near Lake Drive where you left your car across from the Del Dios Country Store.

▶ NEARBY ACTIVITIES

Back at the Sunset Drive trailhead, you can cross the road to see the Sikes Adobe Farmhouse that was built from adobe bricks in the late 1800s and is one of the oldest structures in San Diego County. For more modern fun, go the Westfield Shopping Mall across Via Rancho Parkway, where a variety of shops and restaurants are sure to please.

LAKE HODGES: WEST TRAIL

A leisurely stroll or a fast-paced speed walk—the workout level is your choice on this mostly flat trail that offers views of Lake Hodges.

► DESCRIPTION

The trail heads south from the parking area through a forest of a few mature oaks mingled with eucalyptus—mostly young, spindly trees growing close together. Splashes of sunlight alternate with shade as the trail moves along Lake Drive. The community of Del Dios is on the right, with its aged, unique character and interesting homes with distinct personalities.

At about 0.25 miles, the lake comes into view on the left and one hears the waterfowl chatter. In spring and early summer, the bright yellows and oranges of generously blooming nasturtiums blanket shady stretches along the trail. The bright green leaves on these thriving specimens get as big as dinner plates. In the sunny sections, you'll find yucca, with its ornate, mauve-tinged, white-blooming stalks, and prickly pear cactus with yellow and pink blooms. The peaceful forest atmosphere on this easy trail is conducive to chatting, so this is a good hike to do with someone whose conversation you enjoy.

Continuing to almost the 1-mile mark, you will reach the intersection of Rancho Road and Lake Drive, where the long-established Hernandez Hideaway restaurant is located. Here, Lake Drive ends and the trail dips closer to the lake toward the Windsurf Launch Area, about 2 miles

KEY AT-A-GLANCE INFORMATION

LENGTH: 6 miles

CONFIGURATION: Out-and-back

DIFFICULTY: Easy

SCENERY: View of Lake Hodges

EXPOSURE: Sun and shade

TRAFFIC: Heavy weekend use

TRAIL SURFACE: Packed soil, silt

HIKING TIME: 2.5 hours

ACCESS: Free

MAPS: Distributed by the San Dieguito River Park and online at www.sdrp.org

FACILITIES: Portable toilets along trail

SPECIAL COMMENTS: This easy hike is also popular with bicyclists. Go on weekdays for less traffic.

► DIRECTIONS

Take I-15 to Via Rancho Parkway and head west for about 3 miles to Lake Drive; turn left and continue driving for 0.9 miles and park in the lot on the left (if it is open) or on the street, across from Del Dios Country Store.

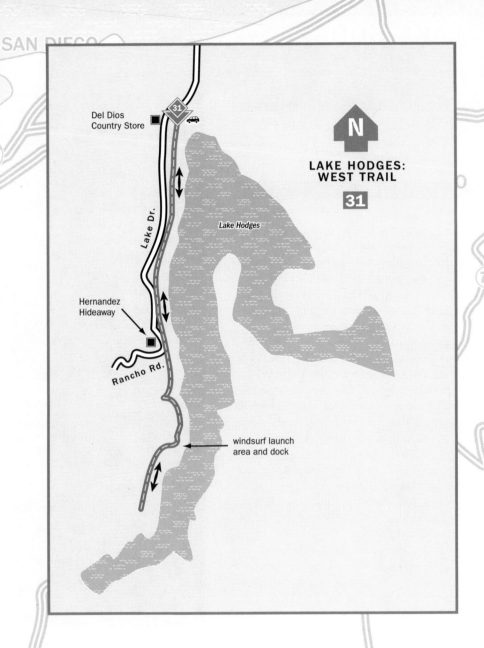

Del Dios
Country Store

N

LAKE HODGES:
WEST TRAIL

31

Lake Dr.

Lake Hodges

Hernandez
Hideaway

Rancho Rd.

windsurf launch
area and dock

from the start. In the off-season you can sit on the metal dock (mind the bird excrement) and let the lapping water rock you while the gentle lake breeze caresses your face. A friendly dog or two might come along, chasing sticks thrown by their masters—local people enjoy the lake nearly every day. There's also a portable toilet nearby. From April to October, group and private windsurfing lessons are offered; the surfers are fun to watch but the activity doesn't compare to from the serenity of off-season. See www.lakehodges.net/aquatic-center for more information about windsurfing lessons.

The single-track trail continues for about another mile. Follow it to the turn-around point then double back, enjoying the last glimpses of the lake that stretches like a rippling blue-green ribbon shimmering in the sunlight.

▶ NEARBY ACTIVITIES

Del Dios Country Store, a fixture in this offbeat, friendly little community, is located on Lake Drive, across from the parking area.

LAKE MORENA TRAIL

KEY AT-A-GLANCE INFORMATION

LENGTH: 4.8 miles

CONFIGURATION: Out-and-back

DIFFICULTY: Easy

SCENERY: View of lake, pine and oak forest

EXPOSURE: Partially shaded

TRAFFIC: Light

TRAIL SURFACE: Packed soil

HIKING TIME: 3.5 hours

ACCESS: $2 per car parking fee

MAPS: Distributed with parking fee at ranger booth

FACILITIES: Rest rooms in campground area

SPECIAL COMMENTS: Watch for snakes, including rattlesnakes; the wide open space of the trail makes for good observation. If you have small children, stay safe and skip the high, narrow Hauser Overlook Trail section; remain on the wide main trail where even pushing a stroller is possible. For more information call (619) 557-5450 or visit www.edweb.sdsu.edu/cab.

IN BRIEF

This pleasant hike through varying landscapes offers view after view of postcard-perfect scenery that makes the 60-mile drive from San Diego worth the time.

DESCRIPTION

From the small dirt lot, walk back around to the gate you passed to park. Access a southwest-bound dirt road, Ward's Flat Trail, partially shaded by cottonwood trees on the right. The route curves, traveling around a finger of Lake Morena, and begins to head northwest. Outcroppings of lichen-encrusted granite rise on the left, some like sheer walls with oak trees seemingly growing right from their craggy faces. Birdsong fills the air.

At 0.7 miles, a granite step stretches out on the right, creating a natural balcony framed by the gnarled branches of an old knotty oak overlooking Lake Morena. The trail climbs very gradually past Indian paintbrush growing in fiery, coral-red clumps; boulder walls soon give way to flat meadows. In spring, yellow daisy-like flowers no bigger than your fingertip carpet the ground and emit a nearly suffocating tangy-sweet scent.

At about a mile you'll notice the connecting trail on the right. Pass it for now; also pass the short, dead-end road on the left that leads to a dilapidated metal storage barn. The trail curves

DIRECTIONS

From I-8 east, exit and turn right onto Buckman Springs Road, continuing west for about 6 miles. Turn right on Oak Drive and travel for another 1.5 miles to Lake Morena Drive. Turn right and drive straight into Lake Morena Regional Park. Pay for parking at the ranger booth, then continue just past a gate on the left (the trailhead), where you'll turn into a small dirt parking area.

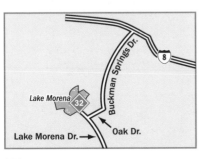

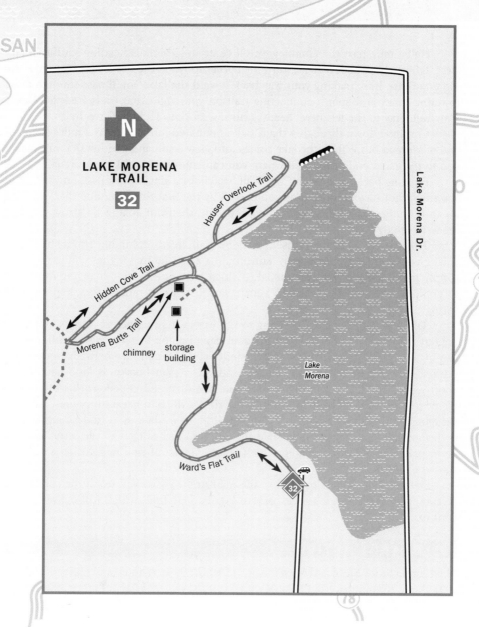

south, heading away from the lake, and moves slightly downhill onto the Morena Butte section of the hike. As you continue, look for a concrete chimney and a few steps—all that's left of a recreation building built some 80 years ago. In the distance to the right, a red-brown rock butte, reminiscent of those in New Mexico, reaches toward the sky. Atop it, freestanding boulders perch precariously along the ridge.

Continue hiking through an area of mature pine and oak that opens into wide, grassy prairies. Although the landscape is varied, the towering pines lend an alpine feel to this segment of the hike.

Half a mile past the chimney, you'll come to side trails heading southeast and west. Ignore these and, instead, turn the corner to reach the northwest section of the Morena Butte Trail, making your way back toward the lake. You'll pass through more towering pines and spot a connecting trail on your right that leads back to Ward's Flat Trail. Stay to the left here, heading northwest onto Hidden Cove Trail.

Continue down through a shady oak-dominated forest. After 0.2 miles from the end of Morena Butte Trail, the lake comes into view again and another 0.4 miles takes you to the gated end of the trail where you can enjoy views of Lake Morena.

Heading back up Hidden Cove Trail, watch for a single-track path on your right. You might not have noticed it as you passed by the first time. But after backtracking about 0.4 miles, you'll discover the path in a washed-out area in a narrow meadow break in the trees.

This narrow path, the Hauser Overlook Trail, heads uphill but is not strenuous. Giving you a bird's-eye view of the surrounding area, the trail invites you to picnic or simply pause to look out over the lake, which reflects the sky—changing from blue to gray according to the weather. Watch, and listen, for rattlesnakes, especially in spring.

The trail continues up, bending to the west where it ends on a rock cliff looking out to the west and down over the dam. Standing on the edge of the cliff, ponder the history of Lake Morena, which includes a 1916 contract between a drought-riddled City of San Diego and Charles Hatfield, a man known as "the rainmaker." Shortly after Hatfield set up his towers near the dam and concocted his secret rain recipe that caused smoke to billow into the air . . . the rain began. It poured for days, deluging San Diego with so much rain that bridges washed away and homes slid off their foundations. Citizens then sued the city for damage to their property! The city never paid Hatfield, reasoning that the rain was an act of God rather than a result of Hatfield's magic.

Retrace your steps downhill to the main trail. When you reach the connecting section, turn right and follow it back to Ward's Flat Trail, which will deliver you to your car.

▶ NEARBY ACTIVITIES

The Campo Stone Store and Museum at 31130 CA 94 is an interesting historical diversion about 20 minutes from Lake Morena; call (619) 478-5707 for more information.

LAKE POWAY LOOP

The Lake Poway Recreation area offers boat rentals and fishing, a walk-in campground, and a grassy picnic area. For day hikers, even busy weekends in this spacious area let you feel close to nature and far from the city.

▶ **DESCRIPTION**

A sense of pride pervades the city of Poway and spills over into its countryside and public recreation areas. With its pristine picnic areas and lake views reminiscent of a European vacation spot, hikers can immerse themselves in the relaxation of a long holiday, if only for an hour or two.

From the parking area, walk north past the office building on the left and look for the trail entrance to the left of the snack bar. You'll head north for several yards and get a view of the boat dock and the lake on your right, to the east. The wide trail, flanked by smallish pine trees that smell like Christmas all year, bends west and leads up a short, steep section before gradually descending northwest. Look for skullcap with purple blooms in spring and summer and wild cucumber and curly dock all growing among the laurel sumac and sage scrub. In spring, watch for fleabane (a natural flea repellent); its lavender daisies with yellow centers grow on spindly stems. White flowers grow almost like tufts of fuzz on holly cherry, a leafy shrub with dark green leaves. In the summer, toyon, a more leathery-leafed shrub, boasts white blooms that change to clusters of red berries to the fall. Blooming sometimes as early as

▶ **DIRECTIONS**

From I-15, take Rancho Bernardo Road and head east. Rancho Bernardo Road becomes Espola Road after about 2 miles. Travel a total of just under 5 miles and turn left on Lake Poway Road. Proceed to the entrance booth and park in the lot.

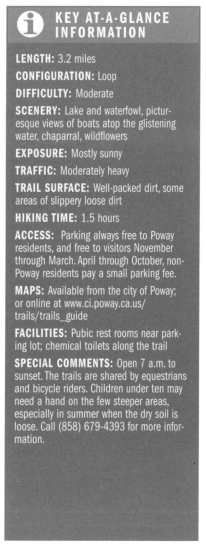

ⓘ **KEY AT-A-GLANCE INFORMATION**

LENGTH: 3.2 miles

CONFIGURATION: Loop

DIFFICULTY: Moderate

SCENERY: Lake and waterfowl, picturesque views of boats atop the glistening water, chaparral, wildflowers

EXPOSURE: Mostly sunny

TRAFFIC: Moderately heavy

TRAIL SURFACE: Well-packed dirt, some areas of slippery loose dirt

HIKING TIME: 1.5 hours

ACCESS: Parking always free to Poway residents, and free to visitors November through March. April through October, non-Poway residents pay a small parking fee.

MAPS: Available from the city of Poway; or online at www.ci.poway.ca.us/trails/trails_guide

FACILITIES: Pubic rest rooms near parking lot; chemical toilets along the trail

SPECIAL COMMENTS: Open 7 a.m. to sunset. The trails are shared by equestrians and bicycle riders. Children under ten may need a hand on the few steeper areas, especially in summer when the dry soil is loose. Call (858) 679-4393 for more information.

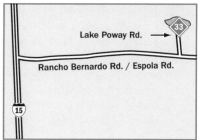

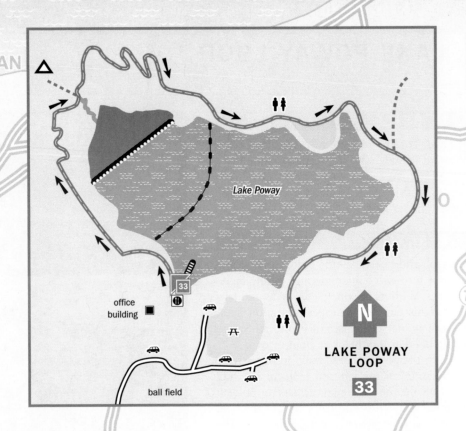

January, blue dicks, a member of the lily family that grows in showy yet delicate clusters atop two-foot, grass-like stems, can also be seen.

At about 0.5 miles, the trail gets steeper and a series of short switchbacks leads you down to the base of the dam. Smaller children might need a helping hand here, especially in dry months when loose ground gets slippery. Look to the northwest for a triangle of rocks peeking between the hills. It's the dam for Lake Ramona, about 4 miles away. When you get to the bottom of the downhill slope, you'll see a water trough for horses, and perhaps a few dragonflies hovering near. A creek runs here at the base of the dam, too, and you'll likely notice the creamy yellow flowers of Hooker's evening primrose during spring and summer. The showy blooms that grow on hairy, reddish stalks may be "dressed to kill," but the name doesn't refer to anything tawdry. They were named for a nineteenth-century botanist.

At about 1 mile from the trailhead, a path on the left leads off to the campground, where there are rest rooms and shaded picnic benches. The trail continues to the right, climbing gradually upward from the dam. At about 1.5 miles in, you'll start to see the dam again. A little farther and the lake is back in view as the trail gradually descends. On weekends, the glistening water is dotted with picturesque rowboats, and you make your way down to the water. On weekends, you'll likely hear laughter drifting across

Boats look peaceful gliding atop the glassy Lake Poway waters.

the lake from the picnic park near your car. As you get closer to the water, you'll hear the clicking and squabbling of the American coot, which gathers in groups on the lake. My family has nicknamed this ever-present bird the American "toot," because its voice is so similar to a child's bicycle horn.

As the trail levels out, you'll see portable toilets to the left. On the right, a short path leads down to a beaching area for boats. You can sit in the shade of a pine tree and watch the water lap at the shore. Several yards forward is another group of portable toilets, and on the lake side of the trail, a shaded bench marked "Pine Point" where hikers and cyclists can overlook the water. With easy access to the beach and rest rooms, this is a favorite picnic spot.

The trail meanders around the northern-most inlet then comes to a fork. Keep heading to the right around the lake and bypass the Mount Woodson Trail opening to the left. You'll start to climb again, but at 2.7 miles, the trail slopes downward and heads past a side trail that leads to the lake's southern shore and the boat dock. Take this if you choose, or head up the trail lined with milk thistle. The spiny plants sprout purple blooms in the summer. When you reach the picnic park, head across the grassy knolls to your car. In the spring, my daughters like to pluck the clover blooms that grow profusely in the lawn, tying them together for a natural chain that brings back childhood memories for me. Press the chains into a book to hold onto the memory of a pleasant day at Lake Poway.

▶ NEARBY ACTIVITIES

Old Poway Park is a historical gem with a museum, an operating steam train, and a Saturday farmer's market. From Lake Poway, turn left onto Espola Road. Drive just over 3 miles to Twin Peaks and turn right. At about 0.8 miles, turn left on Midland. The 4.75-acre park is at about 0.5 miles on the right at 14134 Midland Road. Call (858) 679-4313 for more information.

LAKE POWAY TO MOUNT WOODSON PEAK TRAIL

KEY AT-A-GLANCE INFORMATION

LENGTH: 7.2 miles

CONFIGURATION: Out-and-back

DIFFICULTY: Strenuous

SCENERY: Picturesque view of the lake, interesting boulder formations, wildflowers, and panoramic views

EXPOSURE: Mostly sunny

TRAFFIC: Moderate (heavy on the lake portion of the trail on weekends)

TRAIL SURFACE: Well-packed dirt, some areas of rocky or slippery loose dirt

HIKING TIME: 4.5 hours

ACCESS: Parking is always free to Poway residents, and free to others from November through March; in other months, non-Poway residents pay a small parking fee.

MAPS: Available from the city of Poway; see www.ci.poway.ca.us/trails/trails_guide

FACILITIES: Pubic rest rooms near parking lot, and chemical toilets along the trail

SPECIAL COMMENTS: Open 7 a.m. to sunset. Choose a day in late fall, winter, or early spring to avoid extreme heat on this trail shared by equestrian and bicycle riders. Weekday traffic is low. Call (858) 679-4393 for more information about the Lake Poway Recreation area and its activities.

▶ IN BRIEF

The beautiful and serene Lake Poway Recreation Area is the starting point for this strenuous trail that climbs approximately 2,300 feet to reach the boulder-crested peak of the nearly 2,900-foot-high Mount Woodson.

▶ DESCRIPTION

Head southeast down the dirt road that runs to the right of the lake, where a view of the shimmering water gives the surroundings a relaxed air. Even on weekends, when sports activities and picnickers charge the area with a clatter of excitement, catching site of lazy rowboats atop the glistening water brings a sense of peace. As you get farther from the grassy knolls and the sounds of picnickers, the squabbling of the coots, paddling about on the water in search of food, becomes more noticeable.

The downhill slope changes to a gradual incline at about 0.2 miles, and you will soon pass by the marked Sumac viewpoint and trail on your right. A little further, the route turns right and levels as it heads away from the lake for a few hundred yards then bears left again.

At about 0.8 miles, a junction trail cuts away from the lake loop. Head up the hill's steep, steady grade. After about 0.3 miles, you will see a side trail; ignore it and continue east. On the left is an old dry pond bed—a victim of recent years' low precipitation. The depressed terrain is ready to team with life again once Mother Nature delivers adequate rainfall. The trail levels, continuing

▶ DIRECTIONS

From I-15, take Rancho Bernardo Road east. It becomes Espola Road after about 2 miles. Travel a total of just under 5 miles and turn left onto Lake Poway Road. Proceed to the entrance booth and park in the upper lot.

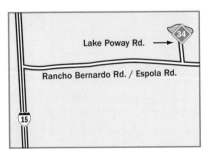

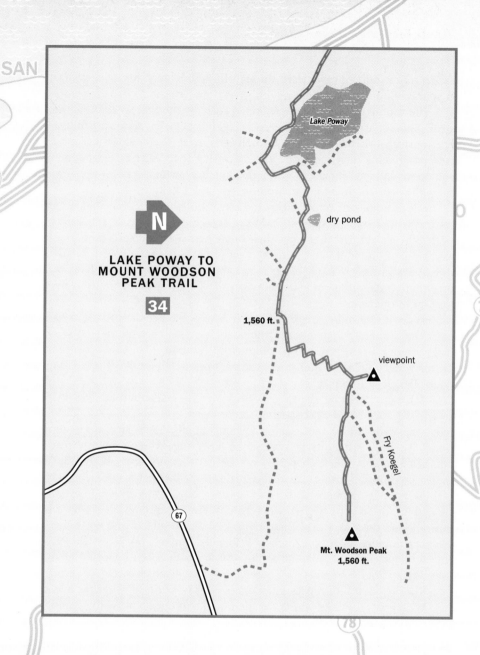

LAKE POWAY TO
MOUNT WOODSON
PEAK TRAIL

34

to a 0.5-mile marker; you have now traveled about 1.3 miles from your start at the lake.

At 1.6 miles, go left where the trail is marked "Mount Woodson" (ignoring the right hand trail). Climb for a short distance, ignoring another side trail, and continue bearing left. A more level section blazes a path through dense laurel sumac forest and comes to another junction. Stay left, heading toward the "peak" (marked). Enjoy the interesting shapes formed by boulder outcroppings on the hillside. From here, it's unlikely you'll spot the narrow trail winding heavenward through those boulders, but pace yourself, you're on your way up.

The sounds of the lake are whipped away by the breezes that offer an updraft to the ravens coasting through the sky. Head northeast for about 0.1 mile and hike a series of steep switchbacks through woody chaparral. The boulders become more and more prominent, encroaching on the narrowing trail. After zigzagging about half a mile up the hill, you'll reach a northerly stretch allowing a view of CA 67 to the east and with what look like toy cars from several miles away.

At this point, the trail is steep and rocky, but a natural stone bench beneath an oak tree is a peaceful resting spot. We've seen bobcat tracks in this area but never spotted the elusive cats that make their home here. Bear left and climb over the boulders that pave the trail. On the right, a set of flat, stepped boulders look almost like a small amphitheater. You'll begin to see the characteristic red limbs of manzanita. After another 0.2 miles, an oak-shaded area lets you view mountains in the east and coast far to the west.

At about 2.5 miles, there is a scenic overlook on the left that can be accessed via a short trail that requires scaling boulders to actually see the view. We usually save this viewpoint for the return trip, and instead continue a few yards past the entry for the marked Fry Koegel Trail and heading toward Mount Woodson Peak (marked Mount Woodson "Trail").

The route levels briefly then begins to climb gradually but steadily. Continue toward a pair of bookend-shaped boulders in the distance. After an additional 0.3 miles, the trail flattens then slants downhill briefly. You'll spot the antennas atop Mount Woodson in the distance, reach an open ridge with a view to the north, then cut back into very thick chaparral and begin to climb again. Manzanita becomes denser, its elevation-loving nature testament to the fact that you're almost there.

At 3.4 miles, a huge, flattish rock appears to block the trail. Step over it to reach the path again on your left. This is a good place to turn around if you're tired, but Mount Woodson Peak is less than a quarter mile ahead, so why not finish? An odd wave-like boulder formation looms. Nicknamed Potato Chip Rock, the boulder features a thin section that juts out at the top. At the peak, find yourself in an antenna forest. Many flattish boulders are perfect spots to picnic or perch.

The downhill return goes much more quickly, but take your time and step with care. With gravity pulling you down the mountain on the rocky, sometimes slippery terrain, you could easily trip and tumble.

▶ **NEARBY ACTIVITIES**

While you're in the area, don't miss a chance to eat at The Incredible Egg, located in the Mercado at 31828 Rancho Bernardo Road. Indoors or on the patio, savor the tastiest of breakfast entrees (served all day). Open daily until 3 p.m. Call (858) 592-7731 for more information.

LAKE POWAY TO MOUNT WOODSON TRAIL (THROUGH WARREN CANYON)

> ## IN BRIEF

The trail runs along the base of the nearly 2,900-foot-high Mount Woodson. Lake Poway makes the start of this sometimes strenuous trail quite peaceful.

> ## DESCRIPTION

Head southeast down the dirt road to the right of the shimmering lake, continuing along as for the "Lake Poway to Mount Woodson Peak Trail" (page 118) for 1.8 miles until you see the sign marked "peak." At this juncture, take a right instead of the left that leads to the peak and heading over hills and dales through a wooded area thick with sumac bushes where wild cucumbers extend their spring tendrils as early as January. Early in the year you may notice wild peonies with their curled ribbon-like leaves. The bowing blackish-red flowers with a fleshy center are often gone by April.

The trail levels for a long stretch. At close to 2 miles from the start, a nice flat "bench" rock appears on the right—a good place to pause to let a breeze caress your skin, or to enjoy the scents of sage and the calls of birds. A short distance further, you may notice another Mount Woodson Peak approach on the left. Stay right (marked "Warren Canyon to CA 67"), and continue east down into Warren Canyon. The route is fairly steep, zigzagging to the left up around some boulders. There's a picnic table on the right at 2.25 miles, just before the trail heads steeply down again. Be careful, taking small, tentative steps so as not to fall. The route will level briefly then

> ## DIRECTIONS

From I-15, take Rancho Bernardo Road east. It becomes Espola Road after about 2 miles. Travel a total of just under 5 miles, and turn left on Lake Poway Road. Proceed to the entrance booth and park in the upper lot.

KEY AT-A-GLANCE INFORMATION

LENGTH: 8 miles

CONFIGURATION: Out-and-back

DIFFICULTY: Strenuous

SCENERY: Picturesque view of the lake, interesting boulder formations, wildflowers, perhaps wildlife

EXPOSURE: Mostly sunny

TRAFFIC: Moderate (heavy on the lake portion of the trail on weekends)

TRAIL SURFACE: Well-packed dirt, some steep (slippery) areas

HIKING TIME: 4 hours

ACCESS: Parking is always free to Poway residents and is free to others from November through March; in other months, non-Poway residents pay a small parking fee.

MAPS: Available from the city of Poway; see www.ci.poway.ca.us/trails/trails_guide

FACILITIES: Pubic rest rooms near parking lot and chemical toilets along the lake trail

SPECIAL COMMENTS: Open 7 a.m. to sunset. Choose a day in late fall, winter, or early spring to avoid extreme heat on this trail shared by equestrian and bicycle riders. Weekdays see very low traffic. Call (858) 679-4393 for more information about the Lake Poway Recreation Area and its activities.

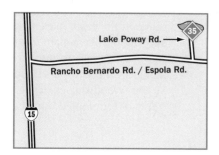

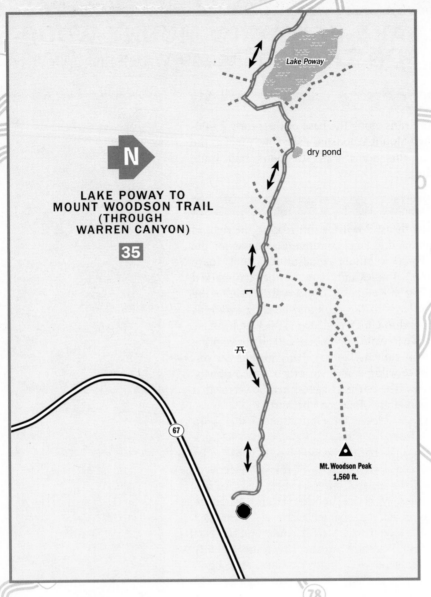

LAKE POWAY TO
MOUNT WOODSON TRAIL
(THROUGH
WARREN CANYON)

35

Lake Poway

dry pond

Mt. Woodson Peak
1,560 ft.

climb for a bit, heading into a series of hills and dales. Huge, round boulders nestle in the earth like colossal eggs; jagged pieces that have broken off lie at odd angles, like a giant clavicle or a hip bone left by an ancient dinosaur.

You'll head through a woody section, tangy whiffs of sage and sumac filling the air. On the left, spot the antenna forest rising above the ridge atop Mount Woodson, evidence of humankind. On the trail, you'll notice the tracks of four-footed inhabitants—deer prints are common along this stretch.

After 3.25 miles, a huge, spreading oak provides a crisp carpet of leaves beneath a dilapidated (as of this writing) picnic table. The cool shade and curling, soft green fern tendrils make this tranquil area that is serenaded by rustling wind and lively crickets a restful place to pause and enjoy the surroundings.

Continuing east, the trail rises up from the woods onto a wide, dry path. CA 67 and its buzzing cars—about a mile and a half away—comes plainly into view. The route will dip down again; although it's only a few feet less elevation, the atmosphere is markedly different. On warm days, you'll notice the temperature drop too. The trail undulates like coaster tracks, embedded boulders lining the path in some spots.

When you pass some massive, two-story-high boulders on the left, watch for a man-made guardrail of smaller rocks stacked alongside the trail on the right. This is the 4-mile turnaround spot. A flattish, saddle back–type boulder just to the left is a good place to get a bird's-eye view of CA 67

Pretend you're Atlas with a rocky boulder "world" on your shoulders at Mount Woodson.

to the west and Mount Woodson Peak to the east. Lie back on the sun-warmed stone, getting a feel for the lizard's life, before heading the 4 miles back to the start.

LAKE WOHLFORD:
NORTH, KUMEYAAY TRAIL

KEY AT-A-GLANCE INFORMATION

LENGTH: 2 miles

CONFIGURATION: Out-and-back

DIFFICULTY: Easy

SCENERY: Native plants, birds

EXPOSURE: Sunny and shady

TRAFFIC: Light

TRAIL SURFACE: Earthen path, leaf litter, sandy

HIKING TIME: 1 hour

ACCESS: Free

MAPS: None

FACILITIES: Rest rooms in the parking area

SPECIAL COMMENTS: Lake Wohlford is open daily from mid-December through the weekend after Labor Day. The area teems with anglers on weekends, but the hiking trails are usually peaceful. Contact the park ranger at (760) 839-4346 for further information.

▶ IN BRIEF

The sparkling blue-green water remains in sight for most of this easy hike along a sometimes unkempt trail on the lake's north side.

▶ DESCRIPTION

Past the rest rooms, spot a sign for the Kumeyaay Trail, which moves east near Lake Wohlford Road for a stretch. Spotty oak shade and the sparkling lake on your right make for a pleasant beginning. The trail crosses some low-lying boulders after a short distance. Look for the telltale indentations in the rock, evidence of days gone by when the area's Kumeyaay Indians gathered to pound acorns into flour.

Just past these boulders, the shade becomes thicker, nurturing poison oak that you'll want to avoid. Tread quietly so as not to frighten the birds; you'll reach large oak trees where herons roost at about a quarter mile. A bench placed beneath the trees overlooks the water; rocks rise from the lake, giving pelicans a place to rest. Cormorants join them, standing with their wings held out to dry in the breeze.

Watch your head for low-growing branches as you continue east, quickly reaching a rocky slope. A few feet ahead, the earthen path resumes, heading uphill toward the right, then back down toward the lake. The scent of sage hangs heavily in the air. Plenty of smooth, rock perches make good spots to sit and watch the water lap lazily at the shore.

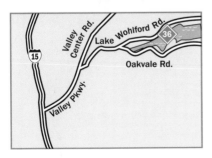

▶ DIRECTIONS

Take I-15 to the Valley Parkway exit. Head east about 5 miles (Valley Parkway becomes Valley Center Road at Washington Avenue) to Lake Wohlford Road. Turn right and drive 2.6 miles, then turn right into the parking area by the ranger office and dock.

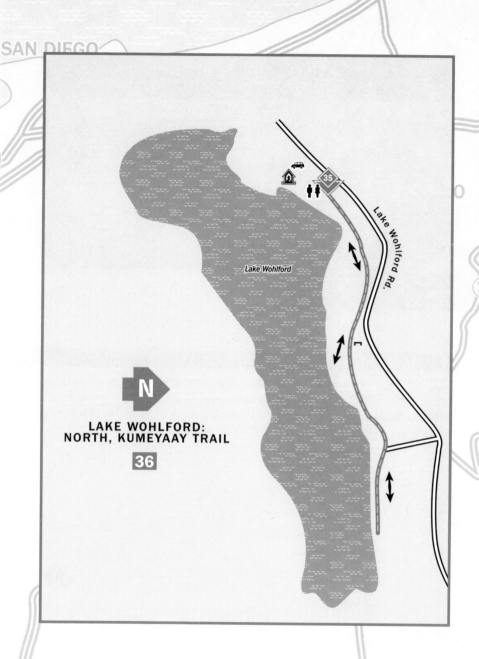

LAKE WOHLFORD:
NORTH, KUMEYAAY TRAIL

36

Lake Wohlford

Lake Wohlford Rd.

At close to half a mile, shade envelops the trail. Gnarled, fallen trees are clumped with tangled vines beneath the living trees that grow densely here.

At 0.75 miles, you'll see a dirt access road heading down from Lake Wohlford Road. A side path heads toward the lake on the right; depending on the water level, you can meander along the shore for another quarter mile or so, watching the birds dive for food, before heading back.

Rustic wilderness overlooks
peaceful Lake Wohlford.

▶ NEARBY ACTIVITIES

Odds are good that you'll find the food tasty at Valley View Casino's Market Square Buffet, with its flavors from around the world. From the lake, turn right on Lake Wohlford Road and travel east then north for about 3 miles to 16300 Nyemi Pass Road, Valley Center. Call (866) 843-9946 for more information.

LAKE WOHLFORD: SOUTH TRAILS

▶ IN BRIEF

Walking these short, easy trails in the dewy morning hours is a feast for the senses.

▶ DESCRIPTION

Find the sign for "Oakvale Trail" to the left of the parking area, and take the narrow grassy path that heads west for 0.2 miles through oak shade. You'll quickly come to a plank bridge placed over a natural rainfall runoff ditch. Be careful of poison oak: The abundant plant is distinguished by its three-leaf pattern, with two leaves anchored opposite one another, and the third having a small stem of its own. It grows in small, bushy clumps in a bigger, almost tree-like form, or as a spindly vine cascading from tree branches. Non-irritating plants such as caterpillar phacelia also grow in lush abundance here. Its dusky white or pale lavender flowers on hairy, coiled stems earned the plant its name.

Over the bridge, the trail narrows, heading through what feels like a mountain-ridge trail. The lake laps gently against the shore about 100 feet away, downhill on the right. Keep your eyes open for cormorants drying their wings on rocks, and blue herons near the shoreline. Look up into the trees above the path too. We saw a pair of herons roosting just a few feet away on our last visit.

It isn't just the treetops that hold interesting sights. This area is a favorite of the funnel web spider. The spiders have woven their nests all

ⓘ KEY AT-A-GLANCE INFORMATION

LENGTH: 1 mile

CONFIGURATION: Out-and-back on each of two short trails

DIFFICULTY: Easy

SCENERY: Native plants, birds

EXPOSURE: Mostly shady

TRAFFIC: Light on weekdays

TRAIL SURFACE: Earthen path, leaf litter

HIKING TIME: 30 minutes

ACCESS: Free

MAPS: None

FACILITIES: Portable toilets in parking area and at the end of Egret Trail

SPECIAL COMMENTS: Lake Wohlford is open daily from mid-December through the weekend after Labor Day. The area teems with anglers on weekends. Go in the early morning on weekdays and the trails are a peaceful delight—especially in late spring and early summer. Contact the park ranger at (760) 839-4346 for further information.

▶ DIRECTIONS

Take I-15 to the Valley Parkway exit. Head east for about 5 miles (Valley Parkway becomes Valley Center Road at Washington Avenue) to Lake Wohlford Road. Turn right and drive 1.9 miles to Oakvale Road. Turn right and travel 0.7 miles to a gated, dirt road that leads to the lake. Park in the dirt area on the right.

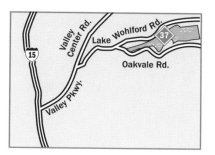

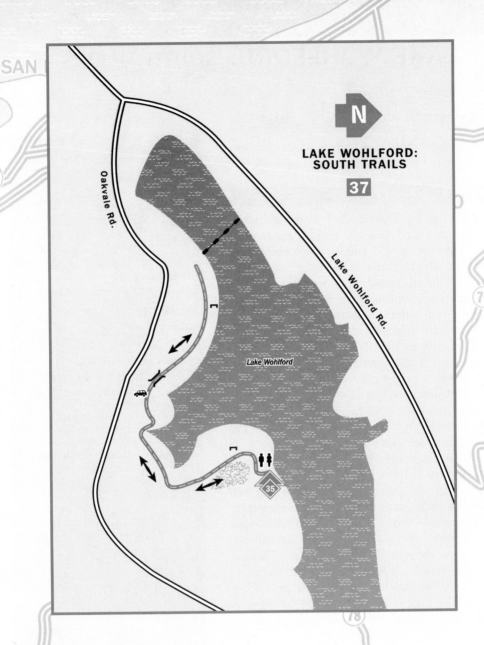

around—small sheets of spider silk lay across the grassy ground. A funnel-like hole extends down into the bush or grass, providing an escape route for the shy resident you're not likely to spot. On cool mornings, dewdrops gather on the silken sheets, creating a uniquely beautiful, almost eerie sight.

At about 0.1 mile, the path narrows even more, heading through lichen-speckled boulders up to a small clearing with a bench that overlooks the water. The trail goes just a little farther, ending abruptly at a clearing before coming to boulders and masses of poison oak.

From here, head back to the parking area, cross the entry road, and access Egret Trail on the right. This northeastward path is wider than the last and has more oak forest. About 100 yards from the entry point, cross a railed plank bridge over a shallow gulch where water flows after rains. Hooker's evening primrose grows here, in its typical showy yellow form, on tall, upright stalks. Another bridge is just a short distance ahead; across it, the trail bends due north.

Wild cucumber grows here, as it does almost everywhere in the county. The inedible plant's bright green fruit is covered in soft, fleshy spikes that dry in the summer, becoming sharp and prickly. This prickly skin peels back to release attractive black seeds that area Native Americans used to gather and polish for necklaces. The vine's dry, inner pod shells lie along the trail. The lacy, oblong, inner pod structure, dropped after the seeds, looks a little like a sea sponge.

A bench overlooks the lake at 0.2 miles where the trail heads through forest. The bushy undergrowth is the perfect habitat for the California towhee, a perky, light brown bird seen foraging in the bushes, using its feet to stir up leaves and food.

Near the end of the hike, many of the trees are bare at the top, providing a good perch for bigger birds. On our last visit, we saw five turkey vultures in one tree. Wondering if the carcass of an animal might be in the bushes below the tree, we watched the big black-brown birds a while. But they were apparently only roosting. They held their red, featherless heads in a tucked position, occasionally spreading impressive wings with silver gray under markings to their six-foot span, as if attempting to dry them in the morning air. Wildflowers grow in rainbow tangles along the last few steps, leading to a portable toilet that marks the turnaround spot. A path leads down to the shore for those wanting to get closer to the water.

Lake Wohlford's trails may be short, but the abundant wildlife makes them a delight. The easy trails are perfect for less-agile hikers. We once brought a family member who was recovering from surgery. He was happy to get back into nature without too much strain.

As you retrace your steps to the parking lot, let the soft lapping of water, the flutter of wings, and the constant *twrp, twrp,* call of the California towhee cast nature's relaxing spell on you.

▶ NEARBY ACTIVITIES

Back on Valley Parkway, a stop at The Stand is a good bet for fresh, locally grown fruits and vegetables.

LOS JILGUEROS PRESERVE TRAIL

KEY AT-A-GLANCE INFORMATION

LENGTH: 1.5 miles

CONFIGURATION: Loop

DIFFICULTY: Easy

SCENERY: Birds, stream, ponds, frogs, waterfowl, trees, and native plants

EXPOSURE: Some sunny and some shady

TRAFFIC: Moderately heavy

TRAIL SURFACE: Dirt and boardwalk

HIKING TIME: 45 minutes

ACCESS: Free

MAPS: None

SPECIAL COMMENTS: In this 46-acre preserve that is the most popular of the sites managed by the Fallbrook Land Conservancy, visitors find it easy to understand the necessity of preserves as cities grow and encroach on nature. Even with busy Mission Road on the west and a housing tract on the east, this space teems with animal and plant life.

IN BRIEF

A pleasant, 1.5-mile loop frames two ponds in this well-managed site that is popular with bikers, dog walkers, and those out for an invigorating walk through nature.

DESCRIPTION

Notice kiosks to the left of the parking lot and head into the preserve just past those. A bench placed right at the start of the trail sets the tone for this adventure—easy-paced with lots of places to reflect.

After the short northwestern stretch that passes sycamore trees and scented sage, a wooden plank bridge appears on the left. Head across the bridge, where yerba mansa grows all around. The flowers' conical centers stretch up above white petals that form the crowning bloom for bright green leaves on red stems. In winter, the plants die back to an ugly matte brown. This westward walk of a few hundred yards takes you closer to Mission Road, which runs along the outside of the preserve. The wooden plank bridge will cross water at some point; how much water depends on the season and rainfall amounts.

Where the plank bridge ends, turn right onto the dirt path. The route heads north alongside Mission Road for close to half a mile, passing a series of short wood plank bridges along the way. This stretch is considered the "nature trail." Dragonflies buzz, birds sing exuberantly, and cot-

DIRECTIONS

Take I-15 north to the Pala/CA 76 exit and go left (west) 4.9 miles to Mission Road, then turn right. After 4.4 miles, you'll see signs for Los Jilgueros Preserve, which is past the high school and just past the Sterling Bridge intersection. Turn right and head down the short dirt road, then park in the dirt- and bark-surfaced lot on the left.

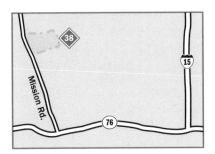

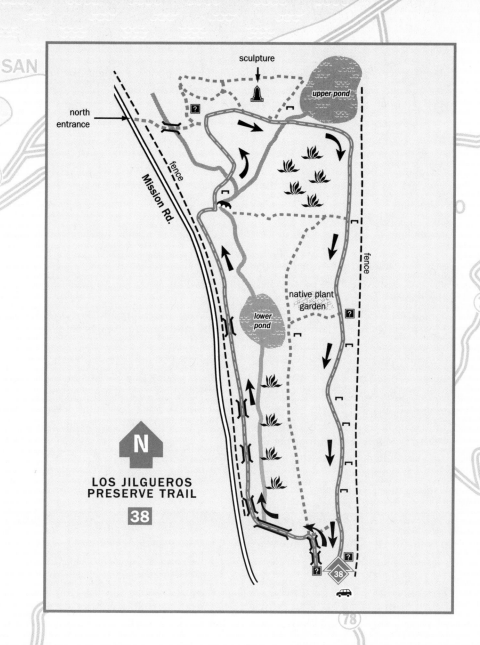

SAN

north
entrance

sculpture

upper pond

fence

Mission Rd.

fence

native plant
garden

lower
pond

N

LOS JILGUEROS
PRESERVE TRAIL

38

tontails hop in and out of the bushes. Thistles reach up, their purple blooms turning to tufts of fuzz as spring becomes summer. At two-thirds of the way in on the nature trail, notice the lower pond to your right. Vegetation makes the pond inaccessible. Stay on the path, respecting the area's designation as a preserve.

The trail bends to the right and continues. Look for another path on the left, heading northeast down into the trees. Take this route where you'll see a concrete silt dam and a bench overlooking the creek. Here, in the shade of the trees, you'll spot frogs lazing in the shallow creek water. Bright orange nasturtiums thrive in this cool, shady environment where spotty sunlight filters down. Butterflies flit about and birdsong fills the air.

After spending time reflecting, cross the small bridge and head left into the open for a moment before reaching the shade of trees again. You'll notice another kiosk with information about the preserve up ahead. Two trails run off to the left of this. One crosses a wooden plank bridge toward the north entrance. The other, a single-track trail, delivers visitors up to the "firescape" garden—which is worth a look for those interested in native California plants that retard fire. If you choose to stroll through the garden, you can still access the main loop from that path later.

Sticking to the main loop trail, walk to the right up the hill (northeast). After a short distance, you will see the upper pond on the left. A short trail on the left leads to a bench shaded by lush pecan trees near the shore. This is a nice place to sit a while and enjoy the birds. Continuing east on the path leads you along the right side of the pond.

The route turns abruptly southward for a long trek. Notice the rusty frame of an old truck and some old farm equipment partially hidden in the weeds on either side, remnants of Fallbrook's history.

You'll come to a kiosk with a huge perennial Matilija Poppy bush growing behind it. To the right of the path is a native plant garden that blooms in a variety of colors in spring. More of the showy Matilija Poppy—which blooms in spring and summer—is planted in the garden. The large, yellow-centered flowers with crinkly white petals have a uniquely pungent scent. A trail leads down around the garden to a shaded bench near the lower pond.

The main loop trail continues south all the way back to the parking area. Benches along the way allow visitors to stop and reflect while enjoying birdsong and the sound of gentle winds.

▶ NEARBY ACTIVITIES

The Museum of Fallbrook History can be reached by traveling north on Mission Road for less than a mile. Turn left on Rocky Crest Road, and the museum is #260 on the left. It's open Thursday and Sunday from 1 to 4 p.m., or by appointment (phone (760) 723-4125). Air Park Road (almost directly across Mission from the preserve entrance) will take you to picnic benches that overlook Fallbrook Air Park, affording views of the afternoon's takeoffs and landings.

LOS PENASQUITOS CANYON
PRESERVE: EAST END TO WATERFALL LOOP

▶ IN BRIEF

Popular for mountain biking and equestrian use, and featuring a year-round creek and waterfall, 3,720-acre Los Penasquitos Canyon Preserve is a favorite of San Diego urbanites looking for an extended backyard in which to exercise. The "no bicycle" off-shoot paths looping out from the main trail offer a wilderness feel in this wide-open preserve in the heart of San Diego.

▶ DESCRIPTION

From the parking lot, head west toward the kiosk and continue on the wide westward trail that is edged with the narrow-leafed mule fat and its cottony pink-tinged blooms in spring. You'll likely encounter bikers and horseback riders on this first stretch of flat trail. On the wide main trail, pedestrians yield to both bikers and horse riders. Horses have the right-of-way, and it's best to stop and give them a wide berth.

At approximately 0.1 mile, go right on the first of several single-track trails marked with yellow signs barring bicyclists. On the narrow path, you'll pass through thick stands of lemonadeberry and buckwheat. At nearly 0.2 miles, prickly pear cactus grows in clusters alongside the trail. As early as February, the pink blooms, curled like onions, begin to unfurl, displaying vibrant, sunny yellow insides. Birds flit about in the brush and, if you're quiet, you might even be lucky enough to spot a coyote on this portion of trail. We witnessed one carrying a bird in its mouth on a recent winter afternoon—despite the heavy weekend-visitor population. The startled animal immediately fled,

▶ DIRECTIONS

Take I-15 to the Mercy Road exit and head west. Black Mountain Road intersects Mercy Road, and runs straight into the East End parking lot and equestrian center.

ℹ KEY AT-A-GLANCE INFORMATION

LENGTH: 8 miles

CONFIGURATION: Loop

DIFFICULTY: Easy

SCENERY: Oak forest, wildflowers, birds, creek, and waterfall

EXPOSURE: Half shady

TRAFFIC: Heavy on weekends

TRAIL SURFACE: Packed river rock, silt, and leaf litter

HIKING TIME: 3.5 hours

ACCESS: $1 parking fee at self-pay station

MAPS: Available by request at ranch house or from patrolling ranger

FACILITIES: Portable toilets at East End parking lot and public rest rooms at ranch house

SPECIAL COMMENTS: Open 8 a.m. to dusk. If you're looking for a private, relaxing hike, don't come here on weekends when the preserve is overrun with bikers, runners, and horseback riders. For more information, see www.sannet.gov/park-and-recreation/parks/penasq.

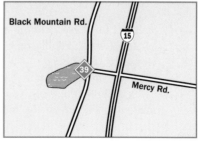

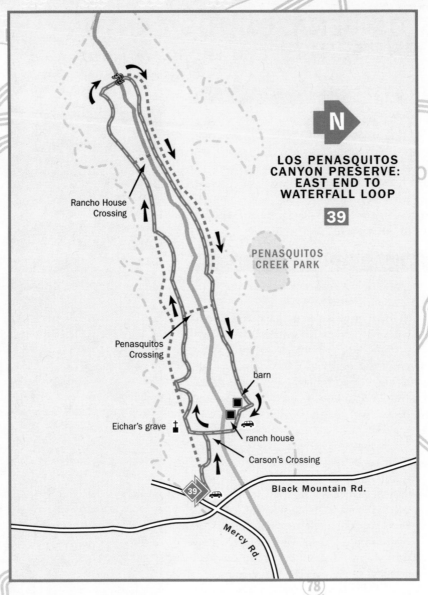

LOS PENASQUITOS
CANYON PRESERVE:
EAST END TO
WATERFALL LOOP

39

PENASQUITOS
CREEK PARK

Rancho House
Crossing

Penasquitos
Crossing

barn

Eichar's grave ✝

ranch house

Carson's Crossing

39

Black Mountain Rd.

Mercy Rd.

as usual for these cunning but shy animals. A few yards past the pale green cactus clumps, you'll come to a wide clearing. A sign indicates the Ranch House creek crossing to the right. Go left onto the cleared path instead, and rejoin the main trail.

Back on the main route, turn right. After a few yards, you'll notice a marker to the left of the main trail. This is the gravesite of Eichar, an individual whose connection to the ranch house isn't completely understood. He died of consumption in 1882. There's nothing much to see here now. The county removed the headstone some time ago after it was vandalized. There is talk of creating a replica, so look for that in the future.

Several yards farther up the main trail is another side trail, marked by a yellow sign. Go right and follow the single track through oak forest. Poison ivy grows thickly here, so remember the "three-leaf" rule and stay on the trail. Through the trees, you'll hear the creek rushing. Queen palms grow in a tangled mass up through Western sycamore trees, their arching, orange-spined, green fronds contrasting with the sycamore's creamy white bark. This short section of trail loops south again, joining the main trail for a few feet, then another sign directs you to the third single-track section. Take this trail for a shadier hike through oak forest and continue for about a mile (passing the northerly offshoot trail leading to Penasquitos Creek Park Crossing). It will loop back out to the main trail once again.

Continue west on the main trail for nearly a mile, passing the offshoot for yet another creek crossing (Carson's Crossing), and head under the power lines. This sunny section of trail will feel the longest, but relief appears in the form of another side trail, marked with a yellow sign. This takes you off the main path for a short distance before looping south to rejoin the main trail. Horses aren't as common this far into the preserve, but you may see some, and their droppings are everywhere. Watch your step—leashed dogs are also allowed in the preserve.

Counting the single-track side trails, you'll have hiked approximately 4 miles when you see a sign marked "waterfall." Head uphill and you'll begin to hear laughter and splashing. A large lava rock formation to the right of the trail marks the spot where stone steps lead down to the water. People often amble along the narrow shoreline for a few yards and picnic here. Watch out for rattlesnakes. We have spotted rattlers swimming across the creek just east of the waterfall—and they slither along the same shore that visitors use.

Using the protruding rocks, agile adults and older children can cross the creek here at the waterfall in a couple of jumps. Stone steps lead up from the water on the other side. Others prefer to head back to Carson's Crossing where there is a footbridge, as at all the officially marked crossings. You may prefer to simply turn back here and retrace your steps out of the preserve.

Assuming you've crossed at the waterfall, proceed up the stone steps on the north side of the creek and turn right (heading east). A marked, single-track trail opens up several yards east. A slower-running area of the creek comes into view amid a chorus of frogs. The trail is in the open here, but after half a mile, mule fat bushes and willows growing on either side of the trail afford some afternoon shade. At 0.75 miles, heading east, one encounters a revegetation area on either side of the trail. Caged oak seedlings tagged with yellow, red, blue, and white strips stretch across the field, their labels flapping like tattered, narrow flags.

At the marker, consider taking the short southward trail about 100 yards to Carson's Crossing. Stop on the north side of the babbling creek in the cool shade of the oaks. Picnicking is peaceful amid the soft whistles of hummingbirds and the cackle of inquisitive crows.

Beauty blooms among the sharp spines of the prickly pear, or "paddle" cactus.

After a restful stop, continue east on the single-track trail that meanders through the oak forest briefly before the trail opens to the sky again. A mosaic of hoofprints is pressed into the path. Layer upon layer, weekend after weekend, this evidence proves that Los Penasquitos Canyon Preserve is popular with riders. Horse traffic becomes heavier closer to the east end of the preserve. Be alert for horses and riders making their way like a clip-clopping train along the path.

About 2.5 miles from the waterfall, the narrow trail connects with the wider main one. Pass the side trail for Penasquitos Crossing. The trail bends northeast, heading past Penasquitos Creek Park, which is outside the preserve. When you spot a white post-rail fence to the right, head south on the side trail and continue past the ranger's storage barn. A pair of playful angora goats is caged near the barn, but fencing keeps visitors from touching the shaggy animals. South, beyond the goats and barn, is the ranch house that George Alonzo Johnson, the second land-grant owner, built in 1862. Francisco Ruiz got the tract as part of the first Mexican land grant in San Diego County in 1823 and built a small adobe house here. Its walls still stand within those of the larger ranch house, which was restored by the county. A gift shop is open Saturday mornings and Sunday afternoons.

Having seen the ranch house, head east again and cross a small footbridge. The trail will lead through a parking area and pick up where the asphalt ends. Go south toward the marked Rancho House creek crossing, and head across the wooden bridge. From here, you'll retrace your steps on the south side of the creek, heading east out of the preserve and to your car.

LOS PENASQUITOS CANYON
PRESERVE: WEST END TO WATERFALL LOOP

▶ IN BRIEF

The creek provides a relaxing riparian backdrop in this popular preserve. The 3,720-acre oasis of nature amid the traffic and city excitement offers a home to wildlife such as coyotes, birds, and rabbits.

▶ DESCRIPTION

Access the trail at the east end of the large parking lot to head through the dense, cool shade provided by sycamore trees. At the kiosk about 100 yards from the trailhead, go left beneath the Sorrento Valley Boulevard bridge. Begin heading northeast, up the hill. The trail soon levels off.

In the spring, you'll spot fuzzy caterpillars also hiking this route. As if racing against the clock, the tiny creatures move quickly, leaving behind smooth channels in the dirt. On a recent visit, we counted 92. Look carefully. Perhaps you'll count even more.

The route descends into the canyon and joins another trail at about 0.6 miles. You'll head right (east) here and soon spot a sign marked "Wagon Wheel Crossing" on the left. Continue past this for now, taking note of the water level. Decide whether you will feel comfortable crossing from the other side or will need to find another route across the creek (other options are described below).

▶ DIRECTIONS

Take I-5 to Carmel Valley Road and drive east for 0.2 miles. At El Camino Real, turn right and continue for another mile to Carmel Mountain Road. Turn right, travel 0.6 miles to Sorrento Valley Road and turn left. Another 0.3 miles brings you to Sorrento Valley Boulevard. Turn left again (at the traffic signal) and go one mile to the staging area on the right.

ℹ KEY AT-A-GLANCE INFORMATION

LENGTH: 6 miles

CONFIGURATION: Loop

DIFFICULTY: Easy

SCENERY: Oak forest, birds, creek, and waterfall

EXPOSURE: Mostly sunny

TRAFFIC: Heavy on weekends

TRAIL SURFACE: Packed dirt, river rock, silt, and leaf litter

HIKING TIME: 3 hours

ACCESS: Free

MAPS: Available online at www.sannet.gov/park-and-recreation/parks/penasq

FACILITIES: Portable toilet at the West End parking lot

SPECIAL COMMENTS: Open from 8 a.m. to dusk. A favorite of many, the preserve sees many bicyclists, runners, and walkers on weekends. If you want a quiet hike, come on a weekday.

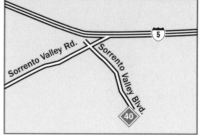

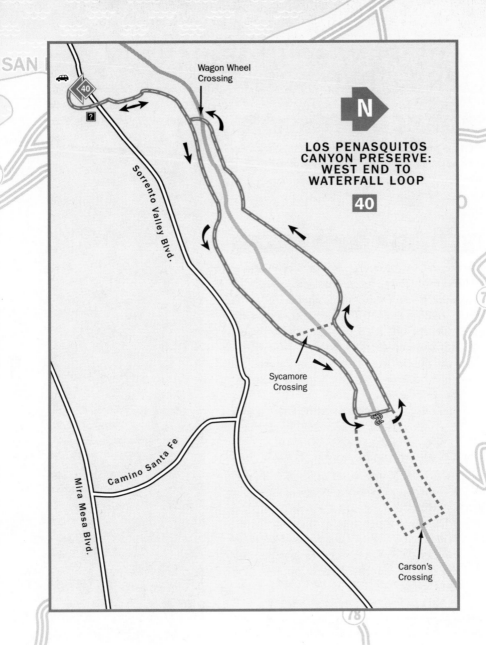

Wagon Wheel
Crossing

N

**LOS PENASQUITOS
CANYON PRESERVE:
WEST END TO
WATERFALL LOOP**

40

Sorrento Valley Blvd.

Sycamore
Crossing

Camino Santa Fe

Mira Mesa Blvd.

Carson's
Crossing

SAN

The route surface changes to coarse gravel and small, smooth river rocks as you continue east. Watch for bright red splashes of California fuchsia and perhaps see coyote scat full of fur—evidence of a thriving canyon population sustained by rabbits and other rodents. In the spring, you may hear pups practicing their yelps from within the off-trail brush, even during the day.

At 1.5 miles, a rocky viewpoint where the trail bends south offers a look up the creek toward the waterfall. The route straightens again, heading into oak forest with lots of shade. Wood roses are among the flowers here. You might also spot the feathery herb, chamomile, growing in clumps midtrail. Where there are flowers there are butterflies, and you'll likely see a variety flitting about here. Bigger river rocks make it easier to carefully cross this stretch.

At about 2 miles, you'll pass the "Sycamore Crossing" path on the left. Check the water level here to help you decide where to cross the creek. To reach the waterfall, continue another mile east on mostly level ground that is open to the sunlight. Rocky in areas, the trail has a variety of sage and mint plants growing alongside it, pleasantly scenting the air. At the waterfall on the left, rock steps lead toward the water. On weekends you'll find bustling activity up and down the creek banks all around the waterfall. Some hikers choose to cross here, scampering across the rocks like agile mountain goats. Others meander upstream then remove shoes to trek across the shallow waters. You could also continue on the main trail for about another half mile to Carson's Crossing where there is a bridge or stop here and return on the same route by which you came. Be wary of snakes that also visit this area. Rattlesnakes are not uncommon anywhere in the canyon but are as attracted to the water as human visitors.

Assuming you've crossed near the waterfall, be careful of poison oak as you head right and up the trail along the split-rail fencing. Head slightly east above the creek, then north back to a wide main trail, where you'll go left (west) to begin the return loop. After several yards, the trail splits right and left. Head left down toward the creek where you get good views of the babbling water as it moves west.

Cross two cement bridges and continue on a path above the creek. The narrow path gradually loses altitude, descending almost to creek level for a time. Sycamores dot the meadow as the trail heads into open space and continues west. The canyon is quieter on this side of the creek. Watch and listen for signs of life lizards, birds, and perhaps a cottontail rabbit hopping along in early morning or late afternoon looking for a snack. Be respectful of any wildlife and plants in the canyon. You'll notice multiple bicycle tire and foot tracks layered along the trail, where visitors do the least damage to this natural habitat. But having planned paths doesn't protect all the wildlife. Occasionally, a creature as fascinating as the seldom-seen millipede lies dead in the middle of the path—the victim of a fast-moving bicyclist.

If you decided on the way out that Sycamore Crossing is your best way across, watch for the sign about a mile from the waterfall. Cross, then take the trail on the south side of the creek back to the beginning. If you decided on Wagon Wheel Crossing, head left at the sign and wade through the water, or find a nearby shallower spot to get to the other side.

Once across, head west for a short distance then south up over the hill. Under the bridge, the mulefat bushes release cottony fuzz in the spring, spilling white bits of fluff into the air where they drift on the breeze. At the kiosk, head right and back to the parking lot and civilization.

MISSION TRAILS REGIONAL PARK: COMBINED TRAILS LOOP

KEY AT-A-GLANCE INFORMATION

LENGTH: 4.2 miles

CONFIGURATION: Out-and-back, with ending loop

DIFFICULTY: Easy, with a more strenuous 1.3-mile climb to peak

SCENERY: Old Mission Dam, waterfowl, San Diego River, views from peak

EXPOSURE: Mostly sunny

TRAFFIC: Heavy

TRAIL SURFACE: Asphalt, sandy soil, packed soil, rocky areas on peak

HIKING TIME: 3 hours

ACCESS: Free

MAPS: Available in the visitor center

FACILITIES: Public rest rooms at visitor center; portable toilets near dam

SPECIAL COMMENTS: If you want an easy hike, skip the 1.3-mile Kwaay Paay summit. For more information about Mission Trails Regional Park, visit the Web site at www.mtrp.org.

IN BRIEF

This nature lovers' mecca in the middle of suburbia is a favorite of hikers, cyclists, and dog walkers.

DESCRIPTION

From the visitor center parking lot, head east down the sidewalk back to the road, which is Father Junipero Serra Trail, the street you entered on. Go left at the gate, which is where the road divides. A yellow-striped curb stretches the distance like a long, lazy snake, keeping cyclists and foot traffic safe on the left-hand side, while allowing cars to travel the one-way road on the right.

After walking on the level road for about a quarter mile, listen for the San Diego River meandering through the trees below on the left. At almost the half-mile point, stone steps lead down to the river. Large flat stones show signs of the ancient Kumeyaay Indians' habitation of this area, in the form of indentations in the rocks. Acorns were ground into flour with a pestle.

Back on the Father Junipero Serra Trail, there is a portable toilet to the right of the road, just a bit farther down. Look up at the vertical rock areas on the left. These rocks are among San Diego rock climbers' favorite climbing spots, and you can often see climbers high above.

At 0.7 miles, a huge rock formation stretches out from the road, extending to the San Diego River. Step onto the warm stone surface and have a

DIRECTIONS

Take I-15 to CA 52 east and drive to the Mast Boulevard exit. Turn left on Mast and drive 0.2 miles to West Hills Parkway. Turn right on West Hills Parkway, drive half a mile to Mission Gorge Road, and turn right. Drive 2.4 miles to Father Junipero Serra Trail and turn right, then almost immediately turn left into the visitor center parking area.

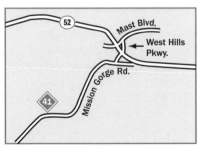

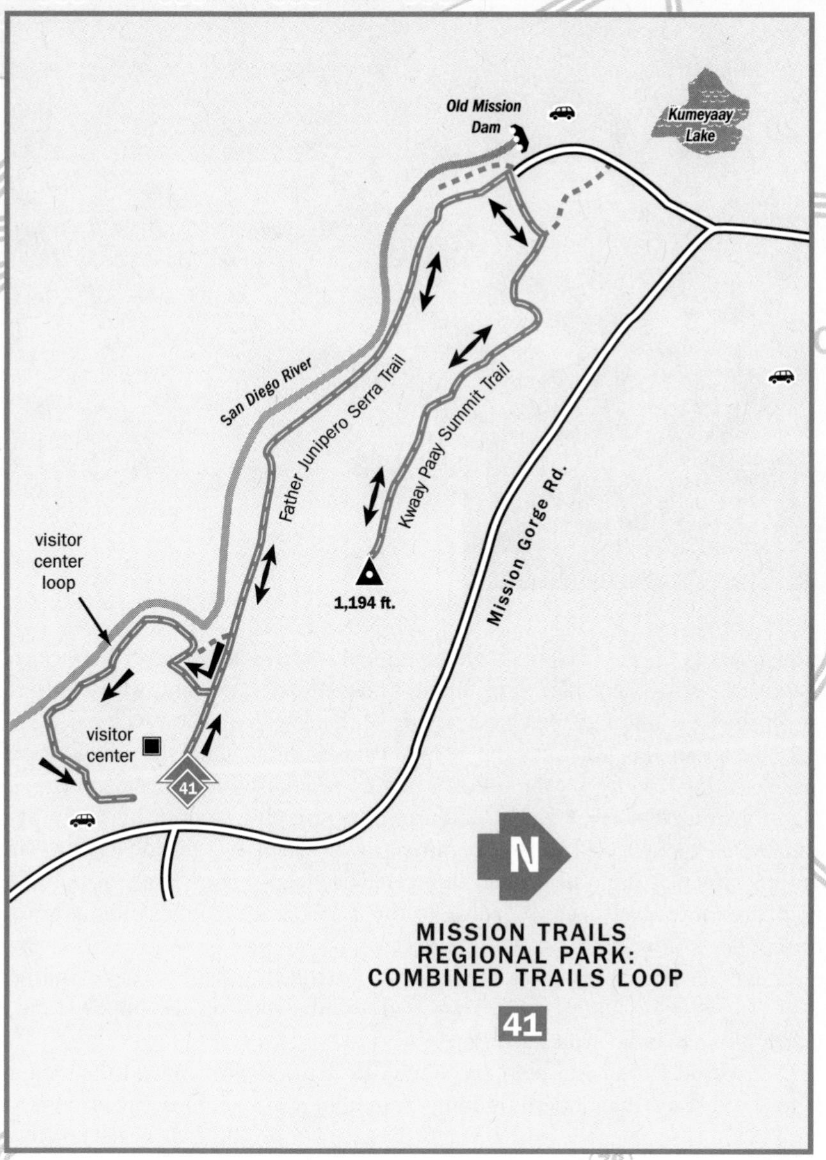

MISSION TRAILS REGIONAL PARK: COMBINED TRAILS LOOP

41

Old Mission Dam

Kumeyaay Lake

San Diego River

Father Junipero Serra Trail

Kwaay Paay Summit Trail

Mission Gorge Rd.

visitor center loop

1,194 ft.

visitor center

41

N

SAN

5

76

78

rest or read the old and new initials carved into a mature oak tree that stretches up to the rock.

Northeast on the trail, there is a wooden bench at just more than a mile. Beyond this, you'll notice a short metal bridge that crosses the river below, and trails leading into the northwest sections of Mission Trails Regional Park. When you reach the stop sign on Father Junipero Serra Trail, look to the right. A narrow trail heads up the mountain to the Kwaay Paay Summit. Head southeast on this uphill stretch for about a quarter of a mile, when you'll come to a trail split. Go to the right and continue uphill, heading southwest now. The eroded trail makes its way up through the chaparral. The bushes

The San Diego River provides a rushing backdrop in Mission Trails Regional Park.

grow taller as the route climbs: white and black sage, lemonadeberry, coast mountain mahogany, warty-stem lilac, and mission manzanita—blooming with light pink flowers in the typical urn shape characteristic of this species—all grow here.

At about 0.8 miles on the Kwaay Paay Summit Trail, the route opens into a mesa clearing. You'll spot the trail starting up again on the other side of the mesa, rising at a suddenly severe grade. Children may use all fours on this steepest section, and even experienced hikers will move slowly when the ground is dry. The loose, gritty soil makes the trail surface slippery. The steep section is about 0.2 miles long, then the route levels again, leading to the 1,194-foot summit where a group of flat rocks offer a view all the way to the ocean.

Retrace your steps down the mountain to the stop sign on Father Junipero Serra Trail. The historic Old Mission Dam is down the road on the opposite side and is worth a quick look if you have time.

Back on Father Junipero Serra Trail, head southwest toward the visitor center. Before you reach the modern building, watch for a side trail leading off into the chaparral. This is your entry to the Visitor Center Loop. The trail bears northwest with some views of the San Diego River, eventually curving to the southwest where the water runs over multilevel stones that make you realize that those popular backyard ponds and falls are modeled after Mother Nature's works. Head uphill, where the trail curves southeast again, leading back to the parking lot.

▶ NEARBY ACTIVITIES

While you're here, the visitor center itself is a worthwhile diversion. On the walkway leading to the entrance, audio panels and information boards offer insight into the sights and sounds of the area's wildlife. Inside the center, video presentations and state-of-the-art exhibits tell the history of the region. A gift shop offers Kumeyaay Indian baskets, pottery, and jewelry, along with books, posters, and other items.

MONSERATE MOUNTAIN TRAIL

▶ IN BRIEF

Serenaded by birdsong, hikers traverse a trail lined with wildflowers, chaparral, and rock formations within 225-acre Monserate Mountain Preserve. At the top, your hard climb is rewarded with panoramic views of mountains in the east and the Pacific Ocean in the west.

▶ DESCRIPTION

Park on the shoulder at the trailhead and walk east on a path lined with wild mustard and laurel sumac. At 0.2 miles, you'll come to a gate, which is open from dawn to dusk. The trail turns south here, then east again through a rock-paved section. The east–south pattern repeats itself several times as the trail heads up the mountain populated by fuzzy red ants. At 0.3 miles, a short slippery area requires careful footing to avoid a fall.

The southward curves on the route afford views of I-15, where the cars now seem tiny. From the rising trail, they are distant reminders of the cares you left behind.

At approximately half a mile, the path heads east at a steady but gradual climb. This straight shot lasts for about a third of a mile, moving through chaparral that becomes thicker. Yucca appears, the pointy green spires encircling the rising shaft with a flame-shaped tuft of ivory blooms. Also along this stretch, find rattlesnake weed blooming in creeping mats on the gritty ground. Flowering from spring through fall, rattlesnake weed is common on the dry slopes of

KEY AT-A-GLANCE INFORMATION

LENGTH: 4 miles

CONFIGURATION: Out-and-back with side trails

DIFFICULTY: Strenuous

SCENERY: View of city of Fallbrook, I-15, mountains, and the West coast

EXPOSURE: Sunny

TRAFFIC: Light

TRAIL SURFACE: Rocky, rutted ground, some slippery, loose gravel, and an asphalt section

HIKING TIME: 3 hours

ACCESS: Free

MAPS: None

SPECIAL COMMENTS: This steep, strenuous climb is not suitable for young children. Check with the Fallbrook Land Conservancy for details about this preserve. Call (760) 728-0889.

▶ DIRECTIONS

Take I-15 north to the Pala/CA 76 exit. Go west 0.25 miles to Old Highway 395 and turn right. Travel 2.6 miles and turn right on Stewart Canyon Road. Pass under the freeway and turn right on Pankey Road, where you'll spot the trailhead immediately on the left. Park on Pankey Road.

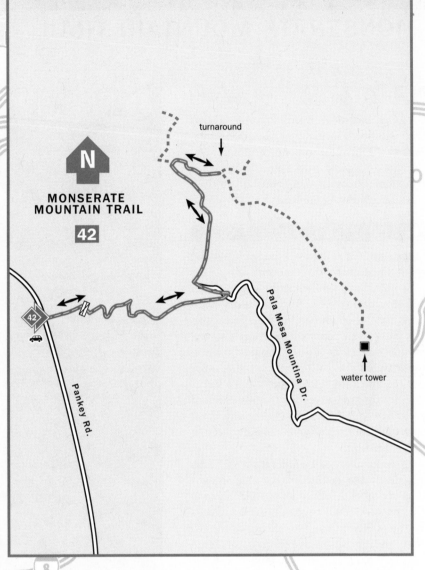

MONSERATE
MOUNTAIN TRAIL

42

turnaround

Pala Mesa Mountina Dr.

water tower

Pankey Rd.

Southern California. The round-leafed perennial was early Spanish settlers' antidote for rattlesnake bites; leaves were pounded into a wet mass and bound upon the wound. Also common on the trail is coyote dung. The dung sometimes contains seeds or fur, showing the diverse diet of this shy creature you're unlikely to encounter on the trail.

At a little more than 1 mile, you will reach an old asphalt road, the end of Pala Mesa Mountain Drive. Turn left and head northwest up the hill. Here, Fallbrook's groves appear like fancy patchwork across I-15. The pavement ends shortly as the road curves more to the north. Now hard-packed dirt, the

Always be watchful for and wary of rattlesnakes since trails pass through their habitat.

trail levels off for a quarter of a mile or so. Be watchful of boulders on the right, and perhaps hurry past. Some of the heavy stones perch precariously above others that have already fallen and now rest, washer-size, along the path. Ornamental grasses grow in profusion here, their foam-pink blooms swishing in the breeze. The trail bends east, where you may notice an offshoot heading north. Whether the section is overgrown (as it has been on my visits) or clearly visible, head east (right) up the hill instead, where the route turns abruptly south (left) for a short distance, then climbs steeply east again to a flat vantage point at about 1,600 feet.

Notice two trails heading off this, the logical turnaround point. One takes you east for a short distance. The other heads southeast for about a mile to a nearby water tower. Retrace your steps carefully back down the hill.

▶ NEARBY ACTIVITIES

An interesting diversion for anyone with a green thumb is Plant World, with potted vegetation, pond supplies, trees of all sorts, lawn and garden statues, and other decor items. You will enjoy looking at—and perhaps talking with—the colorful parrots kept in big outdoor cages. Or, if you prefer, go to adjacent Belle Marie Winery for a little taste testing (www.bellemarie.com/winery). Both businesses can be accessed on Mesa Rock Road, which runs parallel to I-15. Take the Deer Springs Road exit, which is 9.2 miles south of where you turned off the interstate to reach Monserate Mountain.

MOUNT WOODSON EAST TRAIL

KEY AT-A-GLANCE INFORMATION

LENGTH: 3.6 miles

CONFIGURATION: Out-and-back

DIFFICULTY: Moderate (uphill)

SCENERY: Huge boulders and odd rock formations

EXPOSURE: Mostly sunny

TRAFFIC: Moderately heavy

TRAIL SURFACE: Earthen path, asphalt

HIKING TIME: 2.5 hours

ACCESS: Free

MAPS: None

SPECIAL COMMENTS: The continuous uphill cadence with a gain of close to 1,200 feet in elevation makes this hike difficult for some. But less physically fit hikers can turn back anytime. The asphalt route makes for a safe, quick descent.

IN BRIEF

A popular area for rock climbers, runners, and hikers who enjoy an uphill workout; Be sure to bring water any time of year, and on hot summer days, hike in the early morning or late afternoon

DESCRIPTION

The trail begins moving south through oak forest parallel to CA 67, where the car sounds quickly begin dissolving, filtered away behind joyful birdsong and the gentle rustle of wind in the leaves. At approximately 0.1 mile, you'll come to the asphalt route which bears left then back to the right then left again. You'll notice a home, fenced off on the left. Pass by as the road gradually grows steeper. The road is framed with a lizard's paradise of smooth, pale-sided boulders perfect for sunning on.

About halfway up the road (0.9 miles), the view opens to the south, but curves back to afford the northeastern views. All along the road, boulders pile upon boulders. The pale granodiorite surfaces are smoothened by exposure to weather, forming curved shapes within which a good imagination can see a primitive cityscape or animals like the tortoise rock that appears to sleep in the sun near the top. Manzanita finds life within the great rocks, rising from cracks where the boulders

DIRECTIONS

Take I-15 to the Poway Road Exit and drive east until Poway Road runs into CA 67. Turn left and drive on CA 67 for approximately 3 miles. Watch for the fire station on the left. You'll also see a marker sign for Mount Woodson. When safe, make a U-turn (turn into a side road and then make a left back onto CA 67 going the opposite direction) and drive back to park on the southbound shoulder of CA 67, near the marker sign.

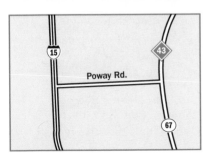

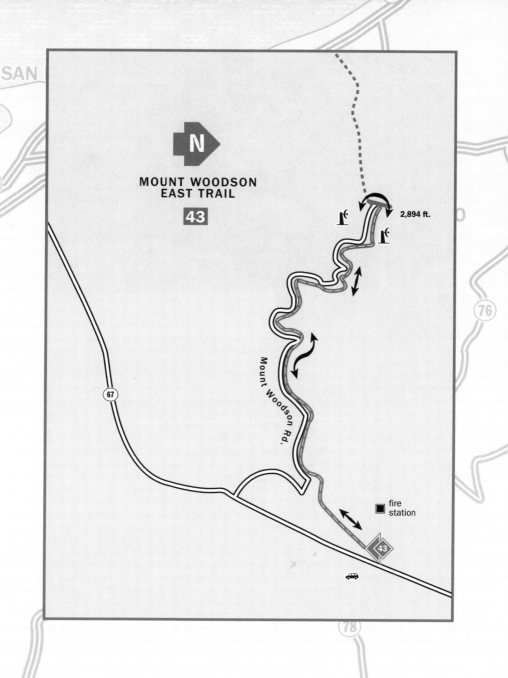

have split apart. Sometimes, the boulders split several times, so they lie alongside one another like a stack of giant chips.

Nearing the top of the mountain, the boulders rise vertically, towering two- and three-stories high and shading the road in spots. Watch for climbers' metal pitons and chalk marks on the rock faces. You'll likely see climbers carrying their ropes and equipment on the hike. Families with children of all ages, and people walking their dogs, are common on this hike,

Watch for "turtle" rock and other creature-feature boulders on Mount Woodson.

too. Runners are also familiar here, their breath a steady puffing rhythm as they run, sweating, up the steep path.

As you huff and puff up the asphalt road, open your mind to the patterns of nature. The Mount Woodson experience, like any other, is what you make of it. Notice the vibrant blue light of sky breaking through repeating green frames formed by the bristly pine branches. Gathered sap glistens like honey on spiky pine needles. The trees cast a mosaic shadow on the wide, pale faces of the boulders that serve as canvas for nature's ever-changing montage of art.

When you reach the crest of the mountain, you can continue forward to a small eastern lookout point amid the shade of pines. Or, take the asphalt road as it begins to descend through a maze of towering communication antennas. Just past the last antenna tower, some big flat boulders provide the perfect picnic spot with views of Poway to the southwest. At nearly 2,900 feet, it's a bird's-eye view, illustrated by the many ravens that hang out here at the top of the mountain.

You'll notice that the road continues southwest. After a short distance, it changes to dirt. If you want to, you can take the trail all the way to Lake Poway (3.6 miles away). That is a hike in and of itself, most often done from the west end.

When you're ready, retrace your steps back down the mountain, bringing the imaginative spirit of watching for nature's artwork with you.

▶ NEARBY ACTIVITIES

For a variety of fast food outlets, restaurants, and cafés, don't head back to Poway Road just yet. Instead, travel north on CA 67 for five minutes into the town of Ramona. The highway becomes the city's Main Street, which hosts a variety of businesses, including many antique stores.

PALOMAR MOUNTAIN OVERVIEW LOOP

▶ **IN BRIEF**

A variety of mountain landscapes include thick conifer forest, creek-side vegetation, and a pond, making this loop a pleasant one for viewing the Palomar Mountain area. Opportunities to see wildlife are abundant—if you're quiet and look closely.

▶ **DESCRIPTION**

From the parking area, you'll see an asphalt maintenance road winding northwest into the trees. Head up this road about a tenth of a mile till you spot the "Chimney Flats Trail" marker on the right. Turn into the dense shade of the forest where the earthy smells of decaying leaves and fresh pines engulf you.

The trail leads down a gradual slope where fallen twigs snap and crackle under eager feet. Dry limbs intermingle with thriving greenery as dappled sunlight dances with shade like gracefully rendered strokes on a painter's canvas. Boulders set in among the trees seem artfully arranged—clusters of large and small ones, with ferns growing up between them like tiny gardens within the bigger landscape.

After about a half mile, the forest opens to a meadow of ferns. The trail narrows to a single-trek path and continues southeast into even denser forest. Squirrels skitter through drifts of fallen leaves alongside the path where towering,

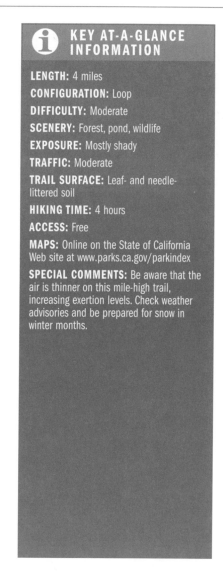

KEY AT-A-GLANCE INFORMATION

LENGTH: 4 miles

CONFIGURATION: Loop

DIFFICULTY: Moderate

SCENERY: Forest, pond, wildlife

EXPOSURE: Mostly shady

TRAFFIC: Moderate

TRAIL SURFACE: Leaf- and needle-littered soil

HIKING TIME: 4 hours

ACCESS: Free

MAPS: Online on the State of California Web site at www.parks.ca.gov/parkindex

SPECIAL COMMENTS: Be aware that the air is thinner on this mile-high trail, increasing exertion levels. Check weather advisories and be prepared for snow in winter months.

▶ **DIRECTIONS**

Take I-15 to the Pala/CA 76 exit and turn right, heading east for about 21 miles. Go left on S6, and drive along the steep, winding road for 6.7 miles. Turn left on "East Grade," then make another immediate left (almost a U-turn, really) on S7 (also marked "Palomar State Park Rd."). Drive 2.6 miles and park in the small asphalt lot on the right.

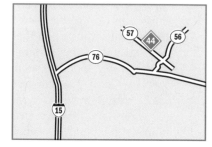

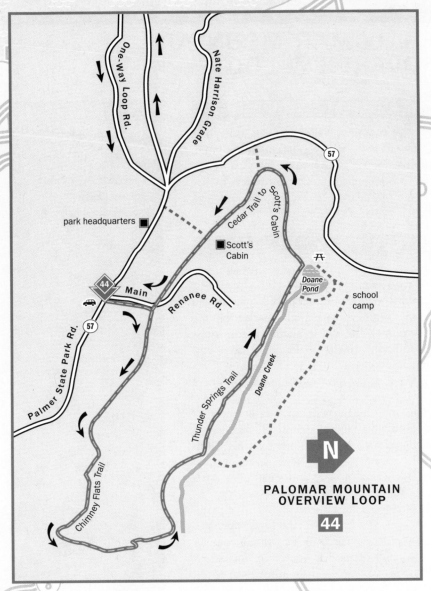

**PALOMAR MOUNTAIN
OVERVIEW LOOP**

44

rough-barked trees play host to pale green moss—growing on the north side of course.

At 0.7 miles, the narrow trail becomes steep, like nature's offered an invitation to run. Be aware that rocks cross the path in spots, and smaller trees have sprung up in the path's center. Going fast you may trip or smash into an unforgiving surface. The trail soon narrows to little more than the width of your foot for a short distance, slanting downhill and making slow the only way to go. The trail bears right then turns abruptly left for a small switchback, then right again, moving north and crossing seasonal Doane Creek.

A short distance ahead, the trail splits. Take the left path, Thunder Springs Trail, which heads northwest, gradually gaining elevation. The thin mountain air may make the slightly upward trek difficult. In the late afternoon, the canopy hides the sunlight.

At a little more than a mile from the start, the trail flattens, heading through open meadow where the grass is golden in fall. As the meadow joins the forest, you'll cross a boggy area where mule deer like to hang out. If you're quiet, you may get a glimpse of them before they see and hear you—and bound off—*boing! boing!*—into the woods.

The route briefly heads uphill again, with gnats often buzzing about, then somewhat steeply downhill again with the creek in view. Doane Pond soon comes into view, and one often sees people fishing along the bank. Frogs escape into the water with a splash then resurface in groups, seemingly as curious as those who stoop to look more closely at their buggy eyes staring back from the murky water. There's a picnic table just past the pond—a convenient place to rest or eat.

To the left of the pond, you'll spot the trail marked "Cedar Trail to Scott's Cabin." Take this steep trail uphill for about 0.1 mile

As the sunbeams penetrate the leafy canopy, *Star Trek* fans may say, "Beam me up, Scotty!"

until it levels out in an area thick with ferns. The route remains level just long enough for you to catch your breath. Tread quietly and watch for deer that sometimes graze just a few feet from the trail. Individually, the trees may look gnarled, bruised, and bent. But viewed from a distance, as a whole, the forest looks flawless, as if every tree weathered the storms of nature (fire, wind, lightning) without a mark.

At the top of the hill, you'll note Scott's Cabin Trail. Turn left, continuing steadily uphill for about a quarter mile until the trail again levels out briefly. You may notice some small offshoot paths to the left, but stay on the main path that now heads southeast. Fallen twigs crunch underfoot as you make your way to Scott's Cabin, which is nothing more than a few rough logs forming the base of the once-tall walls of an early homesteader's cabin.

After the cabin, pass the side trail that marks the way to the ranger station and continue toward Chimney Flats. The leveling route moves through a small meadow dotted with cedars before it splits. Go to the right (the left continues to Chimney Flats) to return to the asphalt road you came in on. Follow it the short distance back to the parking area, keeping an eye out for wildlife. On a recent visit, a bobcat turned to look back at us as he slowly and confidently made his way across the road.

▶ NEARBY ACTIVITIES

As you head back down, look on the right side of East Grade about 0.2 miles from the top: spigots protrude from a stone wall. Visitors routinely stop to fill their bottles with the artesian water.

PALOMAR MOUNTAIN:
FRY CREEK CAMPGROUND LOOP

KEY AT-A-GLANCE INFORMATION

LENGTH: 1.25 miles

CONFIGURATION: Loop

DIFFICULTY: Easy

SCENERY: Cedar and oak forest, squirrels, and possibly deer

EXPOSURE: Mostly shady

TRAFFIC: Light to moderate

TRAIL SURFACE: Loose, leaf-littered soil, asphalt

HIKING TIME: 1 hour

ACCESS: An Adventure Pass ($6 per day), sold at the general store located at the S6 turnoff, is required to park along S6. Otherwise, pay a day-use fee ($12) to park inside the Fry Creek Campground gate.

MAPS: None

FACILITIES: Public rest rooms and picnic tables along the campground road make for convenience.

SPECIAL COMMENTS: Despite its short length, this trail can be disorienting and sometimes difficult to find. Bring a compass and map and bug repellant because the small black flies have no mercy.

IN BRIEF

Fry Creek Trail is a quick mountain hike that leaves the rat-race behind. This trail offers a deep-in-the-woods feel even though it is easy and covers only a short distance.

DESCRIPTION

Being careful of traffic, cross S6 and enter the campground gate. Follow the narrow road about 0.1 mile to the fee station. A large display map depicts the campground and its trail, which begins directly in front of the parking space adjacent to the fee station.

The path begins as little more than an indentation in the leaves, but careful inspection reveals it heading to the right, uphill toward S6. When the trail looks as if it bears even more to the right, you'll need to make a sharp left instead. Find the turn, which is easily missed if you're not watching for it, above some partially buried boulders. Spotting the wooden pole marker a few feet past the boulders assures you're in the right place. If you were to continue to the right, the trail leads back down to the campground road, coming out near the entrance off S6.

DIRECTIONS

Take I-15 to the CA 76 exit and head east (inland). Drive approximately 20.4 miles and note a road (marked "South Grade") forking northeast. Go left onto this road and continue northeast for 6.5 miles to reach a T. Turn left onto S6 and drive approximately 2.5 miles to the Fry Creek Campground. Fry Creek is on the left, but you will need to park in the small turnout on the right side of S6, across from the campground entrance. If you do not have an Adventure Pass, you can pay day fees at the fee station about 0.1 mile inside the park ($12).

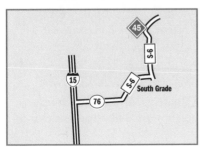

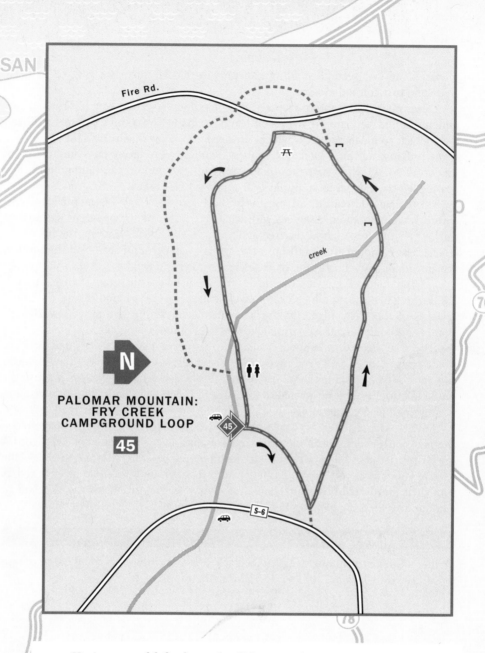

Having turned left, the trail will bear northwest, with markers spaced every few tenths of a mile. At approximately 0.4 miles, the trail crosses the creek bed, which is dry and barely discernible from late summer into fall. A few steps past this, you'll come to a slatted wood bench, which makes a good spot from which to absorb the sounds of a woodpecker in the distance, intent on his work, or the gentle rush of wind through the tree leaves.

The trail undulates over hills and dales for a short distance along a ridge. In the afternoon, sunlight spills from the western sky, filtered through the tops of pine trees and splintered into rainbow prisms. The forest is thicker along this section, holding moisture so that boulders are covered in fuzzy green and rust-colored moss.

Bear right, past another marker, and come upon a second bench. The trail gets difficult to find here among the fallen leaves. A marker on a huge oak tree will lead the way left to a campground, which is where we like to finish this hike. To do the entire trail instead (for a total of 1.5 miles), you'll need to locate the continuation of the loop trail, which is past the tree, looping up and around the campground then bearing left back down to an outlet near the lower rest rooms.

For some odd reason, this relatively short and seemingly simple hike is disorienting. A compass often disagrees with what seems logical and apparent. Because of this, we choose to go left at the tree, making our way down the slope toward picnic tables, past camping sites, and onto the asphalt campground road. We then follow this downhill, marveling at the incense cedars' towering heights.

Along the road, growing up smaller trees, poison ivy turns red, orange, and yellow, looking like benign fall color from a distance. Close inspection reveals the bright splashes of the nasty plant, hiding its irritating oil within the proverbial sheep's clothing and demonstrating nature's lessons of wisdom.

Gray squirrels scuttle about in the dried leaves that carpet the ground adjacent to the road. A dried twig, rolling down the asphalt, sounds like a Native American rain stick or bamboo chimes. We discovered this by accident one day when a melodic sound followed us and we turned to investigate. Fallen twigs are plentiful here. Consider giving one a gentle nudge to start it rolling, musically, down the road.

Where the road levels, near public rest rooms, look to the right and find the alternate longer loop trail's closing stretch ending in a steep descent here, too. A nearby picnic table offers a restful last few minutes before continuing the 0.1-mile back to your car. If you have the time, absorb the surroundings—the incense cedars with their sturdy reddish trunks standing sentry as they reach for the sky, and in autumn, the soothing *plip-plip* rhythm of falling acorns as they hit the ground.

▶ NEARBY ACTIVITIES

Mother's Kitchen restaurant, 2.5 miles back at the S6 turnoff, is a vegetarian haven for hungry souls. Call (760) 742-4233 for more information.

PIEDRAS PINTADAS
INTERPRETIVE TRAIL

▶ IN BRIEF

This easy hike is accessed within the city of Rancho Bernardo. Concentrate on the sights and sounds of the trail and you can *almost* escape the noise and bustle of the urban surroundings and let city tensions melt away.

▶ DESCRIPTION

From the southwest corner of the lot, access the wide, flat trail, which heads south past the first kiosk, which offers general information. Look for a bird list or other flyer put out by the local chapter of the Audubon Society. In this initial quarter-mile section, interpretive signs describe native rock art and other facts about the Kumeyaay Indians who lived here 500 to 1,000 years ago.

Just past the second kiosk, the trail you started on appears to continue southwest. This unofficial trail, like so many others that crisscross the area, has been made by enthusiastic bikers and nearby residents. Follow the plentiful San Dieguito River Park Trail markers whose clear directional arrows help hikers avoid blind routes.

At the first marker, go east. The narrowing trail soon bends southwest through another area with interpretive signs. Here, among the arroyo willow, coastal sage scrub, and chaparral broom, learn how the Kumeyaay used local vegetation. In spring, the scent of low-growing yerba mansa, with its prominent white flowers, will fill the air near the sign describing its use as a cough medicine.

ⓘ KEY AT-A-GLANCE INFORMATION

LENGTH: 3.8 miles

CONFIGURATION: Out-and-back

DIFFICULTY: Easy

SCENERY: Chaparral, trees, Bernardo Bay, birds, a waterfall, and educational panels

EXPOSURE: Sunny

TRAFFIC: Heavy

TRAIL SURFACE: Packed, smooth dirt, with a couple of short rocky areas

HIKING TIME: 2 to 3 hours (depending on how much time is spent reading the interpretive panels and identifying the species they discuss)

ACCESS: Free

MAPS: Free through the San Dieguito River Park; call (858) 674-2270

SPECIAL COMMENTS: Leashed dogs are allowed (although many visitors let them run free). There are many bikers, joggers, and walkers from nearby Rancho Bernardo homes, especially in the early evening and morning. The trail and staging area are open from sunrise to sunset.

▶ DIRECTIONS

Take I-15 to the West Bernardo Drive/Pomerado Road exit. Head west and turn left at the first traffic signal, which is West Bernardo Drive. Follow this for about a half mile, turn right into the Bernardo Bay Natural Area dirt lot (across the street from the Casa de las Campanas retirement facility), and park.

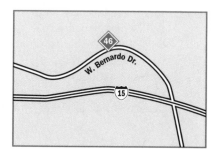

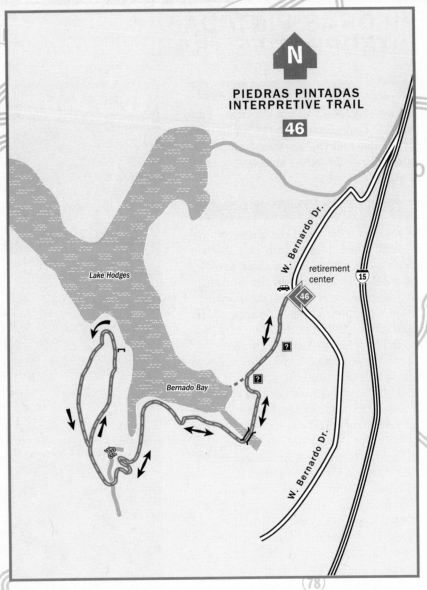

PIEDRAS PINTADAS
INTERPRETIVE TRAIL
46

Lake Hodges

W. Bernardo Dr.

retirement
center

Bernado Bay

W. Bernardo Dr.

You'll recognize the scent as "medicinal," because it does, in fact, smell a little like commercial cough syrup. In fall, the twining growth shrivels to a dead brown blanket that covers the ground.

Continue on to the Green Valley Creek Bridge. Stand here a moment with the natural orchestra of the water rushing beneath you and look to the east where you'll see and hear bustling I-15. When you're rushing down the freeway the perspective is far different from here on this creek bridge, where the wide-open space and the history of the ancient Kumeyaay make the cars and the hustle and bustle of modern life seem insignificant.

Across the bridge, the trail heads northwest, passing Bernardo Bay, where the southwest end of Lake Hodges spills into it. The arroyo willow grows in profusion north of the trail and has been partially submerged in the bay in wet years. Look at the treetops where snowy egrets perch, resting between feeding forays along the shore. Other birds that visit or make this space near the water their home are the belted kingfisher, great blue heron, red-winged blackbird, double-crested cormorant, American coot, and Western grebe. White pelicans have also been spotted, as well as a variety of ducks and Canada geese.

Farther along the trail, a huge oak tree sits beyond a section of pole fencing. There is a space to shortcut past the tree, or you can stop to enjoy a bit of shade on hot summer days. The trail goes over hills and dales then heads south. Beyond the creamy Western sycamores growing to the right, you'll see a year-round waterfall splashing down over the rocks in the distance. Approach it for a better view then zigzag uphill along the boulder-strewn path that appears to lead right into the back-yards of the tract homes just above. Holly-leaf cherry (sometimes called holly-leaf red berry) grows in abundance here. The fluffy blossoms attract bees in the spring. Its bright red summer cherries are edible but hold much more pit than fruit.

The trail heads down again, and a footbridge crosses a stream that feeds the waterfall. Depending on rainfall, the stream can swell and submerge the bridge. Beyond the stream, the path widens again. Head north several hundred yards toward more interpretive signs. Where the trail splits, take the narrower upper path (on the right). Hike up this 0.1-mile ridge loop that moves through large boulders and has a bench from which to view Rancho Bernardo, I-15, and Lake Hodges. Continue down and southwest around the loop, watching overhead for osprey, kestrels, or even a turkey vulture. Red-tailed hawks hunt here. You'll spot them hovering high above the land, then dropping down a few feet at a time, stalking their rodent prey undetected as they ready themselves for the final attack dive.

Reach the loop's close and retrace your steps across the stream, down around the waterfall, and past the bay. If you're heading back at 8 a.m., noon, or 5 p.m., you'll hear the bells at the nearby retirement facility, Casa de las Campanas, which means "House of Bells," heralding your return to civilization.

▶ NEARBY ACTIVITIES

One of Rancho Bernardo's best-kept secrets (not anymore!) is Webb Park, at Bernardo Center Drive and Avena Place. Take a leisurely stroll arond the duckpond and enjoy the tranquil setting.

RANCHO CARRILLO LOOP

KEY AT-A-GLANCE INFORMATION

LENGTH: 2 miles

CONFIGURATION: Loop

DIFFICULTY: Easy

SCENERY: Historic structures, chaparral

EXPOSURE: Sunny

TRAFFIC: Moderate to heavy

TRAIL SURFACE: Sandy soil

HIKING TIME: 1 hour

ACCESS: Free

MAPS: Online at www.ci.carlsbad.ca.
us/cserv/parks/trailmappdf/ranch
carrillo.pdf

FACILITIES: Rest rooms inside Leo Carrillo Ranch Historic Park

SPECIAL COMMENTS: Instead of following the recommendations here, some hikers choose to improvise their own route, entering the historic park through the back gate (open during park hours). Be aware, though, there is no through-way from the park back to the trail.

▶ IN BRIEF

The Rancho Carrillo trails allow visitors to get in touch with nature not far from the sprawl of urban development. As a bonus, the loop surrounds Leo Carrillo Historic Park, a colorful foray into history.

▶ DESCRIPTION

Head past the main Leo Carrillo Historic Park entrance area and find curving asphalt path heading northwest with Melrose Drive on the right. Turn left and continue southwest behind Carrillo Elementary school. You'll notice the rear access gate to the park here, open during regular park hours (see Special Comments in information box). Continue southwest along the path where bougainvillea grows in brilliant fuchsia, soft pink and peach. The hybrid variety that thrives in California descended from the woody Brazilian plant named for an explorer who first noted them in the late 1700s.

Just past the school, the route curves right and comes to a T. Incidentally, the parking area here on the right serves as another trailhead. If you want a longer hike, you could turn right here and head up past the school, cross Melrose Drive and access another approximately 2-mile trail loop. Assuming you decide to save that option for

▶ DIRECTIONS

From I-5, exit Palomar Airport Road and drive approximately 5 miles east to Melrose Drive then turn right. Or, from I-15, take CA 78 west to San Marcos Boulevard (which becomes Palomar Airport Road), travel 4.3 miles to Melrose Drive and turn left. Drive 1.1 miles, turn right on Carrillo Way then quickly right again. Pass through the wrought-iron gate with wagon wheels and film reels, designed by local artist Paul Hobson, and park in the lot on the left

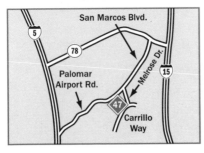

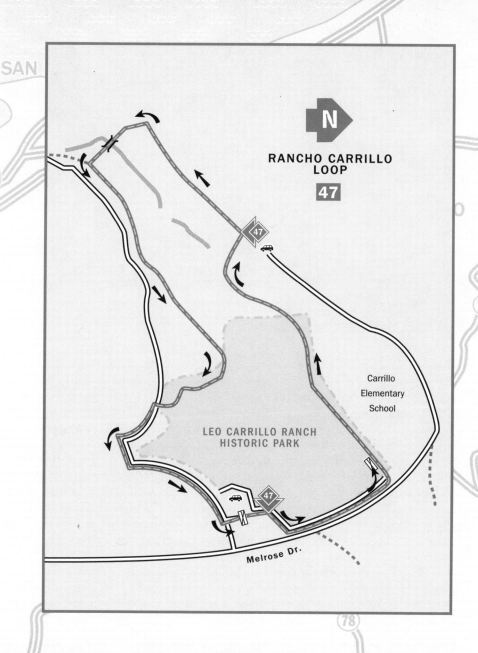

Carrillo
Elementary
School

LEO CARRILLO RANCH
HISTORIC PARK

Melrose Dr.

SAN

another time, make a left on to now earthen path, and begin descending gradually, the city sounds slipping away behind the whirring of humming-birds and the rustling of wind through the brush. *Ahhh*—a bit of paradise surrounded by urban landscape.

On the left, a small fence provides a boundary to the open-space wilderness area with oak trees, fragrant fennel, and dense chaparral. You may hear water rushing or trickling through the canyon, or peacocks scratching about in the bush. A bevy of the colorful birds lives in the Historic Park.

The hardy strains of bouganvillea so prevalent in San Diego County descend from Brazilian plants.

These are breeding descendants of those belonging to motion picture star Leo Carrillo, who acquired the land and constructed his rancho starting in 1937. Watch for baby peacocks in May and June each year.

The trail bears left, and you'll cross a newly constructed bridge, with watershed running below. In the spring and summer, you may hear the call of coyotes still living in the small portions of chaparral and wild lands near new home developments. The youngsters are vocal even in daylight hours. Cross the bridge and turn right. Houses in the Rancho Carrillo development line the ridge, their rear yards backed up the open space and trail system. You'll notice some cement drainage ditches along the trails. It's interesting to see how a little moist mud can collect and support new life—reeds take root, green algae forms a coat on puddling water, insects and frogs come to lay eggs. One has the sense that despite man's encroachment, nature reins supreme.

You've about another 0.7 miles to go before reaching the sidewalk and continuing up to the corner, where you'll head left again and end up back on Carrillo way. Through the reels and wheels motif gate, you can either access your car or visit the historic park.

▶ NEARBY ACTIVITIES

Adjacent to the parking lot, find the entrance to the Leo Carrillo Ranch Historic Park. Once inside, head left to the historic caretaker's cottage, now serving as the visitor center. The free brochure is loaded with historic information, and after seeing the cottage, head down "Palm Lane" toward the hacienda complex. You'll soon understand why this was the film star's retreat, a place to relax and recoup. Perhaps after a leisurely visit, you'll reap the same recuperative benefits! The park operates Tuesday through Sunday; closed Mondays. For more information, call (760) 476-1042.

SAN ELIJO LAGOON TRAIL

▶ IN BRIEF

This easy stroll through nature is a popular with families, walkers, and joggers. People often bring their dogs (on leashes) here.

▶ DESCRIPTION

From the trailhead, proceed west through euca-lyptus forest, where the moist path is home to a variety of toadstools. Hummingbirds buzz in the branches overhead. The younger, spindly trees grow close together here. Their branches chafe one another in the breeze, making a squeaking noise that may have you wondering if an unusual bird is in the treetops.

At 0.2 miles, the trail moves out of the for-est. Lemonadeberry, toyon, prickly pear cactus, bladderpod, and scrub oak line the path. Creep-ing wild cucumber vines twine over the bushes like a lacy veil. At about 0.4 miles, cross the Sta. Helena side trail and continue. Mature pine trees spot the land as the trail gradually climbs. The lagoon soon comes into view on the right, about 50 yards from the path. There are always ducks here, paddling about in pairs. You might also see egrets, herons, and a variety of other birds—295 species have been spotted here at San Elijo Lagoon.

As you continue, sweeping views of the lagoon alternate with areas where thick toyon, sumac, and scrub oak rim the trail. White and black sage grows here, emitting a refreshing scent. The red and yellow of California fuchsia and fid-dleweed provide bright splotches of color.

▶ DIRECTIONS

Take I-5 to the Lomas Santa Fe Road exit. Head east for about 1 mile to Highland Road, then turn left. After about a quarter mile, make another left on La Orilla. Drive 0.1 mile; the trail entrance is on the left. Park in the dirt area adja-cent to La Orilla.

ℹ KEY AT-A-GLANCE INFORMATION

LENGTH: 4 miles

CONFIGURATION: Out-and-back

DIFFICULTY: Easy

SCENERY: Birds, coastal sage scrub, lagoon waters

EXPOSURE: Sunny

TRAFFIC: Heavy

TRAIL SURFACE: Packed and soft sand

HIKING TIME: 2.5 hours

ACCESS: Free

MAPS: Call (760) 436-3944

SPECIAL COMMENTS: This is an ecolo-gical preserve. Leashed dogs only; owners must pick up after them. Although not a traditional horse park where riders trailer in their horses, people from the surround-ing area do sometimes ride here. No bicy-cling is allowed. For more information, visit www.sanelijo.org.

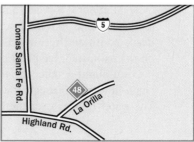

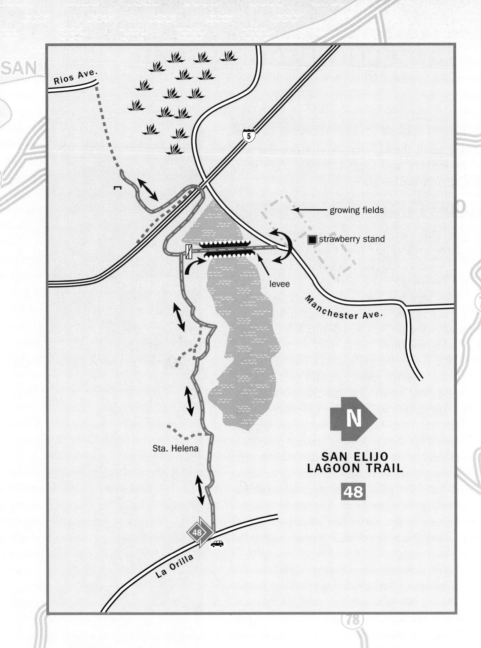

Rios Ave.

5

growing fields

strawberry stand

levee

Manchester Ave.

76

N

Sta. Helena

SAN ELIJO
LAGOON TRAIL

48

48

La Orilla

78

At about 0.8 miles, a side trail loops off to the right. Follow it across a level plain that moves closer to the water. The path comes to a point then heads south and reconnects with the main trail. Go right, continuing west on the main trail. Ice plant grows in the soft sand that slows you down here.

At about 1 mile, the trail comes to a T. Go right, heading around the chain-link pass-through that prevents bicycle access to the concrete levee. The water trickles over the concrete, and bird tracks of varying shapes and sizes form interesting patterns on the cement. Ducks paddle in and out of the marsh alongside the levee as herons and egrets wade and feed in the shallows. The levee trail ends at 0.3 miles. Double back to the pass-through and continue. Pass the point where you turned right to reach the levee. Continue southwest for a short distance and bear right where the trail makes a U-turn, then walk parallel to I-5 on the left for a quarter mile or so.

At the interstate overpass, follow a narrow trail leading under the freeway and emerge on the west side of I-5 where there is a high trail and a low trail. Both trails head south, paralleling the freeway for about 0.2 miles. Runners seem to favor the high trail, which is separated from the low trail by a sandbar. If you choose the low one, notice the millions of shells filling the sand, which has piled high on the left as the water has filled the trail and receded. Pickleweed grows along this stretch that heads west through eucalyptus and willow forest to reach a wooden bench that faces the bird-filled marsh.

From here, retrace your steps back to the car. If you prefer to hike a little longer, continue for another half mile or so to Rios Avenue. Some hikers choose to begin the hike at the Rios Avenue trailhead, taking the trail from the opposite end.

▶ NEARBY ACTIVITIES

When visiting the levee in summer, you may notice growing fields across Manchester Avenue. A strawberry stand there sells the sweet, juicy produce.

SAN PASQUAL VALLEY: MULE HILL TRAIL

KEY AT-A-GLANCE INFORMATION

LENGTH: 10 miles

CONFIGURATION: Thru-hike with a shuttle

DIFFICULTY: Easy

SCENERY: Orange groves, various agricultural fields, old farming implements, dairy cattle, chaparral, and creek

EXPOSURE: Sunny

TRAFFIC: Second half heavy on weekends

TRAIL SURFACE: Packed dirt, some asphalt stretches, muddy areas at times

HIKING TIME: 5 hours

ACCESS: Free

MAPS: Posted at trailhead kiosks for review only; or call (858) 674-2270

FACILITIES: Chemical toilets at East and Ysabel Creek Road trailheads

SPECIAL COMMENTS: The eastern half of the trail sees semi-heavy equestrian use on weekends, while the western end teems with bicyclists and family groups. If you have time for only part of the hike, choose the more scenic eastern half, which is described first here. Otherwise, plan for the full 10 miles, one-way, by placing a vehicle at each end of the trail.

IN BRIEF

This country trail heads though green pastures, past dairy cattle and over a hill then transforms into an urban open space where singles and families exercise.

DESCRIPTION

Orange groves will catch your eye as you head west from the gravel parking lot. You'll pass through several yards of eucalyptus forest where cactus, wild radish, and mulefat bushes grow. Because fields in this area are part of a designated agricultural preserve, the trail makes a left turn and heads south past the orange grove for about half a mile. Watch for farm traffic as you near the end of the southbound trail. You'll cross a wide dirt area that farm vehicles use to access the growing field on your right. The trail picks up again to the right of this wide space. The crowing of roosters from the residence across Bandy Canyon Road fills the air as you head west again on the path along the street. A stretch of trail is fenced, offering some isolation from the usually quiet road.

The trail follows the sod fields and dips below the road to your left. Rusty retired farm

DIRECTIONS

For shuttle, take two vehicles on I-15 to the Via Rancho Parkway exit and head east for 0.2 miles to Sunset Drive. Turn right and go to the end. There is a small parking lot there; you may also park along the road or in the dirt across the street, near the "Sikes Adobe" sign. Leaving one vehicle there, take the second back up Sunset Drive to Via Rancho Parkway and go right. At 0.6 miles you will reach San Pasqual Valley Road. Go right and follow this road for 3.4 miles to CA 78. Turn right again, heading east for 4.4 miles to reach Bandy Canyon Road, and turn right almost immediately to enter the parking area.

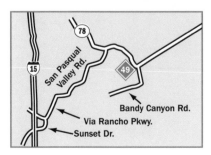

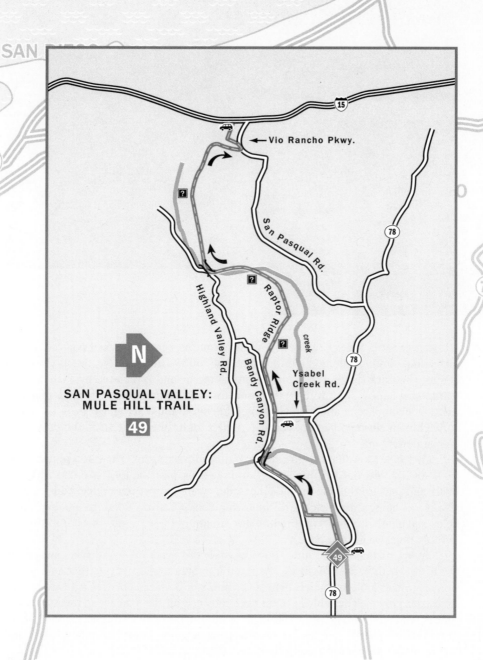

SAN PASQUAL VALLEY:
MULE HILL TRAIL
49

equipment is scattered along the route. After hiking this westbound section for about half a mile, you will find that the fence ends and the trail is interrupted. Keep going along Bandy Canyon Road. You'll stroll past Verger Dairy and get a close-up view of its penned cattle next to the road—always a delight to children who giddily hold their noses against the ripe smell.

Continue for about a quarter mile along the road. There is plenty of room to safely walk along the shoulder until the trail reappears. Cross the

Enjoy the fragrant, trailside flowers. You'll soon pass the dairy with its equally strong smell!

bridge over Santa Maria Creek where castor bean trees grow (the seed pods are highly toxic), and continue along the trail, which still follows the road, but not as closely as before. The thick smell of the dairy begins to recede and is replaced by a fresh, clean scent. The narrow, foot-wide trail heads through fields thick with wild mustard. Another plant that is abundant here is fiddleneck. You'll recognize it by its tightly curled bloom clusters that look like caterpillars, unfurling as the small, bright yellow-orange flowers open.

At 3 miles, you'll come to another trailhead parking lot. There is a portable toilet here—the last one on this hike. Continue west past the lot, cross Ysabel Creek Road, and pick up the trail on the other side, where juniper trees offer shade. Cactus also grows along this stretch. Still following Bandy Canyon Road, trek along flower fields and share the trail with bright black stinkbugs. Roadrunners dash out in pairs, never letting you get too close.

At approximately 3.8 miles into the hike, the westbound trail veers away from the road, which bends southwest. As the trail moves to the right, farther and farther from the road, look to the left, where the sunlight bounces off wrecked cars hidden in the overgrowth. The vehicles must have careened off the road above this spot some time ago. Several yards farther takes you to information panels discussing the history of non-native plants such as the invasive pampas grass. Efforts to remove them and replant native vegetation are also outlined.

Around mile 4, the now truck-wide trail begins its gradual climb, eventually leading to Raptor Ridge, the hike's midpoint. The vegetation changes to chaparral and sage scrub. In spring, flowers bloom all along the climbing trail. Because their tall, spindly stalks almost disappear, unless you're right upon them, the pale blue-lilac clusters of the blue dicks appear to float like puffballs in the air. Popcorn flowers coat the ground like a fluffy snowmelt in spots, and low-growing baby blue-eyes edge the trail, staring sweetly with their dark, blue-purple "eyes" as you pass.

As you near the ridge top, look for orangetip butterflies fluttering about and bicyclists from the western end of the trail, who often turn back just past the ridge. The peak offers a flat viewpoint area and is a good spot to stop for lunch if you're hungry and don't mind sun exposure.

Past the ridge, the trail width narrows to about three feet. The descent on this side is steeper than the way you came. My family likes to run down this side, letting gravity do most of the work. Signs are posted all along this section, warning cyclists to go no more than 5 miles per hour, but there's no speed limit for those on foot!

Nearing the bottom, where old oak forest shades the path, huge, lichen-speckled boulders appear on the left. We've nicknamed one "couch rock" because it is shaped like a big chair. An information kiosk and a picnic bench mark the start of level ground again, leaving about 4 miles to the end.

The trail bends south, following Santa Ysabel Creek for perhaps a mile. Shrouded by thickly growing willows, the creek can be heard, but you will be able to see it only in a couple of sections. After rain, some areas along this stretch get muddy, but the path is two lanes wide, so you can find a dry spot in which to step. You may notice dog tracks here and discover that our canine friends always choose to trudge right through the mud!

At 7 miles, you'll cross the creek and head west on a concrete bridge. Vegetation is being replanted along this strip where cottontails commonly hop about. As you continue along this flat strip, you'll notice planted and fallow fields on the right where crops are rotated from season to season. Perhaps attracted to the corn, deer frequent this area, leaving their tracks behind. The songs of mockingbirds fill the air in this wide-open space. Willows grow in the distance to your left, along the creek, which continues south before rejoining the trail in its westward track.

On the trail, look for a set of information panels discussing birds that are common to the area, such as the yellow warbler and willow flycatcher. As the trail bends slightly to the north for a few uphill yards, then flattens and heads west again, I-15 comes into view. In early morning and late afternoon, gnats buzz along this section.

A sharp right takes the route northward at 8.75 miles, where a series of information panels interprets area history. Make your way north to busy Via Rancho Parkway, where you'll turn left and head along the sidewalk for perhaps 40 yards. Turn left onto a dirt trail, heading south to circumvent the golfing facility's putting green. The path takes you around to the other side, where you'll head west back to your car and the urban side of this country–city hike.

▶ NEARBY ACTIVITIES

The Westfield Shopping Mall across Via Rancho Parkway offers plenty of money-spending opportunities and a variety of restaurants, including fast food on the upper floor.

SANTA MARGARITA RIVER TRAIL

KEY AT-A-GLANCE INFORMATION

LENGTH: 5 miles

CONFIGURATION: Out-and-back

DIFFICULTY: Easy

SCENERY: Lush riparian landscape and dense forest

EXPOSURE: Mostly shady

TRAFFIC: Moderate

TRAIL SURFACE: Packed silt

HIKING TIME: 3.5 hours

ACCESS: Free

MAPS: None

SPECIAL COMMENTS: Open dawn to dusk. Except for a short, slippery section near the trailhead, this is an easy route that is good for families. Smaller children will need lots of help in the slippery area. As always, watch children around water.

▶ IN BRIEF

Mother Nature opens her welcoming arms here, filling visitors' senses with a bountiful harvest of sights, scents, and sounds along the Santa Margarita River.

▶ DESCRIPTION

From the parking lot, head east (away from the road) and enter the trail, which meanders upstream as the water rushes past. After a short stretch, oaks shade the path in a suddenly lush landscape. In spring, milk thistle with large, rosy-purple blooms towers as high as seven feet. A white pattern that looks like spattered milk adorns the spiny, variegated green leaves, giving rise to an Old World belief that the drips of "milk" came from the Virgin Mary as she nursed her infant son Jesus. The plant's species, *marianum,* means "of Mary."

The Santa Margarita River soon comes into view, flowing steadily in all but the driest of years. About 200 yards from the trailhead, the path narrows and climbs 20 to 50 feet above the river while hugging a steep rock slope. Stepping carefully makes it easy to cross this 600-foot section, but be careful of a few slippery spots.

On weekends, it is common to spot unwary hikers trying easier-looking offshoot paths that run level with the river. My family has learned that these sandy shore paths dead-end into thick stands of willow. Some hikers will double back to where they originally went off track. Others, like us, will climb through the bramble and up rocks

▶ DIRECTIONS

Take I-15 to the Mission Road/Fallbrook exit. Head west on Mission Road for 5.1 miles to Pico Avenue, then turn right. Pico becomes De Luz Road after just a few feet. At 1.1 miles, turn right again, onto Sandia Creek Road. A large dirt parking area is 1.2 miles ahead on the right.

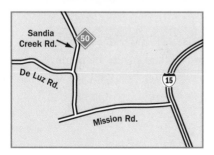

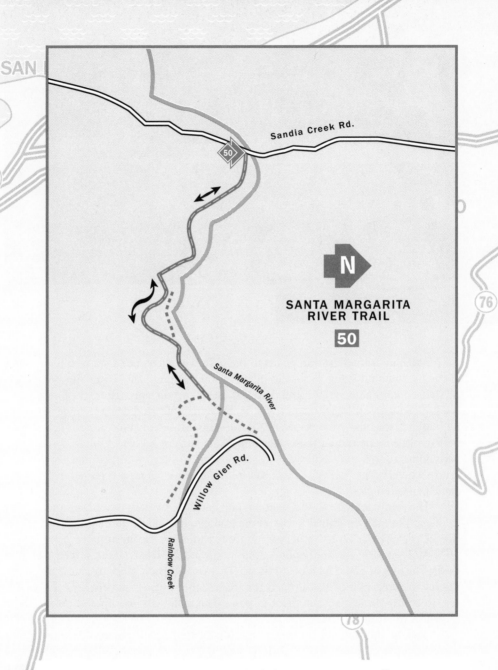

back to the main path above. Some ford the river upstream till it converges with another offshoot path and rejoins the main trail. Save yourself some trouble and stick with the official trail.

The trail evens into a flat silt path through a forest rich in oak and sycamore. Poison oak grows in masses, and wild grape vines twine up through the trees. A variety of colorful butterflies flit through the air, and birdsong echoes all around. The sound of the water gurgles up from the river on the left, which can sometimes be seen from the trail.

The author's son, Henry, riding "eel rock."

At about 1 mile, the trail bends to the right. For a few moments, you'll lose sight of the river behind rising rocks and hills. But the rushing Santa Margarita also curves right, heading slightly more south than east for a short distance. Here, the forest grows thicker, and the path veers closer to the water. Short trails lead down to huge, flat granite boulders that rise from the water. The level expanses of sun-warmed rock are the perfect place to sit and let the whooshing of the current lull you. Children—and perhaps some adults, too—will want to venture out to play on a rock that looks like a giant stone eel. The "eel" pops its head from the water, its mouth poised in a sinister smile beneath a glossy "eye."

The eel rock fuels the imagination, and back on the path other large rocks seem to take on human or animal form. As the trail climbs slightly, moss grows heavily on the rocks at whose bases feathery ferns grow, adding to the mystique.

At 1.4 miles, the trail splits. Continuing on the left trail for several hundred yards, clusters of boulders block passage. This is a pleasant place to picnic if you are careful to avoid poison oak. Watch for snakes, too, but it's mostly lizards you will see. In spring, lizards scurry about in pairs. The male will bob up and down, doing push-ups to attract his mate.

Back at the trail split, take the right-hand trail uphill out of the forest into a more barren landscape. You're likely to hear the roar of many honeybees along this route, which crests, then descends, bearing left back down toward the water. Ignore the offshoot trails on the right and continue to the left along the Santa Margarita River, which disappears then reappears beyond an area of luxuriant foliage. The rushing gurgle can be heard whether its source is visible or not. Also nice is that there are fewer people on this leg of the trail. Many hikers turn around back at the split, so you're likely to have the route to yourself.

As you walk, watch for wild gourds growing in sunny meadows along the trail. At 2.5 miles, the trail splits again. A sign identifies "Willow Glen" on the left and "Rainbow Creek" on the right. This is the turnaround point for the 5-mile out-and-back hike.

If you want a little more adventure, continue along the route on the right that leads to Willow Glen Road about 1 mile away. The left-hand trail ends a short distance ahead. Regardless of your choice, pause for a while in the cool shade near the water before heading back.

▶ NEARBY ACTIVITIES

Just 20 minutes from Fallbrook, the Antique Gas & Steam Engine Museum is located at 2040 North Santa Fe Avenue, Vista. The museum is open daily. Call (760) 941-1791 for more information.

STELZER PARK LOOP

KEY AT-A-GLANCE INFORMATION

LENGTH: 2.2 miles

CONFIGURATION: Loop (with some back-track)

DIFFICULTY: Moderately easy

SCENERY: Chaparral, wildflowers, birds

EXPOSURE: Mostly sunny

TRAFFIC: Light

TRAIL SURFACE: Packed dirt

HIKING TIME: 2.5 hours

ACCESS: $2 day-use self-pay

MAPS: Available at ranger station

FACILITIES: Rest rooms near ranger station in Stelzer Park

SPECIAL COMMENTS: Best visited in fall and spring when lakeside temperatures are moderate

IN BRIEF

This serene family park in the trees provides a starting point toward the dry, upper trails where lizards reign and hawks keep eyes peeled for a meal.

DESCRIPTION

The ranger station adjacent to the parking lot hosts a small museum room with animal and plant specimens as well as historical information. It's worth a quick peek if you have time, and may help you identify vegetation or animals from your hike.

To the right of the ranger station, enter the park through a small gate and turn immediately right onto a shady path. The route leads down through oak forest alongside Wildcat Canyon Creek. The trail crosses a couple of footbridges as it meanders west. Wild grapevines twist up through the trees that allow the sunlight through the dense canopy only in patches. At 0.3 miles, the trail grows rocky and large flat boulders pave the path. Watch your step here. Some stick up at awkward angles.

At half a mile, the trail halts its westward route, ending at a picnic table in the shade. The trail turns left and begins heading uphill. After climbing 0.1 mile, a wooden observation deck with benches allows another opportunity for rest, this time in full sun. From this vantage point, the cars zipping by on Wildcat Canyon Road look tiny. Watch overhead for hawks taking advantage of the canyon's wind currents to soar above the landscape with little effort.

DIRECTIONS

Take I-8 east to CA 67 north. Turn right on Willow Road and travel about 1 mile east to Wildcat Canyon Road. Turn left (north), drive approximately 1 mile into entrance, and park in the lot.

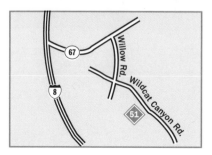

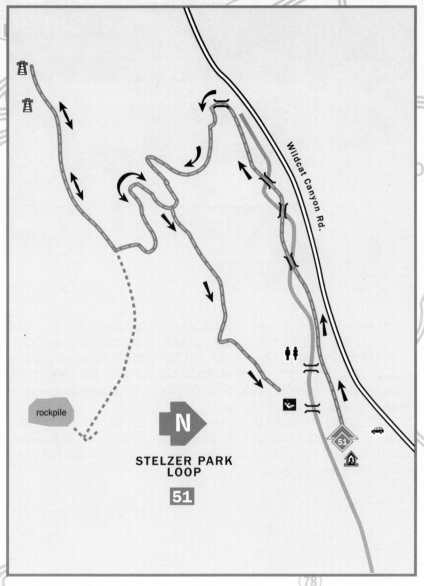

STELZER PARK
LOOP

51

rockpile

Wildcat Canyon Rd.

Past the observation deck, the trail levels for a short distance then becomes semi-steep again. Footing is fairly easy though, since the ground is packed. You'll come to a trail intersection at 0.9 miles from the entrance. Go right and head west uphill. You'll catch the easterly Stelzer Ridge route on your downhill return. The trail bends east and west again, and comes to a T. Choose the right route, which leads gradually uphill through pleasant terrain filled with honeybees, spring flowers, and interesting rock formations, to two electrical towers where a resting bench awaits.

Be respectful of the horned lizard, whose fairly docile nature has contributed to rarer sightings in San Diego.

The left-hand choice isn't recommended for casual hikers. It heads half a mile up to a rock pile with a decent vantage point, but the route is so steep and slippery that all but the most agile, experienced, and daring will be on hands and knees to get there. Coming down is also very difficult and requires crab walking, which still results in dangerous sliding—unless you're one of the many lizards that are accustomed to the dry, slippery terrain here.

After sitting a while under the power towers, retrace your steps to the intersection you passed earlier. This southeastward Stelzer Ridge Trail leads back down to the shady oasis of the park, where you will make your way past the playground and a quiet birdbath area to the gate.

SUNSET CLIFFS PARK TRAIL

▶ IN BRIEF

Some people live in the San Diego area their entire life without knowing about Sunset Cliffs Park, which isn't a park in the grass-and-picnic-tables sense at all. A stroll here allows a firsthand glimpse at the power of the sea, witnessed in the erosion that formed the cliffs here.

▶ DESCRIPTION

The first scenic view is from your car. Driving toward the site, you'll see the Pacific Ocean stretched out, an expansive blue-gray blanket with floating beds of kelp like tufted, decorative knots.

From the parking lot, the trail begins as a wide, safe southbound route lined by boulders and some pole-and-chain fencing; the path soon finds itself along open cliffs for nearly half a mile. You'll turn east toward Point Loma Nazarene College then west again over small hills and dales and coastal safe scrub. Lemonadeberry and non-native castor bean grow here.

Don't think you're too close to civilization to see wildlife. On a recent visit, a large bull snake slid along the trail. The route meanders back toward the coast and more exposed, eroding cliffs. The stones roughened by powerful wind and waves are interesting to see. In the winter months, you may glimpse gray whales migrating south. You'll likely see surfers hanging ten (or wiping out!) in the waves all year long.

If you haven't had enough of the ocean view, take the narrow walkway that extends for quite a distance along Sunset Cliffs Boulevard heading north. Join the others—throngs of people in the

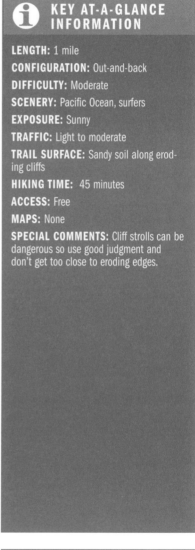

ⓘ KEY AT-A-GLANCE INFORMATION

LENGTH: 1 mile

CONFIGURATION: Out-and-back

DIFFICULTY: Moderate

SCENERY: Pacific Ocean, surfers

EXPOSURE: Sunny

TRAFFIC: Light to moderate

TRAIL SURFACE: Sandy soil along eroding cliffs

HIKING TIME: 45 minutes

ACCESS: Free

MAPS: None

SPECIAL COMMENTS: Cliff strolls can be dangerous so use good judgment and don't get too close to eroding edges.

▶ DIRECTIONS

Take I-8 west and exit at Sunset Cliffs Boulevard. Heading into Ocean Beach, stay to the right and continue 2.5 miles to a parking lot at the corner of Cornish and Ladera Streets.

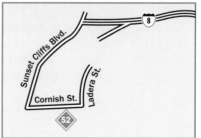

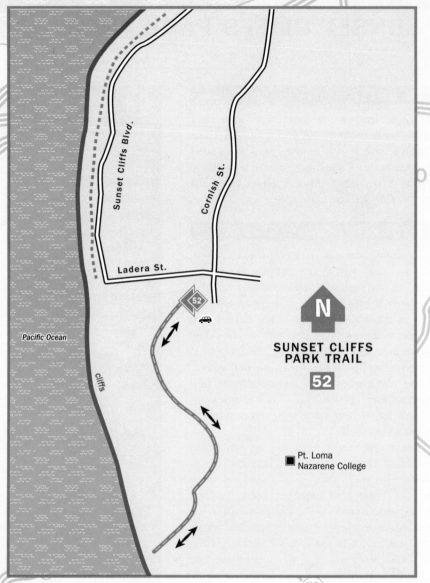

**SUNSET CLIFFS
PARK TRAIL**

52

Pt. Loma
Nazarene College

summer months—as they enjoy the salty, cool Pacific Ocean breeze and the beauty of a California sunset. If you're watching at just the right instant, you might glimpse what is known as the "green flash"—the last glimpse of sunlight making a blue-green flash on the sea.

The eroding cliffscape is
beautiful—and dangerous.

▶ **NEARBY ACTIVITIES**

An Ocean Beach favorite for Mexican food for decades, find Nati's at 1852 Bacon Street for a lively atmosphere and patio dining. Or opt for takeout at Poma's, a much-loved Italian deli with huge sandwiches. Poma's is across the street from Nati's at 1846 Bacon Street. Reach them both by heading back up Sunset Cliffs Boulevard to Niagara Street. Turn left and travel a couple of blocks to Bacon Street where you'll spot them on opposite west corners.

SWEETWATER RESERVOIR: RIDING AND HIKING TRAIL

KEY AT-A-GLANCE INFORMATION

LENGTH: 4.5 miles

CONFIGURATION: Out-and-back

DIFFICULTY: Moderate

SCENERY: Views of the reservoir, birds

EXPOSURE: Sunny

TRAFFIC: Light to moderate

TRAIL SURFACE: Rocky soil

HIKING TIME: 3 hours

ACCESS: Free

MAPS: Available free at ranger station, or order online at www.sweetwater.org

SPECIAL COMMENTS: In warm weather, the area around Sweetwater Reservoir is hot, dry, and dusty, so pack plenty of water. Horses and their riders are often present.

IN BRIEF

The reservoir stretches out, a cool blue strip in the arid land—and a tempting taboo for heat-weary hikers.

DESCRIPTION

Walk uphill a short distance past the ranger station and spot the trail opening on the left. After a level sprint, the wide, rocky route begins a very gradual descent heading southeast. This first part of the hike is uneventful. You may see ravens resting atop the dike, calling out (to you or to each other?) as people pass. Other birds may flit about, but there is little else of interest on this first stretch.

At 0.6 miles the trail makes a fairly abrupt turn to the right, heading northeast past the vernal pool area. The sensitive habitat is cordoned off for its protection. The trail continues along with the boundary fence (a tall chain-link) on the right. At 0.9 miles, the trail bears abruptly left. You'll spot an information kiosk a short distance ahead—on recent visits there have been no brochures available. Turn right at the kiosk, climbing an eastward stretch for about a quarter of a mile.

The reservoir comes into better view at this point—tempting refreshment on hot days, but off-limits.

The route begins heading downhill, then zigzags uphill and to the right, away from the reservoir. The route begins gradually descending again after a quarter mile.

DIRECTIONS

Take I-5 to the E Street/Bonita Road exit and head east on Bonita Road. At 3.2 miles, continue straight and continue east on San Miguel Road for 1.1 miles. Turn left onto Summit Meadow Road. Drive approximately 0.1 mile and turn left into day-use parking on the left, just short of the ranger station.

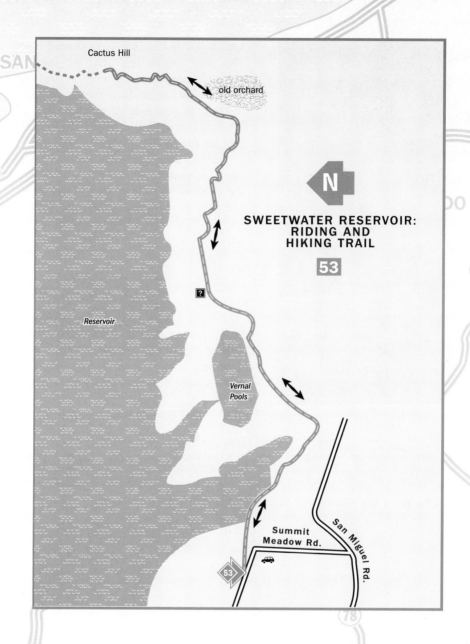

Fragrant fennel and pepper trees dot the surrounding hillsides, and a peaceful hush falls over the land. After another third of a mile or so, you'll head uphill again, staying along barbed wire to the right. A short, very steep section gives way to nice flat trail. You'll see spindly castor bean plants, but the fennel is what scents the air—a licorice-like aroma.

At 1.75 miles from the trailhead, you'll reach a hulking pepper tree close to the trail. Its boughs provide a hidden shelter reminiscent of a kid's

A picturesque view of the pristine reservoir from the turnaround point on Cactus Hill.

fort. A low branch serves as shaded bench. This tree marks the start of the "Old Orchard" portion of the trail (on the official map). Pepper trees shade the path for some distance as you keep along the fence, first heading downhill and then up over rolling trail for another quarter mile or so.

At 2 miles, the route becomes dry and open to sunlight again, climbing in steep switchbacks up the hillside. The path is rocky here, with loose, slippery spots. Be careful of cactus growing along the trail here—alive with colorful blooms in the spring, but always prickly! At the top of Cactus Hill, you'll find a picnic table beneath a shade structure overlooking the sparkling waters of the reservoir.

At 2.3 miles from the trailhead, this viewpoint is a good place to turn back. However, if you're still up for a hike, the trail continues almost three miles, ending past the reservoir near CA 94.

▶ NEARBY ACTIVITIES

At 4035 Bonita Road, the Bonita Museum is a free opportunity to learn more about the history of the Sweetwater Valley. Days and hours of operation are limited. For more information call (619) 267-5141.

SYCAMORE CANYON/GOODAN RANCH OPEN SPACE PRESERVE LOOP

▶ IN BRIEF

This peaceful hike leads you through both Sycamore Canyon, a 1,700-acre wilderness area nestled between Poway and Santee, and bordering 325-acre Goodan Ranch. The diverse landscape is especially beautiful in mild spring or fall weather when wildflowers or autumn leaves add color. Devastated by the 2003 wildfires, this area is a wonderful example of how the earth regenerates after fire.

▶ DESCRIPTION

From the staging area, don't pass through the main gate at the southern end of the parking lot. Instead, head up a southeastbound narrow trail on the left, to reach a ridge path overlooking Sycamore Canyon. In the spring, notice the bright yellow-orange splotches made by California poppies, and the drifts of white created by masses of popcorn flowers.

As the trail continues southeast, it goes first uphill and then down, then northeast, and down and around to the southeast again, helping you'll understand why hikers, bikers, and horse riders are allowed to go only one way on the opening 1.7-mile stretch. It's safer when all traffic moves in one direction on this narrow, rutted trail where areas of loose dirt mean slow going and slippery footing. Bikers even get off and walk their cycles in some spots along the first half mile.

Despite short uphill stretches, the trail generally descends for 0.75 miles or so to Martha's Grove and levels. Dense shade from the massive

ⓘ KEY AT-A-GLANCE INFORMATION

LENGTH: 6.4 miles

CONFIGURATION: Loop

DIFFICULTY: Moderate to semi-difficult

SCENERY: Oak forest, canyon views, chaparral, wildflowers in spring

EXPOSURE: More sunny than shady

TRAFFIC: Moderate

TRAIL SURFACE: Packed dirt, leaf litter, river rock, and some rutted areas

HIKING TIME: 4.5 hours

ACCESS: Free

MAPS: Available from the park ranger

FACILITIES: Portable toilet at Goodan Ranch trailhead

SPECIAL COMMENTS: Open from 8 a.m. to 5 p.m., October through March, and 8 a.m. to 7 p.m., April through September. A walking stick is helpful; be conscious of ticks in spring and summer. The trail is shared with horseback riders and bicyclists, so follow the posted right-of-way rules.

▶ DIRECTIONS

Take I-15 to Poway Road and travel northeast 5.2 miles to Garden Road. Turn right on Garden Road and drive east for 1 mile, then go right onto Sycamore Canyon Road, and drive southeast 2.3 miles to the staging area and park.

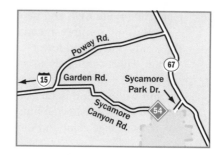

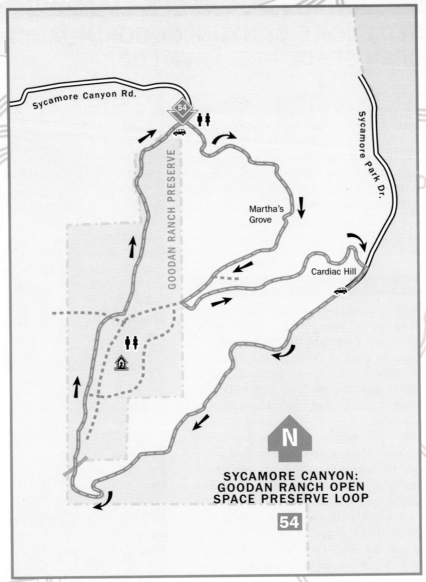

**SYCAMORE CANYON:
GOODAN RANCH OPEN
SPACE PRESERVE LOOP**

54

old oaks embraced the level trail before the fire—and will again. Coast live oaks regenerate quite well, and new growth is sprouting.

Heading southwest, continue through the wooded section. Before the fires, the words "enchanted forest" were good descriptors for this quarter-mile wooded section. Hikers are likely to again see wild cucumber vines twisting up through the trees, the prickly green, inedible fruit hanging above the path. Monkey flowers and wild California fuchsias add fiery spring and summer color, inviting yellow and black swallowtail butterflies to flit from bloom to bloom. In the fall, the oak trees change color and drop their orange-brown leaves to carpet the ground.

The autumn tones eventually change to drab gray litter in winter. Oak forest continues near the trail, providing some shady areas interspersed with sunny ones.

Listen for the repetitive, bouncing-ball sound of the wrentit, the call of raucous crows, the buzzing of bees, and the gentle rushing of a breeze. The trail opens to a meadow. Continue past a narrow offshoot that you'll spot on the left at 1.3 miles from the trailhead.

At 1.5 miles, the trail intersects with another. Turn left here, heading southeast for a short uphill stretch on a truck-wide trail, then bear left again and ascend a mile-long stretch of trail framed by scrub oak and grassy meadows. Watch for tiny tricolor flowers shaped like badminton birdies in the meadows. Colored white, lilac, and yellow, these flowers, named "shooting stars," hang upside down, their tiny petals stretching back. The climb grows steeper near the top of this route nicknamed "Cardiac Hill" for its sustained climb.

Shooting Stars add color along the path.

At the top of the hill, turn right onto the service road and head toward the staging area. This particular parking and staging lot is open only on weekends. Pass through it and pick up the trail from the southern edge of the lot. The path lined with river rocks and framed by chaparral stretches upward, then down, for several short sections heading southwest. The trail bends almost due west then descends another half mile into the canyon. Smooth-sided river rocks through here vary in size from walnut to watermelon. The smaller, loose, round rocks can roll as you step, so be careful not to slip and fall on this slow-going downhill stretch.

At the bottom, pass through an area where oak trees grow and turn right onto the wider, flat trail. Head to the right (north) for about 200 yards, then turn left, move past the stream (often a trickle) and make another left where you'll enter Goodan Ranch Preserve property. The trail moves through stands of oak, serenaded by crickets in the morning and late afternoon for about 0.75 miles. A turnoff point used to lead to a ranger station, historic water tower, and other historic buildings—all were destroyed by the 2003 fire. A new building is in the works, so if you need to make a pit stop, a rest room will likely soon be built. Otherwise, continue forward on the narrow uphill trail where you may see cottontails hopping about. The route gradually bends to the east, reaching a trail junction after another quarter mile.

Don't turn right or left, just continue straight and keep heading north through open, rolling meadows dotted with sage, sumac, and chamise bushes—watch for signs of new growth. This green, fertile land was once a working ranch and is now jointly managed by the cities of Poway and Santee, the California Department of Fish and Game, and the County of San Diego Parks and Recreation Department.

The last 0.6 miles moves gradually uphill on a wide trail where beetles scuttle about, hawks fly overhead, and mourning doves coo in the late afternoon. The chorus of nature caps off a rewarding hike as you approach the staging area where you began.

▶ **NEARBY ACTIVITIES**

After hiking on hot days, nothing beats an ice cold Slurpee, which you can get at the 7-11 on the corner of Garden and Poway Roads. One mile west on Poway Road, a Smoothie King is an alternative source of refreshment.

THREE SISTERS WATERFALL TRAIL

▶ IN BRIEF

A trio of waterfalls known as the Three Sisters is the focal point of this hike that starts out dry and dusty.

▶ DESCRIPTION

Head west past the gate on the fire road leading through chaparral that is quickly recovering after the fall, 2003 firestorm that raged through San Diego's backcountry. After approximately 0.2 miles, the route passes through sparse oak forest, not situated close enough to shade the wide, rutted path. The trail begins to narrow and gradually move downhill. In the spring, the ground is carpeted in color from a rainbow palette of wildflowers, attracting an almost equally wide range of butterflies and moths.

You may hear a scuttle and see a lizard scurrying into the brush. The horned lizard, sometimes called "horny toad," is prevalent in this area, even though it has largely disappeared in San Diego. The docile little lizard with horns looks like something out of the dinosaur era, but its sluggish nature has made it vulnerable. If you do spot one of these small horned reptiles, remember how few remain and what a rare privilege you've been given. Respect its beauty and leave it alone.

▶ DIRECTIONS

Take CA 78 east past Ramona and Santa Ysabel; turn right on Pine Hills Road. After about a mile and a half, turn right onto Eagle Peak Road and follow it for 1.4 miles. The road bears left; after 0.3 miles, go right on Boulder Creek Road and travel south for about 8 miles (the pavement ends after 3 miles). You'll spot the trailhead where Cedar Creek Road intersects Boulder Creek Road from the west; park in the small turnout, or alongside the narrow road.

ℹ️ KEY AT-A-GLANCE INFORMATION

LENGTH: 3.5 miles

CONFIGURATION: Out-and-back

DIFFICULTY: Moderate; final optional section to falls is strenuous

SCENERY: Waterfalls, oak trees, mountains, wildlife

EXPOSURE: Mostly sunny

TRAFFIC: Light

TRAIL SURFACE: Packed dirt, last 0.4 miles are loose dirt and brush

HIKING TIME: 3.5 hours

ACCESS: Free

MAPS: None

SPECIAL COMMENTS: This hike's remote location means few people know about it; the last section of the hike is a nearly vertical drop, though, so many turn around before reaching the actual waterfalls.

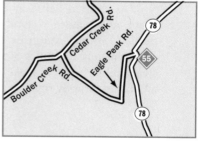

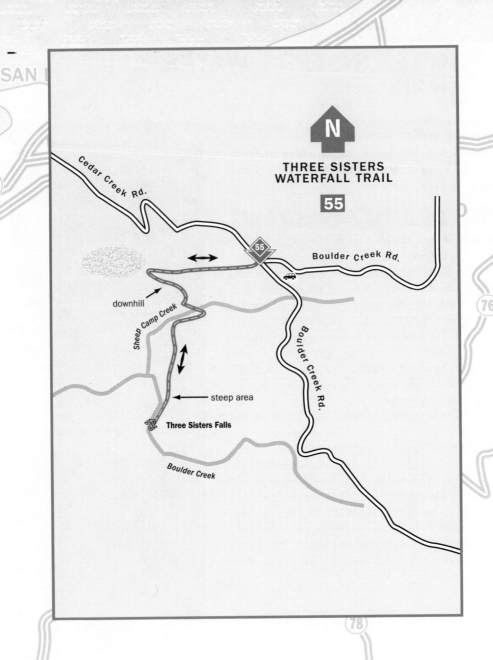

THREE SISTERS
WATERFALL TRAIL

55

Cedar Creek Rd.

Boulder Creek Rd.

downhill

Sheep Camp Creek

steep area

Three Sisters Falls

Boulder Creek Rd.

Boulder Creek

SAN

At close to half a mile, you'll start to hear the waterfalls toward the south. At 0.6 miles, a stand of tall oaks provides shade. You'll see a trail on the left, leading southeast down the hill. Follow this downhill route for approximately 0.5 miles along the ravine that opens on your right. A few steep, slippery places make for generally slow passage, until the trail levels and turns abruptly right.

Continuing, the hike takes on a different atmosphere, heading through shady oaks. You'll cross Sheep Camp Creek (when it's running) and move along the trail above it for a time. Be careful of poison oak along this shady stretch. The three-leafed plant grows in thick clumps that twine up over tree branches and form canopies that hang low over the trail. You'll need to pay attention overhead as well as where you step, being careful none of the extending vines brush against you on this narrow, shaded trail.

After walking approximately 0.2 more miles, the route heads uphill, alternating sun with shade. In the fall, the trees' changing color set the land to crimson and gold. In the springtime, the bright red flowers of Indian paintbrush stroke the air along the path, which leads uphill for a short distance, then opens into a small meadow.

From this open area, you can look down upon the cascading Three Sisters Waterfalls, or sit on small boulders if you need a rest. A narrow trail leads off to the left. Follow this carefully downhill. Some areas are gritty and rocky with 50 to 60 percent grade, causing even the most surefooted to slip, so go slowly.

After approximately 0.2 miles, the trail abruptly drops to a nearly vertical descent. This is where most hikers turn around, even the promise of cool waterfalls in the distance not enough reward to climb precariously on the steep trail—and rightly so. This final, strenuous section isn't for everyone. If you choose to turn-around here, you'll have logged in 3.2 miles when you return to the trailhead.

If you decide to continue forward, the short, perilous section will have even experienced, agile hikers grabbing at closely growing bushes for security. At the bottom, hikers can marvel at how much shorter the 450- to 500-foot section looks than it did from up above.

The final stretch to the falls may require pushing aside some bushes since relatively few hikers make it this far, and the primitive trail to the left becomes overgrown. Masses of poison oak grow here, so be careful what you touch. Make your way the final 0.2 miles along this route. Here at the Three Sisters Waterfalls the sound of the pounding water is deafening, silencing all worrisome thoughts and troubles that may have clung to you from the clamour of civilization you should have left back at your car.

If you climb up onto the slippery rocks around the waterfalls, step carefully so as not to fall. The middle fall is the most magnificent, with approximately 60 feet of water cascading into a long, curved pool.

Even if you choose not to make the final trek down to the falls, don't feel disappointed. The three falls are also impressive from the meadow up above.

▶ NEARBY ACTIVITIES

If you time your travels to drive out of the area as the sun begins to set, keep your eyes peeled for deer. They're often seen grazing on the hillsides just a few feet from Boulder Creek Road. Wild turkeys are also common. Be sure to roll down the windows so you can hear their telltale *gobble-gobble*.

TIJUANA ESTUARY TRAIL

ℹ KEY AT-A-GLANCE INFORMATION

LENGTH: 3.5 miles

CONFIGURATION: Out-and-back

DIFFICULTY: Easy

SCENERY: Marsh plants, birds

EXPOSURE: Sunny

TRAFFIC: Moderate

TRAIL SURFACE: Mostly fine gravel

HIKING TIME: 2 hours

ACCESS: Free

MAPS: Free trail map at the visitor center

FACILITIES: Visitor center with store, museum, and rest rooms

SPECIAL COMMENTS: For more information contact the visitor center at (619) 575-3613 or visit the Web site at www.tijuanaestuary.com.

▶ IN BRIEF

A birder's delight, the Tijuana River National Estuarine Research Reserve is a biological preserve within the city of Imperial Beach. Flat paths make the reserve a walker's haven for nearby homeowners and nature lovers who come for rare glimpses of endangered year-round residents and the migrating shore birds that winter here.

▶ DESCRIPTION

Although San Diego is well known for its beautiful beaches, the estuary's 2,500 acres of intact coastal wetland prove that there is more to the city's coastline than just surf and sun.

From the visitor center, head east on the sandy path past the entrance for the North McCoy Trail, which is a short, dead end overlooking a tidal channel. Continue southeast toward the opening to Grove Avenue. If you're lucky, you'll get a glimpse of a great blue heron. My family has often seen one or more of them standing in the field just south of the path. Startled, the bird spreads its blue-gray wings to an impressive six feet and takes off in a slow motion lift. It will land again several yards away, as if wanting to stay safe yet close enough to watch visitors pass.

A wooden footbridge traverses the bend at Grove Avenue then settles onto the dirt start of the southbound River Mouth Trail. Pass the backyards of several tract homes. At 0.75 miles, Iris Avenue meets the trail, marking another entrance

▶ DIRECTIONS

Take I-5 south to Coronado Avenue in Imperial Beach and head west; Coronado Avenue becomes Imperial Beach Boulevard at the 13th Street intersection. About 2 miles from the interstate, turn left on Third Street, which will curve onto Caspian Way; park at the visitor center on the right.

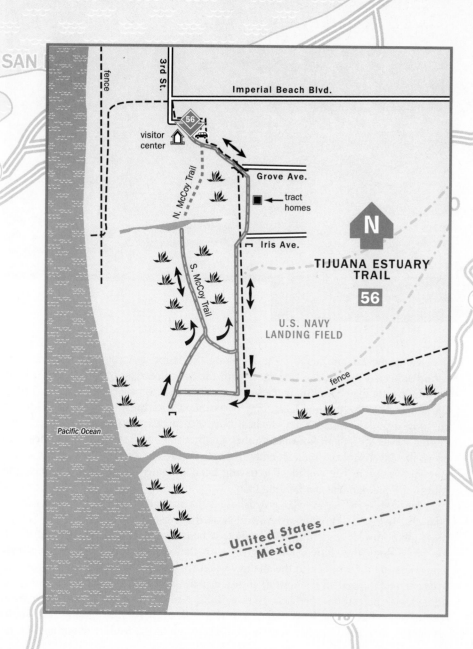

point for visitors. A shaded bench provides a brief resting spot here where the U.S. Navy Landing Field fence starts and the trail widens, changing to a fine gravel surface. Mallards routinely gather on the other side of the navy's chain-link fence. They paddle in water that gathers in a shallow ditch at the edge of the landing field. Maybe the water looks better than the reedy pond that's on this side of the fence—or maybe it's the "greener" government grass that attracts them!

At Tijuana Estuary, the birds explode like nature's fireworks.

Continue for another 0.75 miles along the fence and you will reach a westbound side trail that leads off to meet with the South McCoy Trail. Don't turn here. Keep following the chain-link fence south until cut logs force a right (westward) turn. On sunny days the Pacific Ocean may be visible across the vast fields of California buckwheat and lemonadeberry bushes, but on overcast weekends, you'll hear the roaring waves for half an hour before they finally come into view at this southeastern tip of the River Mouth Trail. Monday through Friday the sudden view of the ocean may surprise you, the sound of it having been drowned out by the comings and goings of helicopters at the landing field.

Head west, where even on gray fall days the sunlight glints off the waters of the tidal channel, and the calls of birds such as the Western grebe fill the air. Several yards of southwest-stretching trail leads to a bench—a good place to sit and watch the birds along the shore. Snowy egrets with their bright yellow legs wade slowly along, jabbing their bills into the shallow water to feed. The light-footed clapper rail, which is endangered in California, strolls in pairs and trios along the shore that is riddled with holes from the birds' probing bills. Nearly 400 types of birds have been seen here, including the least tern and brown pelican, which are endangered. Books sold at the visitor center offer more in-depth facts about the wildlife mentioned in the center's free brochures.

From this southernmost tip of the trail, the Bull Ring located just a couple of miles south in Mexico is visible, resembling, from this distance, a great stone monolith rising from the earth. The reserve is the terminus for the 1,734-square-mile Tijuana River watershed. Only one-third of the watershed lies in the United States. The other two-thirds are in Mexico, including most of Tijuana and all of Tecate. Managed cooperatively with the U.S. Fish and Wildlife Service and the California Department of Parks and Recreation, the Tijuana Estuary is located entirely on U.S. land.

After a breather, take the trail behind the bench; it leads north to the South McCoy Trail, which continues north for about a mile past marshes and wetland areas. A bench placed halfway along the trail faces west to overlook the wetland where a variety of waterfowl sounds like a chorus of kazoos. On the east side of the trail, wetland birds such as the snowy plover, black-bellied plover, and killdeer gather en masse. Bring binoculars to catch sight of all of them—there are sometimes thousands. Their coloration blends with the marsh, making them difficult to spot at first glance.

The smaller tern varieties are prey to the American peregrine and other large falcons populating the area. The terns sometimes put on an amazing flight show. Looking like a fireworks display, large groups of terns take off from the marshy feeding grounds. They school like fish, and, flying with their darker topsides to the sky, tilt and change direction to display their snowy undersides. The erratic movement serves to confuse predators. The mass of terns fly away and then back, dipping close to the path, the whirring of so many wings in flight a deafening roar.

Retrace your steps and turn left (east) onto the first side trail you come to. This takes you back to the chain-link fence, where you'll pass the ducks again and make your way north to the footbridge, then west back to the visitor center where permanent exhibits educate guests about estuarine ecology.

▶ NEARBY ACTIVITIES

If you enjoy fishing, try tossing a line over the Imperial Beach Fishing Pier. No fishing license is required here. Or catch a good meal at the Tin Fish, located at the end of the pier. You might also get an exciting view of dolphins romping in the Pacific Ocean while you eat. Open daily. Call (619) 628-8414.

TORREY PINES STATE RESERVE:
COMBINED TRAILS AND POINTS LOOP

KEY AT-A-GLANCE INFORMATION

LENGTH: 1.7 miles

CONFIGURATION: Loop

DIFFICULTY: Easy

SCENERY: Sweeping view up San Diego's coastline and the rolling Pacific Ocean; dolphins, chaparral, and wildflowers; California gray whales from December through February

EXPOSURE: Sunny

TRAFFIC: Heavy

TRAIL SURFACE: Silt

HIKING TIME: 1 hour

ACCESS: There is a $4 parking fee ($3 for seniors), payable at the ranger booth or at visitor center.

MAPS: Available in kiosk boxes or in the visitor center. For more information, see www.torreypine.org.

FACILITIES: Pubic rest rooms are located in the upper parking lot.

SPECIAL COMMENTS: Open 8 a.m. to sunset; visitor center opens at 9 a.m. The trails are for foot traffic only, and no pets are allowed. Use common sense when it comes to bringing children since portions of the trail run along steep cliffs. No food is allowed in the reserve, so confine your picnics to the nearby beach. Bring binoculars for a better look at passing whales and dolphins.

▶ IN BRIEF

With a cool ocean breeze and sweeping views of the Pacific, Torrey Pines State Reserve is a favorite coastal exercise spot.

▶ DESCRIPTION

The dusty silt trail starts behind the public rest rooms at the south end of the parking lot. Head west through chaparral on the flat route framed by pole-and-cable fencing. After about 0.1 mile, the route heads right and splits off in two directions. Choose the rightmost option, marked "Razor Point," and follow it north for a short flat stretch, gradually bearing left. Steps on the left lead a short distance up to Red Butte, opening to an attention-getting coastal view. Be careful on the wooden steps leading down the other side, where the trail turns abruptly right, then left (west) again.

You'll gradually head down on easy north-south switchbacks. Watch for whole families of quail running through the bush in the summertime. There are likely squirrels here, too. Accustomed to people in this busy reserve, they are almost fearless. With a shake of its bushy tail, one may "guide" you along, running ahead then stopping to wait until you get closer before it runs ahead again.

At approximately 0.3 miles, a bench faces northwest for an angled view of crashing ocean waves framed by valley walls. A short distance

▶ DIRECTIONS

From I-5, take the Carmel Valley Road exit and head west to the traffic signal marked "Camino del Mar." Turn left onto the road, which, despite signage, is considered "N. Torrey Pines Road" if you turn left. Continue driving about 0.7 miles to the entrance on the right. To park closest to the trailhead, drive through the visitor center parking area and cross the road for additional parking.

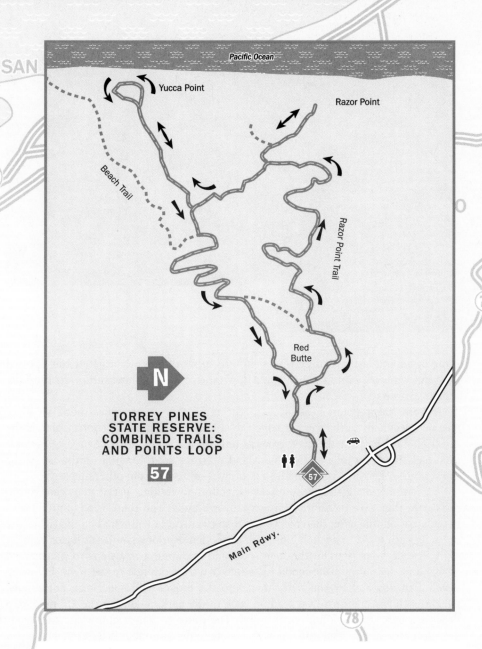

Pacific Ocean

Yucca Point

Razor Point

Beach Trail

Razor Point Trail

N

Red
Butte

TORREY PINES
STATE RESERVE:
COMBINED TRAILS
AND POINTS LOOP

57

57

Main Rdwy.

further, head right (west) off the main trail to get to Razor Point. Pole and cable fencing adds minimal security here where the route runs along the steep cliff. Pass a short view trail on the left and continue as the path bends north. The constant wind has eroded the cliffs into interesting patterns.

After a short distance, you'll come to Razor Point, with its wooden viewing deck. There's a bench, but more visitors opt to stand at the deck's railed edge where the breeze is refreshingly cool in summer, and chilling to the core in winter. Below, the ocean rolls in a hypnotic rhythm. On the beach, strands of kelp slide in the surf, forced first toward the open sea then back to the

The forces of wind and water create artwork erosion in the cliffs at Torrey Pines State State Reserve.

shore again and again. During winter months, pods of gray whales are easily spotted from this vantage point as they migrate down the coast. Dolphins surf in the breaking waves year-round.

From Razor Point, head back to the main trail, which offers good views of gnarled specimens of the tree for which this reserve is named. The Torrey pine is the rarest pine in the United States, growing only on the small strip of San Diego's coast from Del Mar to La Jolla and on the island of Santa Rosa 70 miles northwest. These trees' needles needles grown in clusters of five—different from other pines.

Continue in a generally southeast direction down long, tiered steps carved into the earth, then cross a short boardwalk over a gully. The route heads uphill, with tiered steps adding ease, then comes to the marked Yucca Point Trail on the right. The 0.2-mile path leads to a small loop with a wooden overlook similar to Razor Point's.

Retrace your steps to the main trail and continue a few steps to the marked Beach Trail. If you're in the mood for a longer walk, continue to the right, following Beach Trail down along the water then into the Broken Hill and North Fork Trails, which reach the main roadway leading back to the parking lot. For the 1.7-mile loop described here, turn left and head uphill. The route switchbacks upward and heads away from the beach. Near the top, you'll come to the bottom of Red Butte, which you passed earlier on the other side. Take the flatter, left-hand route. Pass the trail marked "Razor Point," and continue to the familiar ground leading up toward the parking lot.

▶ NEARBY ACTIVITIES

Instead of turning back toward the freeway at Carmel Valley Road, consider heading north on Camino del Mar, which runs straight through town. A plethora of shops and eateries makes this a good choice for an impromptu stop.

VOLCAN MOUNTAIN PRESERVE

▶ IN BRIEF

Leave your worries and city mentality in the car and enjoy the utter silence and beauty of Volcan Mountain.

▶ DESCRIPTION

Nature author John Burroughs once said, "One has only to sit in the woods or fields, or by the shore of the river or lake, and nearly everything of interest will come round to him, the birds, the animals, the insects."

Nowhere more than at Volcan Mountain does this thought ring true. Walk quickly and you may see nothing more than tracks, but wait patiently and wildlife ventures into view.

From your car, walk up the gravel road (past homes with fruit trees) to the creative main gate, designed in part by renowned artist James Hubbell. After pausing to look at a colorful tile compass that adds to the artsy feel of this entrance, enter the preserve, where the stillness of nature wipes away the worries of the day.

A dirt road heads north, climbing a semi-steep grade for about a third of a mile before curving east. Mule deer tracks are common here. Raccoons and mountain lions are among the other

ⓘ KEY AT-A-GLANCE INFORMATION

LENGTH: 3 miles

CONFIGURATION: Out-and-back

DIFFICULTY: Moderate

SCENERY: Possible wildlife sightings, oak forest

EXPOSURE: Sunny and shady

TRAFFIC: Moderate

TRAIL SURFACE: Packed soil; can be muddy after rain or snow

HIKING TIME: 2 hours

ACCESS: Free

MAPS: Viewable on kiosk near gate

SPECIAL COMMENTS: No horses, dogs, or bicycles are allowed in the preserve; this well-kept trail features undisturbed wildlife and vegetation. For more information or to find out about docent-led hikes that go further into the preserve, visit www.volcan mt.org.

▶ DIRECTIONS

Take I-8 east to the Japatul/CA 79 exit and turn left. Drive 2.5 miles and turn left onto CA 79 north toward Julian. Continue on CA 79 for approximately 21 miles where the road comes to a T. Turn left and head on Main Street through the town of Julian. Main Street becomes Farmer Street after passing through town (less than a mile). After 2.2 miles, turn right onto Wynola Road, travel 100 yards, then turn left onto Farmer Road. You'll notice the preserve sign on the right. Park here on the road's shoulder.

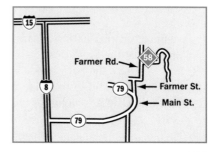

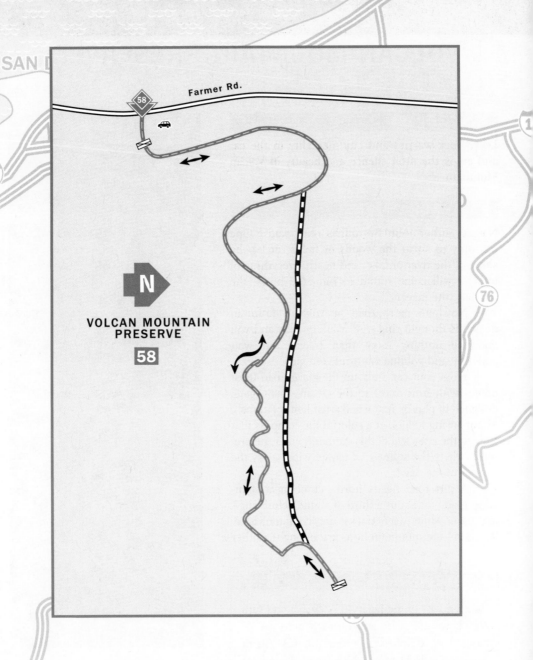

animals in this habitat. Identifying tracks is easy: see the examples and information at the kiosk near the gate.

Where the path bends south, take the stone steps leading to the right up off the road and onto a side trail. A short distance through the trees is a ridge path that zigzags along for a quarter mile or so before entering thicker oak forest.

Continuing to switchback up through the trees, the path is steep in some areas, but only for short distances, offering plenty of opportunities to stop to rest and enjoy the scenery along the way. Mistletoe hang from the branches of ancient Engelmann oaks, sometimes the clumps are so thick you may think a new species of tree grows here—the Mistletoe Tree. Don't let this vascular parasite fool you, however. Mistletoe can't grow on its own; it relies on host trees in order to live.

About a mile from the car, on an eastward bend in the path, the trees open to frame the distant mountains of the Anza Borrego Desert. The hazy, purple-blue image is at first surprising—incongruent with the tree-filled mountain scenery through which you've come.

The oak forest thins a bit, and the path levels out just before rejoining the dirt road on which the hike began. If you're interested in seeing wildlife, this area is a good place to find a log to lean on while you wait quietly for "everything of interest" that Burroughs describes. That may be a deer stepping gingerly through the trees. Or perhaps you'll see a golden eagle soaring through the sky, its keen eyes searching for the movement of a tasty rodent—and probably well aware of your presence in its habitat.

Turn right where the trail meets the dirt road, and follow it another quarter mile or so to a gate where the public trail ends. To return, retrace your steps down the narrow zigzagging path back through the trees and rejoin the road where the trail first cut away. Or, for new scenery, follow the road down the mountain, which is a quicker descent.

▶ NEARBY ACTIVITIES

The Julian Coffee and Tea House at 1921 Main Street, serves wonderful wet-your-whistle concoctions to go or to sip while sitting in a friendly, homey atmosphere. Their hearty sandwiches are big enough for two—but so tasty you'll want one all for yourself. For more information, call (760) 765-1906.

WILDERNESS GARDENS PRESERVE: COMBINED TRAILS LOOP

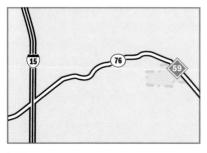

IN BRIEF

The pond, quiet forest, meadows, and hillside scenery make this preserve a relaxing retreat that doesn't require a long drive. Even on weekends, you may be the only hiker on these seldom-used trails.

DESCRIPTION

What's great about Wilderness Gardens Preserve is that there are several individual trails for hikers wanting to make a number of short visits. This description covers three trails that make a loop. This gives you a three-mile trek that enables you to see nearly everything the preserve has to offer.

Peaceful and tranquil best describe the 700-acre Wilderness Garden Preserve in Pala. For thousands of years, this area was used only by Native Americans. The Upper Meadow Trail seems untouched by modern civilization. And when walking along the narrow path, one can almost imagine going back to that very time.

To begin, head west from the parking area across the San Luis Rey River bed, which, in California's drought conditions, is usually dry. A wooden footbridge was put here five years ago when heavy rains washed away the concrete. Except in very wet years, water stays underground, surfacing farther to the east rather than here, but the footbridge remains. Hop on or walk alongside it to enter Pond Trail, which is where the loop begins.

Continue northwest through the shady oaks, cottonwood, and sycamores. You'll pass the exit marker for Upper Meadow Trail on the left. Keep going. About 0.25 miles in you'll see a portable,

DIRECTIONS

Take I-15 north past Escondido. Turn right on CA 76 east and drive about 10 miles, then turn right into the preserve.

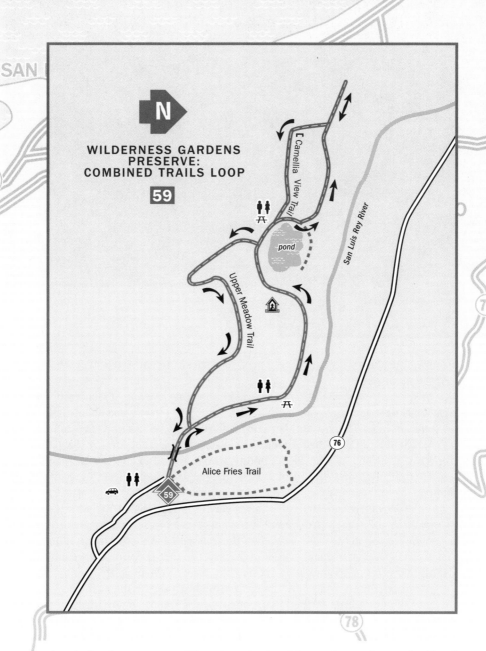

Camellia View Trail

San Luis Rey River

pond

Upper Meadow Trail

76

76

Alice Fries Trail

59

78

chemical toilet rest room. There is a picnic table nearby on the north side of the trail in a small outlet overlooking the riverbed to the north. Stop and listen to the birds in this enchanted place, which was the first preserve owned by San Diego County. Saved from condominium builders in the 1970s, the land represents the county's first attempt to preserve natural habitat and wilderness. Park rangers, along with the statewide organization, Small Wilderness Area Preserves (SWAP), have worked hard to maintain the atmosphere that Ranger Judy Good calls "magical." Continue west toward the pond on this quiet, woodsy trail where poison ivy grows beneath the trees. Posted regulations

Mistletoe hangs in clumps high in the trees along this peaceful trail in the wilderness.

encourage speaking softly, and forbid pets, loud music, or barbecues to protect the pre-serve's natural serenity.

A short distance ahead, a southward bend passes the ranger residence. The trail then heads west again, passing a kiosk with maps and information about ticks, which are common here. There is another chemical toilet to the south of the trail. A picnic table overlooks the man-made pond. The water level is kept low. In the 1950s this property was owned by Manchester Boddy, who intended to cultivate a botanical gar-den. He built the pond as part of a recirculating system to irrigate the camellias he planted. Take the short offshoot that leads around to the north edge of the pond for a closer look at the water. Here, the breeze causes the cattails to rustle softly and stirs up ripples in the sun-glinted water. The rapid music of the elusive wrentit, and the low, vibrating sound of frogs fills the air. In summer, the cattails bloom in long, com-pact clusters that later open, releasing fluffy seeds that the wind blows around like cottony snow. Enjoy the peace before heading back to the main trail.

Head northwest where the trees grow thicker, pass by the Camellia View Trail exit marker, and, a little further, that same trail's entrance. You're likely to see signs of wildlife here along the last 0.25 miles of the main trail. Raccoon and bobcat tracks, perhaps enlarged by gentle rains or nighttime moisture to look like bear or cougar tracks, mark the same trail you tread. Coyotes, deer, possum, and foxes also live here, but their natural shyness makes spotting them a rare occurrence. You're likely to see their droppings, though, and perhaps even get a whiff of skunk scent lingering somewhere along the path.

The trail halts at the end of the forest. Turn around and head southwest back to the Camellia View Trail entrance, now on your right. Enter the trail and head south. My family calls this area the "Tarzan" trail. Old-growth grapevines twist up through the trees. The deciduous vines turn to weathered, knotty ropes stretching up through oak branches in the winter, so no matter what the season, this section looks like a jungle. A rustic bench where the trail curves east provides a resting spot. Just be careful of poison oak amid the tangled foliage. In spring, the camellias bloom all around. In summer, clusters of grapes hang from the vines. The fruit is especially abundant in wetter years. Continuing along the trail, you'll cross a two-foot concrete spillway and then a wooden footbridge over a larger spillway. They were part of the irrigation system designed by Boddy but are now dry. Exit the 0.75-mile Camellia View Trail back near the pond and take the main trail south several yards to the entrance for the Upper Meadow Trail.

The Upper Meadow Trail heads southeast, gradually ascending through the trees along a river rock–lined path. You'll see holly-leaf cherry, toyon, and large boulders covered with sea foam–green lichen. The trail narrows, crosses a split-log bridge over a ravine, then becomes steeper as it briefly heads north. Curving east again, the trail opens up to meadows on the south side then begins to descend. A set of steps made from railroad ties aids you in the steepest section. The ridge path overlooks the pond and the forested area below. Ferns cascade from the steep hillside wall like waterfalls, and moss covers sections of trail, tree trunks, and boulders. You'll hear the wrentit and woodpeckers, and see birds flitting among the trees. The route descends to level ground, meanders through a rocky section, and makes its way back to the main trail. From the Upper Meadow View exit sign, go right and head back across the wooden footbridge to the parking lot.

▶ NEARBY ACTIVITIES

After experiencing the peace and tranquility of nature, perhaps some excitement is in order. At nearby Pala Casino, 5 miles west on CA 76, the shrill sounds of slot machines advertising jackpot winnings will provide a contrast. Even if you don't gamble, Pala has six restaurants that offer everything from Asian food to steaks. The Terrace Room features an exhibition kitchen with 12 chefs preparing more than 60 food items. For more information, see www.palacasino.com.

WILLIAM HEISE COUNTY PARK:
COMBINED TRAILS LOOP

KEY AT-A-GLANCE INFORMATION

LENGTH: 3 miles

CONFIGURATION: Loop

DIFFICULTY: Moderately strenuous

SCENERY: Native plants, trees, birds

EXPOSURE: Mostly sunny

TRAFFIC: Moderate

TRAIL SURFACE: Earthen path, leaf litter, rocky areas

HIKING TIME: 2 hours

ACCESS: $2 day use/parking fee

MAPS: Available from ranger

FACILITIES: Rest rooms in the picnic area near cabins

SPECIAL COMMENTS: Bring a compass to verify you're headed in the right directions. These trails can be disorienting.

IN BRIEF

The variety of landscape and difficulty on this combined-trails loop makes this hike a lot like a planned gym workout. You begin in a scenic forest with a moderate climb, wind your way through a rugged, strenuous portion with panoramic views, and end with an easy cooldown through lush foliage.

DESCRIPTION

Watch for burned areas along the route. Manzanita and other vegetation are amazing in their ability to vigorously regenerate.

From the parking stalls marked "Canyon Oak," head down the hill (southwest). You will see a narrow asphalt road on the right, with signs indicating a youth area, group camping, and the Canyon Oak Trailhead. Turn right onto this asphalt path to reach the trailhead kiosk after approximately 400 yards.

Head left behind the kiosk, up onto the forest trail that continues north through oak forest

DIRECTIONS

Route One: Take I-8 east to CA 79 and travel north past Lake Cuyamaca (about 10 miles) into the town of Julian, then head west through the town to Pine Hills Road.

Route Two: Take I-15 to the Poway Road exit and head inland. Poway Road ends at the CA 67 intersection. Turn left and drive (CA 67 becomes CA 78/79) to Pine Hills Road (approximately 26 miles). Turn right and head south to Frisius Road. Turn left and follow Frisius directly into Heise County Park.

After paying at the ranger booth, continue northwest on the main road to a small day-use parking section on the right labeled "Canyon Oak." The lot is adjacent to campsite 63.

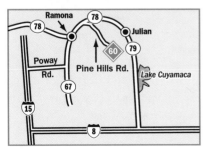

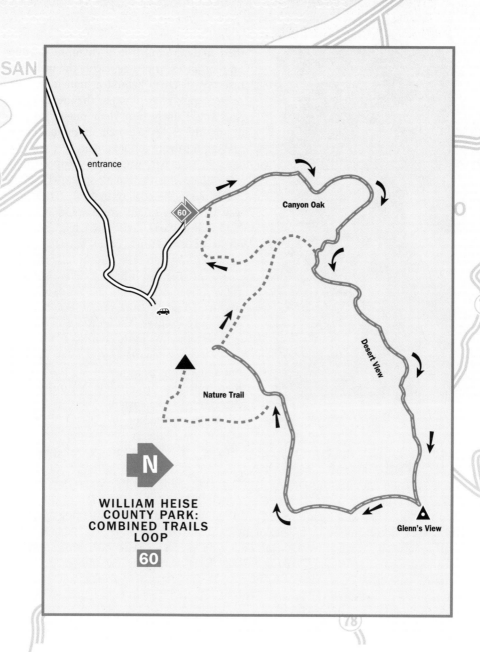

SAN

entrance

60

Canyon Oak

Desert View

Nature Trail

N

WILLIAM HEISE
COUNTY PARK:
COMBINED TRAILS
LOOP

60

Glenn's View

5

76

for a short distance. The gradual uphill slope bends left, moving through thick manzanita forest, then levels out.

As you hike along, the wind rushes up through the mountains, making soft, rustling music in the leaves and grasses it sweeps to and fro. And what's that crackling sound? Is it raining? You might find yourself checking for drops, but the crackling, dripping sound you hear could be cicadas—if you're lucky to visit when the insects are in their active cycle. Look closely at the narrow branches of scrub oaks and manzanita trees for a lacy-winged insect with bulging eyes. The shy cicadas take three years to mature and emerge from

Is that an elephant or a tree?

their underground lives as nymphs, feeding on root juices. If you get close, the inch-long insects will creep behind a branch to hide. As you walk away, though, they relax again. And you'll likely hear their music start up again—the males use their abdominal noise-making organs to attract a mate.

In summer, watch for cupped mariposa lilies with their pink-speckled, yellow petals along the edge of the trail. These give way to tufted, bright green moss at about 0.35 miles, where the route, which becomes moist under a thick cover of trees, bears right heading northeast and uphill. The trail then curves left (northwest) before straightening to lead due north. The forest opens to sky in places, and the trail alternates from wide and leaf-littered to narrow and rocky as it begins bending to the southeast.

At approximately half a mile, the path turns abruptly right for a short distance, then southeast again, moving through hills and dales for another 0.2 miles or so. The connecting point for the Desert View Trail appears suddenly at the bottom of one of the dales. Turn left and begin moving steeply uphill. Split logs are placed at intervals of several feet. This wide, smooth area runs for several hundred feet before jagged rocks protrude into the path—some half covered in pine needles, so watch your step.

Small turnouts serve as viewpoints along this stretch, with a view to the southeast of mountains that seem to go on forever. Butterflies are out in spring and summer. They flutter about in full color but are surprisingly well camouflaged when resting in a pile of dead leaves. Harvester ants are also common on this stretch of trail, as are darkling beetles, walking on skinny legs with their rear ends raised. Many refer to these black beetles as "stinkbugs." On our last visit we saw a pair mating—to the song of birds and the hum of bees, of course.

At more than a mile from your starting point, the trail bends slightly to the left now and again but generally bears right to a junction point at about 2 miles. A short trail to the left leads to the panoramic expanse seen at Glenn's View. On clear days the Salton Sea gleams like a ribbon of silver on the eastern desert horizon.

When your eyes have had their fill of the Glenn's View, go back to the junction point and head carefully downhill (south) along a rocky ridge. A canyon stretches below on the right. The trail eventually levels, curving west to make the loop and hook up with the Self-Guided Nature Trail. Turn right at the marker and head through the lush shade of the Nature Trail.

You'll come out near campsite 91 with a clear head and a desire to return to this peaceful place. Head southwest on the narrow asphalt roads of the camping area and make your way back to the small lot where you left your car.

60 Hikes within 60 MILES

SAN DIEGO

INCLUDING NORTH, SOUTH, AND EAST COUNTIES

APPENDIXES AND INDEX

APPENDIX A:
OUTDOOR SHOPS

Adventure 16
www.adventure16.com
2002 South Coast Highway
Oceanside, CA 92054
(760) 966-1700

4620 Alvarado Canyon Road
San Diego, CA 92120
(619) 283-2374

143 South Cedros Avenue
Solana Beach, CA 92075
(858) 755-7662

Bargain Center Surplus
3015 North Park Way
San Diego, CA 92104
(619) 295-1181

Big 5 Sporting Goods
www.big5sportinggoods.com
1253 East Valley Parkway
Escondido, CA 92027
(760) 480-6860

949 Lomas Santa Fe Drive
Solana Beach CA 92075
(858) 755-5953

8145 Mira Mesa Boulevard
San Diego, CA 92126
(858) 693-4941

16773-B Bernardo Center Drive
Rancho Bernardo, CA 92128
(858) 673-9219

4348 Convoy Street
San Diego, CA 92111
(858) 560-0311

666 Fletcher Parkway
San Diego, CA 92120
(619) 444-8139

3729 Rosecrans Street
San Diego, CA 92110
(619) 298-3350

760 Sycamore Avenue
Vista, CA 92083
(760) 727-2859

6061-A El Cajon Boulevard
San Diego, CA 92115
(619) 583-7930

2301 Vista Way
Oceanside, CA 92054
(760) 757-4154

C & C Outdoors
www.ccoutdoorstore.com
3231 Sports Arena Boulevard, Suite 104
San Diego, CA 92110
(619) 222-2326, (888) 385-3456

Cal Stores
1019 Garnet Avenue
San Diego, CA 92109

4030 Sports Arena Blvd.
San Diego, CA 92110

GI Joes Army & Navy Surplus
544 Sixth Avenue
San Diego, CA 92111
(619) 531-1910

REI
www.rei.com
5556 Copley Drive
San Diego, CA 92111
(858) 279-4400

Sport Chalet
www.sportchalet.com
3695 Midway Drive
San Diego, CA 92110
(619) 224-6777

1640 Camino Del Rio North
San Diego, CA 92108
(619) 718-7070

4545 La Jolla Village Drive
San Diego, CA 92122
(858) 453-5656

Sportmart
www.sportmart.com
5500 Grossmont Center Drive
La Mesa, CA 91942
(619) 697-8160

7725 Balboa Avenue
San Diego, CA 92111
(858) 292-0800

11690 Carmel Mountain Road
San Diego, CA 92128
(858) 673-9700

Sports Authority
www.thesportsauthority.com
390 East H Street
Chula Vista, CA 91910

1050 North El Camino Real
Encinitas C 92024
(760) 634-6690

1352 West Valley Parkway
Escondido, CA 92029
(760) 735-8501

2160 Vista Way
Oceanside, CA 92054
(760) 967-1891

8550 Rio San Diego Drive
San Diego, CA 92108
(619) 295-1682

ONLINE SHOPS

Just Gear
www.justgear.com

Out in Style
www.outinstyle.com

APPENDIX B:
SOURCES FOR TRAIL MAPS

Adventure 16
www.adventure16.com
2002 South Coast Highway
Oceanside, CA 92054
(760) 966-1700

4620 Alvarado Canyon Road
San Diego, CA 92120
(619) 283-2374

143 South Cedros Avenue
Solana Beach, CA 92075
(858) 755-7662

C & C Outdoors
www.ccoutdoorstore.com
3231 Sports Arena Boulevard, Suite 104
San Diego, CA
(619) 222-2326, (888) 385-3456

Map Centre
3191 Sports Arena Boulevard
San Diego, CA 92110
(619) 291-3830

REI
www.rei.com
5556 Copley Drive
San Diego, CA 92111
(858) 279-4400

APPENDIX C:
HIKING CLUBS AND ORGANIZATIONS

Back Country Land Trust of San Diego County
www.bclt.org
338 West Lexington Avenue, Suite 204
El Cajon, CA 92020
(619) 590-2258

Encinitas Trails Coalition
www.encinitastrails.org/join
330 Rosemary Lane
Olivenhain, CA 92024

Fallbrook Land Conservancy
www.sdlcc.org/flc
P.O. Box 2701
Fallbrook, CA 92028-2701
(760) 728-0889

San Diego Natural History Museum's "Canyoneers"
www.sdnhm.org/canyoneers/index
P.O. Box 121390
San Diego, CA 92112-1390
(619) 255-0425

San Diego Sea to Sea Trail Foundation
www.seatoseatrail.org
P.O. Box 19413
San Diego, CA 92159-0413
(619) 303 6975

Sierra Club, San Diego Chapter
www.sandiego.sierraclub.org/home/index.asp
3820 Ray Street
San Diego, CA 92104
(619) 299-1744

San Elijo Lagoon Conservancy
www.sanelijo.org
P.O. Box 230634
Encinitas, CA 92023
(760) 436-3944

Walkabout International
4639 30th Street, Suite C
San Diego, CA 92116

INDEX

INDEX

INDEX

INDEX

NOTES

NOTES

NOTES

NOTES

NOTES